Communication Research
and Broadcasting No. 11

Editor:
Internationales Zentralinstitut
für das Jugend- und Bildungsfernsehen (IZI)

Educational Programmes on Television – Deficiencies, Support, Chances

Contributions to an International Symposium organised by the Internationales Zentralinstitut für das Jugend- und Bildungsfernsehen (IZI) and the Bayerische Landeszentrale für neue Medien (BLM)

Edited by
Manfred Meyer

K·G·Saur
München · New Providence · London · Paris 1993

Editor of the series:
Internationales Zentralinstitut für das Jugend- und Bildungsfernsehen (IZI)
Rundfunkplatz 1, D-80335 München,
Tel. (0 89) 59 00-21 40, Telex 52 107-0 brmd, Telefax (0 89) 59 00-23 79

Responsible:
Paul Löhr

Editor of this issue:
Manfred Meyer

Editorial assistance:
Sylvia Ortlieb, Rosemarie Hagemeister

Editorial collaboration and linguistic advice:
John Malcolm King

Translation of German contributions:
Geoffrey P. Burwell

Translation of French contributions:
Norman Jones

A German edition of this book will be published later this year under the title
„Kultur- und Bildungsprogramme im Fernsehen −
Defizite, Unterstützung, Chancen.
Beiträge zu einem Internationalen Symposium".

Die Deutsche Bibliothek − CIP-Einheitsaufnahme

**Educational programmes on television : deficiencies, support,
chances** ; contributions to an international symposium /
organised by the Internationales Zentralinstitut für das Jugend-
und Bildungsfernsehen (IZI) and the Bayerische Landeszentrale
für neue Medien (BLM). Ed. by Manfred Meyer. − München ;
New Providence ; London ; Paris : Saur, 1993
(Communication research and broadcasting; No. 11)
Dt. Ausg. u.d.T.: Kultur- u. Bildungsprogramme im Fernsehen
ISBN 3-598-20210-5
NE: Meyer, Manfred [Hrsg.]; Internationales Zentralinstitut für das
Jugend- und Bildungsfernsehen <München>; GT

Contents

5

Chapter 4: Cooperation and Partnership: Media Integration and Shared Responsibility

Chapter 5: Alternative Ways of Offering and Financing Cultural and Educational Programmes

PART II: Background Information

Introduction

About this book

This book contains most of the contributions to an International Symposium that took place in July 1992 on the occasion of MediaNet '92, an event that had been introduced as 'the international network of audio-visual and interactive media and programmes for information, culture and education'[1] – formerly known as the Munich International Media Market.

The symposium took place under the title "Cultural and Educational Programmes on Television: Deficiencies and Chances in a Competitive Media Environment". Since this book does not intend to represent what is commonly understood by the proceedings' of a conference, we felt free to change the title insignificantly.

We ignored the aspect of cultural programmes for intrinsic reasons to be explained later, and left out the 'competitive media environment' simply for editorial reasons and on the sound advice of our librarian who often enough has been irritated by mammoth titles and subtitles. Instead, we re-inserted the word 'support', as it is the core issue of most of our contributions.

Most of our speakers had been invited to talk about support media, supportive actions or measurement, and back-up activities for programmes that were conceived as educational television programmes in a rather narrow sense. They were either concrete series of broadcasts directed to schools of various levels, or programmes for adult viewers who purposefully seek information, aim at developing certain skills or want to increase their knowledge continuously in a more or less systematic way.

When cultural programmes on television were referred to during the conference, they were not mentioned as concrete examples of, say, magazine formats conveying information on cultural events or artistic achievements. As in the general discussion at least in Germany, culture was something beyond entertainment, news or 'infotainment' and sports, something which the public service organisations claimed to reflect and the private or commercial broadcasters were said to ignore and simply leave out.

A joint venture

Our conference was a joint venture. It was organised by the 'Internationales Zentralinstitut für das Jugend- und Bildungsfernsehen' (IZI) in close cooperation

---

[1] MediaNet, Internationale Münchner Filmwochen GmbH (Ed.): Offizieller Katalog/Official Catalogue MediaNet '92. München 1992.

with the 'Bayerische Landeszentrale für neue Medien' (BLM), the umbrella organisation under public law for private broadcasting in Bavaria.

The BLM is one of the regional institutions that were created in each of the Federal Laender in Germany, charged with monitoring and controlling private broadcasters in order to keep their actions in compliance with the media legislation. Readers familiar with the broadcasting scene in the UK would best understand their function within the German system by thinking of the former Independent Broadcasting Authority (IBA).

Initially, both partners were separately in contact with the organisers of MediaNet i.e. the 'Internationale Münchner Filmwochen GmbH', until *Eberhard Hauff*, its General Manager, proposed a joint conference in view of apparent similarity of the purpose and target audiences aimed at.

There were, however, some slight differences in conception at the beginning. The BLM had proposed a conference that put more emphasis on cultural programming and on cultural aspects of the duopoly of public service and private broadcasting organisations.

The IZI was already heading for what was intended to be a 'closed' workshop for educational broadcasters, with particular reference to functional aspects and the organisation of educational broadcasting, such as concrete measurements and strategies to promote educational television programming, to create higher awareness and increased acceptance for it, to develop back-up and support media and activities Most of our speakers were already contacted before the two partners met for the first time.

Cooperation was established rather late in the process of preparation, and changes in the conception of the conference caused concern about the pending load of organisational work.

There were even voices that doubted the possibility of effective cooperation between an Institute affiliated to a broadcasting organisation such as the BR known for its firmly adhering to the public service idea, and an institution that was often said to 'represent' private broadcasting, but which in fact is effectively running, licensing and supervising it.

However, without great difficulty a compromise was achieved regarding the structure for the conference: the three sessions already prepared by the IZI, concentrating on support and back-up for educational programming, were preceded by an introductory session on 'Cultural and Educational Programmes and the Dual System' that was more of interest to the BLM people. A final session on possible 'Alternative Ways of Offering and Financing Cultural and Educational Programmes' was worked out together; the closing session was devoted to a Panel Discussion on 'Future Developments' in the field.

10

This gives me the opportunity to express my gratitude towards the partners from the BLM. Apart from the fact that their financial engagement in connection with our common untertaking was quite respectable, we owe thanks to *Dr. Wolf-Dieter Ring*, the President of the BLM, who also gave a keynote speech in the opening session, to our direct contact persons *Johannes Kors* and *Dr. Wolfgang Flieger*, as well as to a flock of efficient and untiringly friendly young ladies that helped to establish communication between the two houses.

The aims of the conference

It was agreed upon that, due to technological innovations and political developments, broadcasting legislation had undergone substantial changes in most European countries, and that, as a result, both the public service broadcasting corporations and the state-controlled broadcasting organisations have lost their monopoly, thus being forced to compete for the public's favour with private broadcasting companies.

For many broadcasting organisations, however, no changes have taken place in the legally founded programme assignment with its three remits − information, entertainment and education. On the other hand, similar demands are being increasingly made on private companies.

The following questions have arisen from this development:

− How can cultural and educational programmes, often conceived only for specific minorities, manage to continue in this dual system with a competitive character?
− What strategies and methods have been and are being developed in the production departments to reach the target groups they are aiming at, e.g. culturally interested minorities or groups with special information needs?
− What chances do cultural and educational programmes have on the audio-visual media market?

These considerations led us to the formulation of the objectives for the conference, as listed in the information distributed.[2] The aim of this event was

− to stimulate discussion on the chances of cultural and educational programmes in dual broadcasting systems;
− to exchange information on the experience and activities of European and non-European broadcasting organisations in a competitive situation;
− to propose support measures and activities to enhance the awareness for, and acceptance of, educational programmes, especially those relevant for attaining objectives of national or regional educational policies.

---

[2] Cf. Press Release, App. B, pp. 273−274

11

Cultural and educational programmes in a dual system

In general, the division of this book is orientated to the proceedings of the conference. The first chapter mirrors the opening session, starting with an introductory statement by *Wolf Feller*, the Director of Television at Bayerischer Rundfunk, who also chaired this first session.

It is followed by two explanations of opposing positions: the discourse 'On the Situation of Public Service Broadcasting in Dual Systems' by *Albert Scharf*, the Director General of Bayerischer Rundfunk and currently President of the European Broadcasting Union, and the rejoinder of *Dr. Wolf-Dieter Ring*, President of the BLM, who talks about 'Private Television and Public Responsibility'.

At the conference we were to owe thanks to *Alfred Payrleitner*, Head of the Main Department Science and Education, not only for having stepped in to replace ORF's General Secretary *Kurt Bergmann* at very short notice. In his brilliant essay that closes the first chapter he provides a refreshing reminder that there should be a junction, as it were, between media policy considerations ('What do the Media want?') and the necessarily crucial question for all programme makers working in the new competitive media environment: 'What does the audience want?'

Taking stock of educational broadcasting

The three chapters that follow — including the corresponding background information in Part II — could be seen as an attempt to reflect the state of the art of educational broadcasting. As chapter headings, we adopted the groupings introduced to structure the conference, despite considerable overlapping. Moreover, cross-references would be possible between almost all contributions to the chapters on 'Public Service Broadcasting and the Market Situation' (Chapter 2), 'Strategies for Increasing the Acceptance and Effectiveness of Educational Programmes' (Chapter 3) and 'Cooperation and Partnership: Media Integration and Shared Responsibility' (Chapter 4). The articles in Chapter 2 could also be grouped under the heading School Television, and the ones in Chapter 3 under Continuing Education.

Most of our contributors were contacted through a connection that had proved to be a starting point for fruitful cooperation in our field: The Working Party for Educational Programmes of the European Broadcasting Union (EBU). I have reported on its purpose and the scope of activities of its members elsewhere.[3]

---

[3] For example in the summary of results of a survey 'On the Situation of School Television in Western Europe'. In: M. Meyer (Ed.): *Aspects of School Television in Europe. A Documentation.* München: Saur 1992; pp. 17 – 54.

It was no coincidence that the first topic-related session on 'Public Service Broadcasting and the Market Situation' was chaired by *Armin Veihl*, a Senior Officer at the EBU Permanent Services Division in Geneva who has acted as Secretary to the Working Party for decades. We are indebted to him for his splendid advice on many occasions while the conference was being prepared.

One of the keynote speeches for this session was delivered by *Léa Martel* from BRTN, currently President of the EBU Working Party. Dedicated to European dimensions, she went beyond her experience as Director of BRTN's Educational Broadcasting department in her talk on 'Culture, Education and Training: New Challenges to Public Service Broadcasting'.

Under the heading 'BBC Education and the New Broadcasting Environment' we rightly expected a profound presentation from the British Broadcasting Corporation (BBC). Their work was respectably represented by the joint contribution of *Brian Wright*, Head of Educational Broadcasting Services, *Jean Nunn*, Head of Educational Developments and Information, and *Robert Seatter*, the Manager of Information and Promotions for BBC Education.

For our purposes here we have printed their papers under separate titles: 'BBC Education and the New Broadcasting Environment' (Brian Wright; pp. 55 – 59), 'Extending and Supporting the Educational Use of Broadcasts' (Jean Nunn; pp. 60 – 67), and 'BBC Education: The Role of Marketing' (Robert Seatter; pp. 68 – 73).

With BBC Education, probably the most renowned, at any rate by far the largest education department (as it was then) of all broadcasting companies in Europe was represented. In the meantime, BBC Education has been reorganised, now constituting a directorate of its own[4], which is a true indication that educational broadcasting is far from showing signs of decline, at least in the UK.

Of the few broadcasting organisations that have specialised in educational programming in Canada, TVOntario is certainly the most interesting one. We had invited *Olga Kuplowska*, Managing Director of Policy, Research and Planning, and *Judith Tobin*, Director General of International Affairs, who jointly presented 'TVOntario's Educational Programming: Reaching the Market of Millions'. In this book, it is Olga who explains the 'Working Model', whereas Judith reports on marketing activities and international liaison.

---

[4] See chart showing the 'Outline structure of the new directorate' appended to the BBC Education background information on p. 237, the latter depicting the situation as of June 1992.

Educational broadcasting organisations

In Europe too, we find organisations that have been exclusively created to provide educational broadcasting: in the Netherlands and in Sweden. I have referred to them as 'educational broadcasting organisations'.

In the Netherlands, these organisations are *Nederlandse Onderwijs Televisie* (NOT), a foundation whose only function is to produce school television programmes and supplementary print material, as presented by *Henk Jacobsen* ('Promoting and Marketing School Television Programmes in the Netherlands'; pp. 120 – 123)), and the *Teleac* Foundation. The latter, a producer of multi-media courses for adult education comprising television and radio programmes as well as all sorts of other educational media and learning aids, was introduced by *Henny van der Eng* who is Head of their Programme Support Department ('The Multi-media Conception of *Teleac*'; pp. 141 – 145).[5]

Sweden's educational broadcasting organisation calls itself *Utbildningsradion* (UR). Its task is to produce radio and television programmes for classroom use at all levels including kindergartens, for preschool children at home, for distance education students, for adult education, and for the general public. UR was represented by the Head of its Programme Department Foreign Languages, *Rolf Horneij*.

Strategies for school broadcasting

With *Christopher Jones* and *David Lee* we had invited two senior education officers who worked at the headquarters of the Independent Television Commission (ITC) until recently. They had already contributed to the book 'Aspects of School Television in Europe', showing their expertise in field research, information provision, and liaison with the education community.[6]

Chris Jones reported on 'Strategies for Increasing the Acceptance and Effectiveness of School Television', David Lee spoke about 'A Professional Network of Support: Education Officers and Effective Liaison'.

---

[5] To complete the picture: with the *Radio Volks Universiteit* (RVU), originally founded as a radio service of the Dutch Federation of Adult Education Institutes that started TV broadcasts in 1983, there is a third educational broadcasting organisation in the Netherlands. RVU's focus is on permanent education for everyone, on stimulating active participation in the community, and on imparting basic knowledge to understand the world.

[6] Cf David Lee: Ears to the Ground. ITV Liaison Activities with the Schools Audience. In: M. Meyer (Ed.): *Aspects of School Television*. pp. 167 – 195; Christopher Jones: Keeping Track with KEY – A Database for School Television Programmes and Support Media, ibid., pp. 221 – 226; and Christopher Jones: What Do Teachers Expect from Schools Television?, ibid., pp. 462 – 476.

Moreover, with *Paul Martin* (Central TV) and *Rolf Horneij* (UR) two specialist producers were won who could draw upon their long-term experience as specialist editors in subject areas that were either very difficult to tackle, e.g. Science and Mathematics for pupils (Paul Martin: 'Support Activities for Science and Maths Programmes') or particularly popular among the adult audience, i.e. 'Learning Foreign Languages by Television' (Rolf Horneij: 'The Role of Back-up Material').

Another glimpse overseas was permitted by *Yoshiyuki Fukushima*, Head of NHK's School Broadcast Programme Production unit, who introduced 'Activities in Support of Educational Programmes in Japan'. The Japanese public service broadcasting organisation NHK is undoubtedly the most outstanding and prolific provider of educational programming for all kinds of purposes in Asia, and we learnt that there is intensive cooperation with other companies in the field of educational broadcasting, e.g. with TVOntario.

Cooperation and partnership

To open this chapter, *Dr. Hans Paukens* reports on the experience gained at the Adolf-Grimme-Institut, a specialised institute of the German Adult Education Association, well-known on account of the Adolf Grimme Award and renowned for its media work, in 'Cooperation with German Broadcasting Organisations'

It was our intention to include an account of the present state of *Telekolleg* in this part of the conference as a second contribution from Germany. *Telekolleg*, however, was reported on the very same day, at almost the same time during another workshop organised by CEDEFOP.

The following contribution, therefore, is *Henny van der Eng's* report on 'The Multimedia Conception of *Teleac*', the Dutch educational broadcasting organisation already mentioned.

That outside organisations and partner institutions can be commissioned to provide back-up material in the same way as television programmes is the daily experience of *Derek Jones*, the Editor Support Services at Channel 4, which in itself is an interesting model for organising broadcast programming ('Commissioning Television Programmes and Back-up Material: The Model of *Channel 4*'). He describes the manifold ways of getting close to, and keeping in touch with, those parts of the audience that want more than just news and entertainment in their leisure life, and who willingly take more advantage of a TV Channel if it is skilfully and competently offered to them.

What parts of the audience want, what especially young people appreciated if offered from the media, is often more than the right kind of information. It may be a need

15

for immediate and personal advice on how to proceed in a given situation or in view of a pressing problem that was met with in a programme. It might even be a cry for help. To provide this type of feedback to the audience normally exceed the resources and possibilities of a broadcasting organisation.

In 1975, the BBC founded a not-for-profit organisation whose task was exactly this – to provide further assistance and help whenever needed and demanded as an outcome of broadcast presentations that are likely to involve social actions, such as the provision of information leaflets leading to social services and help agencies, of helplines, dial-and-listen offers, telephone conferences, outreach activities etc. 'Broadcasting Support Services – A Joint Enterprise' is reported upon by its Director Keith Smith.

What happens to all these support materials and back-up activities? Who uses them, who writes off for back-up literature or rings a helpline? What do they think of the back-up materials or services requested? Do requesters take any further action as a result of the back-up? – These are questions that can only be answered by research. Rosemary Bristow, Manager in the Special Projects section of BBC Broadcasting Research Department, went to the trouble of gathering the scarce research literature that was available and uniquely summarised the findings on 'Public Attitudes Towards Back-up Activities'.

Alternative ways

All broadcasting activities mentioned so far were programmes broadcast on-air over terrestrial networks. In a session titled 'Alternative Ways of Offering and Financing Cultural and Educational Programmes' we sought to consider the possibility of disseminating programmes via satellite or cable.

One example of offering cultural programming is ARTE, the – still much disputed – European Cultural Channel which was launched in May 1992 as a joint venture of the French and the German Government but is open to the participation of other partners. At present, its programmes are transmitted via satellite and fed into local cable systems. The background and the peculiarities of ARTE are elucidated here by Dietrich Schwarzkopf, its Vice-President, who asks 'The European Cultural Channel – Cultural Programming Without Borders?'

In France, all school television programmes are transmitted over the regional channels of France 3, the former FR3, but they are produced by a non-broadcast organisation, i.e. the Centre National de Documentation Pédagogique (CNDP), a national centre associated to the French Ministry of Education.

The CNDP is also charged with many other tasks in addition to, and beyond programme production, such as providing information, publishing magazines, producing audio-visual materials for all educational areas, and promoting the use of new forms of technology in education. Its main stronghold is probably that it serves, and is assisted by, a network of 116 regional, departmental and local centres for 'documentation pédagogique'.

In 1990, *Pierre Trincal* became its new Director General. He willingly consented to come to Munich to explain his new concept for the gigantic organisation. 'Technology Support for the French Educational System' also includes the system *Éducâble*, an 'image bank' with more than 7,000 films to be made available on request via a cable network.

With the invitation of *The Discovery Channel* we originally intended to present a real success story directly from the USA: the story of a cable company offering nothing but high-quality educational and cultural programmes that gained more than 50 million subscribers. However, initial arrangements failed due to a baby being born and a young production company being launched. We owe thanks to *Nick Comer-Calder* who himself was busy assisting the birth of *The Learning Channel*, a child of the European branch of the Discovery Channel, for talking about 'really useful television', as he sees it in his contribution *'The Learning Channel* and *Discovery Europe:* Educational Programmes via Cable'.

At this stage, the conference programme also included the talk on 'Cultural and Educational Programmes on Public Service Broadcasting and Private Television – A Programme Analysis' which was a summary of a piece of research commissioned by the BLM to Prof. Dr. *Hans-Jürgen Weiß* from Göttingen University. In the meantime, Professor Weiß has published his paper in a specialised journal[7], and there was no time left to translate his extensive report and present it in this context.

A guide to educational broadcasting institutions: Background information

The organisers of MediaNet wanted the symposium to be open for all visitors and vendors of the exhibition and to the participants of all satellite events schedules during the market days, since entrance was covered by a general fee.

This meant that we had no idea what the nature of our audience would be like, a question that was asked by many of our speakers. In fact, we had to expect

---

7 Cf. Hans-Jürgen Weiß: Kultur und Bildung. In: Media Perspektiven, 11/1992, pp. 733–749.

fluctuation and occasional customers, with a lot of people coming and going, or even constantly changing audiences, from visiting school classes to the interested public that usually turn up at these kinds of events in the late afternoon after work.

These preliminaries are mentioned here because they bear on the nature of our contribution to this book to some extent. For the reason mentioned and to save time in an overloaded schedule we urged our contributors to leave out, as far as possible, any factual information on their organisation, such as foundation and history, basic objectives and scope of activities, statistical figures on programme output and utilisation etc..

We also asked them to concentrate on essential issues such as support mechanisms, partnership arrangements etc., and to show as much audio-visual material to illustrate their points as possible.

We intended to gather this kind of prospectus or directory information well in advance in order to have it translated into either English or German, and possibly into French. The idea was to leave the little time left over for the presentation rather than for reading to the audience what they could read themselves. Another advantage hoped for was that late-comers or 'swappers' could be given these background information leaflets in the moment they entered the session hall.

We found out that we had an unexpected multiplication effect this way. Many persons passed by just for information material and did not bother to follow entire talks, and weeks later we received letters requesting the 'documentation distributed at the conference'.

This explains the organisation of this book: The first part contains most of the papers presented or transcripts of oral presentations given, some with understandable shortcomings when the spoken word had to be converted into readable print. This was difficult in cases where people used transparencies to structure their talk and spoke rather freely about their subject, inserting some programme clips here, slides made from print material there, or even pages or spreadsheets from a computer programme or a data-file.

In the second part we compiled all the background information and contact addresses that were made available during the conference, properly corrected and updated in those cases where considerable changes came into effect later in 1992.

The most noteworthy of these changes took place in the UK, where BBC Education, a former subdivision with obligations to report to both the television and the radio directors, was turned into a Directorate of its own, having at its disposal, among other things, its own subsidiary company, Educational Publishing.

Acknowledgements

My special thanks, therefore, have to go first of all and foremost to the contributors to our conference and to this book. The circumstances resulting from our somewhat experimental way of handling the organisation described above meant that we had to demand more assistance from most of them than would have been necessary if we had only had to publish papers presented and formulated well in advance and ready for printing. Everyone was extremely helpful and appreciative of the situation, and I can only hope that this book as an outcome of our common efforts reflects what they had in mind when they came to Munich to make their points.

As always we depended on the skill and expertise of our translators and linguistic advisers. I should like to acknowledge the efficient and extremely helpful assistance of *John Malcolm King* and his language services company in editing most of the English texts, and to *Geoffrey P. Burwell* and *Norman Jones* for excellent translations into English from German and French, respectively.

Particular thanks go to Ms *Sylvia Ortlieb* who was employed part-time as my assistant for the organisation of the conference. I appreciated her organisational talent and her ability to work independently as much as the sense of calm she radiated even in the most hectic moments.

Finally, I owe thanks to my colleagues in the Institute. Without their helpful cooperation neither the conference nor this book would have been possible.

Munich, May 1993   Manfred Meyer

PART I

Contributions to the Conference

Chapter 1:
Cultural and Educational Programmes and the Dual System

Wolf Feller

Cultural and Educational Programmes and the Dual System – Some Preliminary Remarks

Before I introduce this morning's speakers, allow me to make a few basic preliminary remarks. The situation at the outset is characterised by two quite contrary quotations. If we look up Article 4, Paragraph 1 of the Bavarian Broadcasting Act, we find the programme remit defined as follows:

"The broadcasts of the Bayerischer Rundfunk serve the aims of education, instruction and entertainment. They shall be supported by a democratic attitude, by cultural responsibility, by a human point of view and objectivity and take Bavaria's special features into account . . . "

In contrast to this is the statement made by a person responsible for the programme of Sat 1, one of our private channels:

"We do what goes down well with the viewer – that is the natural law for private broadcasting. On no account can minority programmes be taken into consideration here."[1]

How, then, can cultural and educational programmes, often conceived for minorities only, continue to exist in this dual system with a competitive character?

---

[1] Quoted from the *Nürnberger Nachrichten* of March 29, 1985.

Let me dwell, if you will, for a moment on our so comprehensive public service remit. We are obliged to transmit programmes for all viewers who pay their licence fees. That means we have to make not only programmes that attract the mass audiences but also those orientated to minorities. Anyone whose programmes fail to attract the majorities is soon unable to do anything for the minorities either. In the end, the question as to the right to exist would very soon and quite rightly be put to a broadcasting service that is financed by licence fees but whose programmes only address a fraction of the population.

Bavarian Television sees itself as a cultural institution rooted in the country: but for our participation, many cultural events in Bavaria would not exist. So the Bayerischer Rundfunk is – unlike commercial broadcasting organisations – a medium of Bavarian culture and at the same time a culture institute. It is the wide variety of programmes broadcast by public service stations which in turn makes the large number of private stations and programmes possible.

But since the same demands are by no means made of the private broadcasting stations, the picture of the supposed 'competition' is distorted. Cultural and educational programmes are an essential part only in the case of public service broadcasting; a fact which is sometimes overlooked.

Interestingly, in the judgement of the Federal Constitutional Court of the 4th November 1986, which was chiefly concerned with clarifying the position of public service and private broadcasting, the word education did not appear. The judges replaced the term education by 'cultural responsibility'. This can be interpreted to mean that the Federal Constitutional Court at that time wanted to break away from the narrow definition of education, to jettison the idea of reducing the remit to pure instructional programmes and to turn to the broad area of the humanities, as Rainhold Merkert concludes: Learning remains exciting if people can choose for themselves what they want to learn.[2]

The German media researcher Peter Nowotny, on the other hand, observed:

"The view that educational broadcasts should face up to the competition in the general programme rivalry and justify their existence seems to be growing . . . It is no longer adequate to argue by referring to the educational remit. What applies to the future for the systematised forms of learning in the integrated media, educational series and course programmes is that they must make a greater effort to improve quality and efficiency."[3]

I must, however, express my strong disagreement with a statement I found in the booklet *MEDIANET'92 Information* which attempted to explain the subject of our session. It said there:

---

[2] Cf. *FUNK-Korrespondenz*, No. 18, April 29, 1992.
[3] *FUNK-Korrespondenz*, No. 25 of 20th June, 1991.

"While the *attractiveness* of informational and educational programmes presented by public service broadcasting is *declining*, the programmes of the private stations dealing with culture and education leave much to be desired."[4] The latter statement is, of course, correct, but it is no longer possible to assert so generally that the attractiveness of the educational programmes is declining.

It is right, on the other hand, that the educational programmes have become more journalistic, react more quickly to events and also use the possibilities offered by entertainment. Thus the series *Alles Alltag*, an educational programme on the Ten Commandments, is presented exclusively in the form of professionally produced feature films. Professional actors have long been used in school and continuing education programmes as well; the formats 'reportage' and 'documentation' have become accepted in this section.

The responsible producers are moving away from the curriculum-oriented planning that used to be usual in their programme strategies. We often choose for broadcasts a form of presentation which could certainly be described as experimental; the use of all the means of graphic presentation – including computer animations – is almost a matter of course.

In the dual system, cultural programmes have a chance if they provide important information on cultural events in society and if they continue the discussion in the programme on what is being discussed in society. However, cultural programmes must not concern themselves for the most part with elitist subjects.

Talking about 'elitist': Who actually wants cultural broadcasts, who looks at them? Allow me here to refer to a few figures from the large-scale representative ARD/ZDF study *Kultur und Medien* (Culture and Media).[5]

Only 12.7% of all Germans can be described as belonging to the 'culturally-interested core audience'. Around 11% have practically no contact with culture in their neighbourhood and in the media, and 31.3% are 'occasional users' of culture; they are to be found most frequently among the 30- to 49-year-olds. The study described 45% of the population as 'entertainment orientated', which applies especially the 14- to 29-year-olds.

Another finding of the study indicates that ". . . the cultural reality beyond popular culture is virtually 'ignored' by the commercial channels, especially RTL plus, SAT 1 and Tele 5".[6]

---

[4] Cf. *MediaNet '92 Informationen*. München: MediaNet – Internationale Filmwochen GmbH, p. 22.

[5] Berg, Klaus; Maletzke, Gerhard; Müller-Sachse, K.-H.: *Kultur und Medien. Angebote – Interessen – Verhalten*. Eine Studie der ARD/ZDF-Medienkommission. Baden-Baden: Nomos 1991. (Publication Series *Media Perspektiven*, Vol. 11)

[6] Cf. *Der Tagesspiegel*, June 23, 1991.

But let me also refer here to the fact that so-called 'interested minorities' of television viewers expressed in *absolute* figures are quite considerable: Every cultural television broadcast no doubt reaches far more viewers than, for example, the staging of a play or opera can. From that point of view, the competitive character exists not only with regard to the commercial stations but also has to be seen in the overall context of a society's cultural institutions.

In a competitive environment, however, producers of cultural and educational programmes have to show even more consideration for the needs of the recipients. For example, it is currently very important to familiarise the people who will be mobile in the Europe of the future and have to work in different countries with the appropriate languages and living habits of their European neighbours.

Thus our colleagues at the BBC are, for example, producing programmes for European secretaries; with the magazine *Euroklick* we have created a journalistic educational programme which deals exclusively with subjects from the European world of work.

The Bayerischer Rundfunk plays a decisive role in developments that are important in media politics and in culture such as EINS PLUS and the Franco-German culture channel ARTE.

Cultural and educational programmes – they should not be seen in too narrow a framework – are the 'staple food' of a public service system and are, as the example of Bavarian Television shows, in the meantime also seen as genuine alternatives to the conventional programme offerings, when one thinks, for example, of programmes we transmit at 8.15 pm on Saturday evenings. These include series such as *Der Gelbe Fluss* (The Yellow River), *Die Seidenstrasse der Meere* (The Silk Routes of the Seas) and *Der Regenwald* (The Rainforests), programmes which inform and educate, but which through the attractive packaging of the contents can also fascinate large audiences.

Albert Scharf

On the Situation of Public Service Broadcasting in Dual Systems

In almost all European countries today two different broadcasting systems exist side by side. I am deliberately avoiding the expression "dual system". Although it has become widely accepted, it is wrong. Nowhere is there a really dual system. One would understand by dual system that one sector could replace the other. But that is precisely not the case. Thus for both sectors of such a system there is, on the one hand, a guarantee of independent developments – depending on its own conception – but, on the other, this also results in awkward problems.

And this brings us to the situation of public broadcasting. This term implies for me institutions like the BBC in Britain, France 2 and France 3 in France or the RAI in Italy and Sveriges Radio in Sweden, to name only a few examples. Apart from the niceties of the legal structure, our position on the so-called market, which has arisen as a result of such parallel broadcasting concepts, is the same. This position is as difficult as it is fascinating. The broadcasting landscape has changed, but not the task of those who were here before and still are here – and according to the whole concept are to stay here, because their task, their mission, was never more important than it is now.

It is the task of these public service broadcasters – as it says succinctly in the rulings of the Federal Constitutional Court – to guarantee a basic provision. By this one understands not only the staple intellectual food, the bread and water as it were, which is indispensable for living in a cultural society. Basic provision is far more. It means ensuring the best possible broadcasting provision in all areas, for all sections of the population, throughout the country and in the comprehensive classical spectrum of the broadcasting remit, as it was similarly once descriptively defined by the Federal Constitutional Court: information – culture – entertainment.

This task of the public service broadcasters has not changed; but the audio-visual environment in which this task has to be fulfilled now and in the future certainly has. On the one side, broadcasting as a public service in the broadest sense of the term: a service for everyone, i.e. for large and small audiences, depending on the contents, the occasion and the target group. On the other side are the broadcasting companies which are geared towards economic success and commercial profit. I am not criticising that, for this other concept is legitimate. It is only different, it is a basically different concept.

Our programme planning has to appeal to everyone: all strata and all interests of society. For those others it is imperative to design their programmes with a constant eye to mass appeal in order to finance the system — as is consistent with a commercial market.

Some time ago a German politician asked in the course of a conversation with the programme directors of one of the major American networks: "What criteria do you use to decide which programme you are going to make?" The executive vice president responsible replied: "That is quite simple: the question is 'Does it sell to a big enough audience'." Big enough here refers to the financing and greatest possible profit.

Education and culture 'don't sell', it is said. The average audience ratings for broadcasts labelled as cultural or educational programmes are no incentive for the advertising industry and not adequate for them to finance a programme commercially — apart from exceptions where there is interest in certain programme strands. What is interesting for advertising is what attracts 20 or more per cent of the viewers. Here from the start cultural programmes only stand a chance in very exceptional cases.

Even if they reach one hundred per cent of their target audience — of all potential viewers perhaps three to five per cent, more rarely as many as ten per cent, switch on their television sets. That is not enough to do business with. Nevertheless, this audience — as we know, and as the legislation also recognises — is important. This section of society, too, demands that its interests should be served by radio and television and this section also wants relaxation, entertainment, sport . . .

It must therefore be the task and ambition of public service broadcasting to reach this audience in the best possible way. Not in order to provide itself with an alibi, but because this is an essential part of its task and because it is important for society that mass media also impart culture and that culture is incorporated into societal communication. Incorporated into that kind of communication of which the audio-visual media — unfortunately or thank heavens — are nowadays the most prominent producers, and that far beyond what other communication institutions such as theatres, universities, schools, adult education centres and scientific societies can achieve. Of course, anyone wanting and having to perform this service must not be pushed aside into an esoteric ghetto of the culturally-minded, of minute splinter audiences.

If we want to reach small varied target audiences with cultural interests we also have to offer programmes which appeal to majorities; majorities from which the smaller audience entities then emerge. For it must not be forgotten that the maximum four or five per cent who watch an opera on television are also potentially contained in the 51 per cent who saw the European Cup Final.

And, as we all know, especially through the programmes with a mass appeal, channel connections come about which hold people over and beyond their own interests and which no longer result in that selection which the remote control theoretically makes possible.

One wants to see something different on the channel on which one has experienced the mass-appeal programme: information and also education and culture. In the discussion on media politics it is occasionally said that public service programmes should be mainly determined by culture, whereas commercial programmes should be entertaining. This phrase is foolish and would, in the last analysis, lead to culture being finally ousted altogether from audio-visual broadcasts.

In the United States we have experienced how a different concept, which did not perform this service for everyone as described, came into being, gained in strength over the decades and finally had a monopoly. And how a complementary system was introduced there, in the reverse order from us in Germany, which was intended to back up the commercial programmes in order to offer what the latter did not achieve and were unable to achieve on account of their financing strategies. This, however, did not turn out to be a great success.

We had a chance to do it the other way round: to establish the commercial system which was complementary to what already existed and covered the entire spectrum of societal interests. Offering programmes with a mass appeal does not mean having to join in doing everything that is possible or usual. When I unquestionably support the idea that the public service programmes must continue to be in a position to attract majority audiences – that means also offering entertainment, sport or feature films in the most attractive way possible – it still remains essential that their own profile has to be demanded of them: quality in form and contents and not adapting to that level which apparently is inevitable for commercial reasons. This is by no means meant as a reproach to the taste of the programme directors concerned; it simply has to be seen as a logical conclusion from the law under which they have taken up their work.

We must not try to win this contest in the area of mass programmes on the lowest level. What is important for public service broadcasting is that it has an alternative to offer at practically every time of day. The alleged obsession of the public service broadcasting stations that is repeatedly pointed out to fill up every frequency and every channel with something or other to oust other broadcasters is a completely false representation as far as the motivation is concerned.

When the ARD has a chance to offer a major joint national television programme designed to have a mass appeal and at the same time to back up this joint programme in the Third Programmes with the above-mentioned cultural elements, this occurs with the claim that altogether the whole spectrum of the classical broadcasting assignment is being fulfilled. This is fulfilled from another point of view and in an effort to offer different types of broadcasts and these at different times of the day with alternative contents and other types of programmes.

It is not the intention to compete, at the same time, against the feature film, the talk show or whatever else it may be just in order to offer competition by means of another public service programme to, let us say, ten commercial broadcasters in the hope of being better or worse than these others. This is an important element of the position which public service stations have to contribute to the discussion.

The same applies to Eins Plus or 3 Sat or ARTE: in each case a different programme for an audience which is observably or presumably different, even if it is not an audience that can be brought together in masses.

Moreover, culture and education cannot be so clearly separated from the other tasks of public service broadcasting, from information and entertainment as much of the polemics in media-politics seems to insinuate. All parts are elements of a uniform assignment vis-à-vis society. At this point one should really discuss the different ideas of the terms culture and education. But only a few points can be mentioned here.

Article 4 of the Bavarian Broadcasting Law – as an example of similarly worded tasks of public service broadcasting corporations – shows that there is more to it than merely stating the categories education, information and entertainment. Something is added which applies to all three elements of this task: a democratic attitude and cultural responsibility. And this also applies to entertainment programmes, for example the presentation of sport or whatever it may be.

Humaneness and objectivity, the specific character of one's home region, the characteristics of one's origin, the experience of life in one's surroundings – to impart all this independently of the saleability of the goods or ability to purchase them as cheaply as possible on the world market is also a task of public service broadcasting. To offer a programme in which someone feels at home, where the homeless person finds a home, to put it in rather exaggeratedly philosophical terms – this, too, is a constituent part of the cultural function of such a service to society.

Culture and education is therefore not to be understood formally and not too narrowly. Education is presented not only in programmes which have previously been generally described as educational programmes: a term which is possibly now used to a lesser extent as a collective term for instructional programmes, teaching programmes, school broadcasting, school television, Telekolleg, language courses and the like. Certainly the function of such programmes within the framework of the overall task should not be underestimated. These programmes were – and continue to be – the tasks of public service broadcasting because they have filled in gaps in the existing educational system which nobody else could have covered in a comparable time and with comparable effort.

But that is only one aspect under the heading of education by the broadcasting media. Our own language usage leads us, so I believe, to narrow down what has been set us as our task.

As obvious as it may be that the organisational patterns of the broadcasting corporations contain a department for culture and in addition a department for politics and current events, music or drama, it always has to be considered how a little culture and education in a programme providing political information or even in a family series can be transferred to the audience in these other areas as well: cultural responsibility as a principle for shaping the entire programme.

It is precisely at this point that our own considerations have to begin under the given circumstances when we know that in the competition with programmes of a different kind and objective we have to show an independent profile, an independent identity, an unmistakable image, as it is occasionally put. In reality education occurs in a wide variety of ways in broadcasting. In reality culture (hopefully) manifests itself not only in programmes which are put on by the Culture Departments. The whole programme, including entertainment, should be a contribution to the culture of society.

And now to come to a notion which makes it clear what little importance I attach to formal categorisations: for me education is the always uncompleted result of a constant process of experience which is fed by the differently intended and even unintentional elements and factors. Education cannot be learnt in some courses or years of apprenticeship. Conversely, education will never come about without imparted and acquired knowledge, without a realisation of what can be experienced.

So education as a constant process of experiencing — applied to the media — presupposes a constant effort on the part of broadcasting to impart such values of an extremely varied kind as result from experience. And here the fact that what is seemingly unintentional, not at first recognised by the recipient of our efforts as educational experience, can and at best should bring about education. This occurs in every kind of broadcast and in all areas. Culture therefore has to be interlaced and dovetailed with every programme and programme strand, as is, or should be, the case in the reality of societal life.

One could even express it more generally: a highly respected Italian diplomat of the old school wrote at one point in his memoirs that for him the whole discussion revolving around the term education was something strange. For in the end education — based on an appropriate upbringing and experience in life — was, he wrote, only acquired taste. A somewhat superficial term, one would say today, but this sentence, it seems to me, contains much that should induce us as a cultural medium to reflect.

It is what we can find in the 1891 edition of the Brockhaus encyclopaedia as "gesellige Bildung", which means something like "education to achieve sociability". There it says — expressed here somewhat more simply — that education calls for understanding and knowledge which allows one to pass judgement on everything that concerns a person as a participating world citizen. It requires a sensitivity and purity of feeling, a rapid and correct appraisal of the circumstances, an effortlessness and exercise of the mind in dealing with a multiplicity of forms, in short a subtle tact which is capable in conversation of attaching to each thought the right frame of reference, the most attractive meaning, the most fitting expression and the brightest colour.

One may feel that this quotation is old-fashioned or merely amusing; but if we turn it into modern language I could imagine that here we find precisely the independent profile of programmes for everyone which are accountable to the public: namely, to promote, to mould and shape society in its spirit and style and taste. An eminently cultural task and an eminent profile in contradistinction to programmes with other objectives. And for me that is, expressed briefly, the task of public service broadcasting in this competition, characterised by antagonisms, for the public in a pluralistic society. Let us hope that we do not amuse ourselves to death, but remain a discriminating, open cultural society.

Wolf Dieter Ring

Private Broadcasting and Public Responsibility

The German television programmes reach about 70 per cent of the population every day. During the prime time evening hours alone, some 30 million adults watch the television programmes. No other mass medium, nor any other cultural institute, has such a mass audience every evening, i.e. in the core leisure time of the population. For millions of people television is still the Number One leisure pastime, in spite of a decline in certain sections of the population.

The significance of television in our communication and leisure society is still unbroken. Television series determine fashion and *Zeitgeist*, impart behaviour patterns and social models and are capable of determining the way we spend our leisure time. Television shapes opinions, societal thinking and acting and has a direct influence on the development of political objectives.

When private broadcasting was introduced into Germany, television also became an important economic factor. Based on the audience ratings of the programmes, the advertisers are offered the chance to transmit commercials for payment. In order that they may provide the appropriate evidence of success, the private broadcasters are primarily dependent on programmes with a mass appeal.

This realisation and the possible negative effects on the quality of television led to a fierce debate which continued between the opponents and advocates for decades as the introduction of private broadcasting approached. The upshot is that a dual broadcasting system consisting of public service and private broadcasting came into being which in the meantime has been accepted by a broad audience of viewers.

Whether the range of programmes, the quantity of which has meanwhile greatly expanded, also entailed an improvement in quality is assessed in different ways, and this is hardly likely to be surprising. According to an analysis carried out jointly by ARD and ZDF media researchers the profile of the public service television is shaped quite clearly by its function to provide political and current information and to form opinion and give guidance.[1]

The profile of private television is, on the other hand, no less clearly determined by its function to entertain. The cultural performance of the private stations is

---

Cf. Darschin, Wolfgang; Frank, Bernward: Tendenzen im Zuschauerverhalten. Fernsehgewohnheiten und Fernsehreichweiten im Jahr 1991. (Tendencies in viewers' behaviour. Television viewing habits and coverage in 1991.) In: *Media Perspektiven*; -/1992/3 (March); pp. 172–187.

limited – according to the analysis – almost exclusively to the distributive exploitation of cultural goods produced elsewhere.

The relationship of culture and television – or, rather, the understanding of culture – is increasingly becoming the private television critics' criterion for the distinction between the programme profiles of public service and private programmes. Neil Postman is no doubt the most popular representative of the thesis of cultural decline as a consequence of the introduction of private television, which, however, he has deduced from the model of the purely commercial American television market.

This kind of cultural pessimism is, however, not a feature peculiar to our times. Whenever culture is presented in new forms, this phenomenon is encountered – it happened, for example, when entertainment was first broadcast on radio in Germany in 1923. A debate on culture soon set in which differed little from the current one. Reduced to a brief formula, the contents of this discussion can be reduced to simple terms by referring to the contrast between 'mass culture' and 'elite culture'.

But in essence the cultural debate, often conducted aggressively, is also concerned with questions of power distribution in our communication society. Especially when I bear in mind that private television programmes have to rely more on entertainment than on educational programmes I can agree with the statement of the Director General of the ZDF, Professor Dieter Stolte, which implicitly no doubt refers to public service television:

"Television cannot – at least in its main programmes – be solely concerned with showing only elite culture which then finds very few viewers, nor can it present only mass culture, which is measured by the extent of its dissemination, but it must endeavour to avoid both the dangers and one-sidedness of elite culture and those of popular culture."[2]

The public service broadcasting corporations and the private companies reverse the emphasis they put on these respective cultural approaches. The legal basis imposes different assignments on them. The public service corporations have an absolute obligation to provide information and education which they have to fulfil in the interests of all. Only in this way can the funding by means of licence fees be justified. Apart from this, they can also attract regular viewers by offering entertainment with a mass appeal.

In contrast to this, the emphasis of the private broadcasters is on entertainment programmes, sport and 'infotainment'. This accentuation does not and must not

---

[2] Stolte, Dieter: Fernsehen und Kultur. Anmerkungen zu einem problematischen Verhältnis (Television and culture. Comments on a problematic relationship.) In: Walter Nutz (Ed.): *Kunst, Kommunikation, Kultur*. Festschrift zum 80. Geburtstag von Alphons Silbermann. Frankfurt am Main (et al.): Peter Lang 1989; pp. 203 – 219.

reclude the possibility of private television companies also offering cultural programmes which have less of a mass appeal. In addition to general minimum requirements, ensuring that the programmes are varied and balanced is an obligation of broadcasting financed by advertising revenue.

This has been established by decisions of the Federal Constitutional Court and also reappears in the regulations of the latest inter-state agreement of the governments of the Laender on broadcasting in the united Germany[3] as well as in the individual laws of the Laender relating to the media and broadcasting. According to the former, as high a degree as possible of balanced diversity has to be ensured in private broadcasting as well. A 'full programme' within the meaning of the inter-state broadcasting agreement is ,, . . . a broadcasting programme with diverse contents in which information, education, advice and entertainment constitute an essential part of the overall programme".[4]

According to the programme principles of this inter-state agreement on broadcasting, the full private programmes are meant to contribute an appropriate proportion of information, culture and education in order to present the diversity in the German-speaking and other European countries. In addition, full television programmes should contain a considerable share of their own productions as well as commissioned and joint productions from the German-speaking and other European countries.

Although no percentage rates for programmes or productions have been laid down, the terms of the agreement make it quite clear that in private television the three programme areas information, education and culture have to be given adequate consideration apart from entertainment. The German broadcasting system thus clearly differs in its private form from the purely commercial system in the USA. The framework of regulations laid down in the inter-state broadcasting agreement applies to both areas of our dual broadcasting system.

In the case of the public service corporations there will be no increase in the superficiality of the programme, because then they would lose their special privilege of being funded by licence fees. On the other hand, the precautionary measures taken for private broadcasting prevent it from covering only the entertainment area.

The *Landesmedienanstalten* − the control bodies of the individual Laender for private broadcasting − are well aware of their public responsibility and must in future pay greater attention to their role as guardians. In the competition for market shares and audience ratings we cannot allow questionable ways of holding on to

---

3 Staatsvertrag über den Rundfunk im vereinten Deutschland (Inter-State Agreement on Broadcasting in a United Germany) of 31.8.91.
4 Ibid., Section 2, Paragraph 2.

the viewers to be resorted to. In this connection key words such as sex and violenc' have to be mentioned. How seriously these problems are being taken in the meantim' by large sections of the public I can see from numerous letters we have receive' from a great variety of groups and organisations, especially in recent weeks.

Private television addresses a broad public. Every evening the private stations no' reach a prime time audience of 10 million adults. They thus have an obligatio' towards the public. In future we shall make more use of the sanctions provide' by the inter-state agreement on broadcasting whenever a breach of existing legislatio' occurs. Over and beyond the area of pure infringements of the law, it will in futur' be a question of the private broadcasters becoming more aware of their publi' responsibility than hitherto. It is one of the duties of the *Landesmedienanstalte'* to sharpen the eye for journalistic responsibility.

The symposium ,,Cultural and Educational Programmes on Television – Deficiencies and Chances in a Competitive Media Environment'' also fits into thi' context. We have quite deliberately and with pleasure prepared this event togethe' with the *Internationales Zentralinstitut für das Jugend- und Bildungsfernsehen* (IZ' because in this area we can certainly see chances for both systems which have no' yet been taken advantage of. We are hoping that this symposium will provide man' ideas and suggestions for improving the acceptance of existing programmes, bu' above all for possible new ways of offering cultural broadcasts on television.

For thousands of people engaged in the cultural sector television is today alread' their main source of income. It is important for the further development of televisio' to contribute towards safeguarding the existence of this potential by increasing th' number of our own and commissioned productions and to expand this creativ' potential by stepping up our efforts in vocational and in-service training. It is her' that the great chance lies for present and future television broadcasters in ' competitive environment.

Alfred Payrleitner

What do the Media Want? –
What does the Audience Want?

It seems to me to be a lucky coincidence that at the end of this session a media practitioner from the monopoly country per se, Austria – the only one remaining among the Western democracies – has been given an opportunity to address you on both the future intentions of the public service broadcasting stations and on the assumed or already recognised viewers' wishes.

I do indeed come from a kind of land of milk and honey – so it appears, at least –, from a public service paradise: for apart from terrestrial broadcasting from abroad and the satellite and cable programmes, which we in Austria are also faced with, of course, the ORF has so far been used to acting like the only star in the show. It is incredible but true that until recently ORF Television with its two channels had a market share of over 80% – I repeat, 80%.

This situation can be explained by several circumstances: firstly, by the geographical location of our country, whose mountains in the west make it very difficult for German-language programmes to penetrate directly, while in the flatter, eastern part we are surrounded by competitors who use other languages. Secondly, Austria is far too small for the transmission of independently produced, full private programmes. This, in turn, encourages the country's political parties to continue to adhere to the domestic broadcasting monopoly; only in the private radio sector does anything seem to be happening.

In spite of and because of this, we are, however, fully aware that this public service Utopia is an outdated model and that even the ORF is in for a drastic and epochal change. Or rather, we are already in the midst of this upheaval, the pollsters furnishing us with clear data: in satellite and cable households, which, together with the areas in Austria accessible terrestrially from abroad, already account for half of all television households, the Austrian share of the market has in recent times dropped from 80% to currently 42%.

Added to this is the clear example of our German sister stations – reason enough to wake up from all the monopoly dreams. By the end of this decade or even earlier it can be expected that Austria will in fact be fully supplied electronically with competitive German-language programmes. So we assume by projecting the development hitherto that by 1997 83% of the Austrian television households will already have the necessary means of receiving foreign stations. That is probably sufficient to start worrying about what we should and what we can do – and how both can be brought into line with what the public wants.

In my capacity as responsible Head of the Main Department Science and Education I shall express some of the realisations we have come to as a result of concrete experience, and not of speculations and conjectures. In this connection, I am drawing on ORF's Infratest findings and a comprehensive market research study which we commissioned in the autumn of last year on the problems of imparting culture by broadcasting.

Realisation No. 1

The times of euphoria about popular education by television are over. The hope that television might turn out to be a new kind of electronic royal road to learning, something like a funnel into which you fill the educational programme at the top and the completely enlightened and responsible citizen comes out at the bottom, was naive and mechanistic.

That applies in particular to everything that smacks of school in any way: the mass medium television and school have gone separate ways. It is true that inasfar as television has a public service remit they do have related functions, but can only fulfil them in a complementary way at best.

Our responsibility is not to be education officials, but television journalists who have to bear in mind, in addition to the relevance of what is offered, above all our craft, the way in which contents are imparted. We are stimulators, we motivate people to take an interest in knowledge, no more – but that alone is difficult and expensive enough.

It cannot be any more than that, because not only the laws of the market but also of perpetual psychology and television drama are opposed to what is merely connected with school. School television as we know it up to now is a concrete example: as from the autumn of this year it will lose its morning and late afternoon broadcasts; although they have been going on for decades they will be discontinued on account of the proven indifference of the viewers. This is being done in agreement with the Ministry of Education, which has realised that it is senseless to try to reach individual target groups by the mass medium of television.

Minorities who are willing to learn can avail themselves of the old familiar video disc, which can be interrupted and repeated as required, or the exciting new world of CDI, the interactive disc, which allows interactive navigation. In other words questions can be asked not only on a hierarchical but also a horizontal level. As most of you probably know, a single CD contains as much information as you can type onto 350,000 sheets of paper — a veritable treasure trove of ideas for the next decade, which should ensure the permanent occupation of thousands of teachers and popular educators.

I can only recommend everyone to grant themselves the intellectual pleasure of searching for terms, persons or events in one of the latest electronic encyclopaedias, and that with the chance of being able to narrow down what you are looking for not only from the text but also using sound quotations and pictures. Individual and group use is replacing collective use. But what this offers is more specific and can be tailor-made.

Realisation No. 2

We thus have to abandon the idea that we can reach and thereby educate everybody equally well and equally efficiently. Television and the other media as well fail if someone cannot or does not want to educate him or herself. We have to accept this; there is no other choice.

Realisation No. 3

Should there be such a thing as 'cultural socialisation' — and, of course, there is — it is largely determined by the home. About three-quarters of all respondents interested in culture interviewed in the above-mentioned study also had culturally-interested parents, one-third of whom were themselves active in art or science. (Most of them, by the way, gave reading as their most frequent cultural pursuit.) They found the programmes offered by television to be an interesting and essential additive, a stimulating extra.

In this connection the effect of the school can, by the way, only be perceived very ambivalently — some felt that it motivated and supported them to educate themselves, while others reported on off-putting experiences. In all cases it no doubt depended on the quality of the particular teacher as to what the educational endeavours did or did not achieve. From the age of 16, it also turned out, cultural socialisation has only little chance, since by that time the way ahead is already programmed.

Realisation No. 4

The influence of the electronic media on cultural socialisation lags far behind the above-mentioned formative effects. Sound radio culture is well and truly beaten by the television programmes. Pure cultural programmes are only listened to by those extremely interested in culture – it would be pointless to deceive ourselves on that.

Conversely, this phenomenon can also be interpreted positively: once somebody is culturally formed, he or she is usually quite satisfied with the appropriate special programmes offered by the mass medium; and the question is reproachfully asked again and again as to why what was broadcast was not presented in far more detail and much greater depth; or complaints are made about the programme being transmitted too late or too early. Thus a greater division into various qualified minorities can be observed – one could also remark that we are living in a kind of information class society.

All in all, it is the expression of the fact that the fine-sounding briefs of the various broadcasting laws alone are not sufficient. The legislator wants the education of young people and the public generally to be spread, adult education in particular to be promoted, cultural matters to be imparted, but to achieve this two are necessary, the communicator and the recipient – and the latter is not placed under any obligation by these laws.

In Austria the situation is still further aggravated by the fact that the ORF can neither attract people with the bait of academic degrees nor threaten them with bad exam marks – thus we are not familiar with the established institution of the *Telekolleg I* and *Telekolleg II* which to your great credit you run here in Germany.

Although the ORF wanted to set up something similar along the lines of the Open University 20 years ago, this never came about because of political requirements and endless squabbling among the parties on how they were to be represented proportionally. At that time we would still have had an unchallenged monopoly. Today, faced with an explosive increase in competition and with advertising providing a 52% share of our total revenue, we cannot even start to think about programmes like the Telekolleg. The only option we have is to *secretly persuade* people to take in information and consume culture, with constant competition from innumerable other 'persuaders'.

The obvious question is what has happened to the positive aspect. The same market studies and our Teletest, which, unlike in Germany, also gives marks for quality, furnish quite clear information on how, in spite of everything, the public, or certain sections of the public, can be reached. At this point I have to correct the title of this paper 'What does the audience want?' It is not so much a matter of *what* the viewers want, but of *how* they want to have it. On no account do they want it in any form of instruction or like a school classroom.

Max Scheler realised this decades ago, and without any reference to television: Education, he wrote, does not take place where it is explicitly aimed at, such as

n school, but preferably behind the educator's back, in other words when it is
ot explicitly intended. When education is provided seemingly free of any purpose
nd without any finger-wagging, it is accepted. At least then it does not get in the
vay. Education, Gerd Bacher once put it, has to come ‚from behind', in other words
reep into one's consciousness more or less by cunning, insidiously.

`he ORF's cultural study from the previous year confirms this. If those interested
n culture and education are asked what they long for, they first mention the
presenters or, rather, what people apparently miss in the ORF's usual presenters,
amely 'easy-going, humorous, casual but at the same time well-informed and
ompetent behaviour'. They want a pleasant appearance, clear, good language and
lothing appropriate to the broadcast, self-confidence, 'without any affectations
r smugness' and without the presenter pushing himself too much into the
oreground.

`he subject of culture should remain the chief concern. Competence should be
ombined with an easy-going manner, sound knowledge with clear language. Just
s interesting are the ideas of the 'ideal cultural broadcast' per se. In this connection,
vhat is looked for is that two values should be aimed at – 'democratic' and
relaxed'. Democratic, it turns out on closer questioning, also refers to the manner
f imparting culture – it should not be done condescendingly, from the person
vho knows to the person who is ignorant, but in a 'democratic way'.

t is precisely those interested in culture who apparently have the feeling that they
re manipulated and indoctrinated by an authoritarian manner of presentation.
`hey always want several people with different attitudes to be allowed to speak;
here should be more pros and cons. They also want to hear what the visitors to
 gallery say, how they disagree with one another, but not preconceived value
udgements.

ll that is reason for hope, since it indicates that it is often only mechanical
ifficulties that have up to now resulted in our failure to impart culture. Education
as to be seen as a perfectly natural part of normal journalistic broadcasts, for
xample, of the news services, and I am proud that the news about culture is part
f our daily programme *Zeit im Bild*, and that has now been the case for almost
 quarter of a century.

culture and education – the terms merge into one another, that is why I use them
lternatively – have to become a ritual that is taken for granted, a habit. It is this
egularity that the viewers want and on which they insist – and that is the reason
hy they first recall the daily *Kulturjournal* when they are asked about this subject.
t is also interesting that all those culturally interested who were interviewed by
s do appreciate the transmission of operas and plays, but almost always prefer
 be personally present in the theatre or opera house. According to the motto:

If it's live, then it's best to be there in person. I regard this as a completely understandable and proper reaction.

This clearly illustrates what media people have long known and what in German countries is apparently so difficult to put into practice: both those especially interested in culture but also the average public certainly do not like to be given a reason to be annoyed when they watch television in the evening wanting to remain with one programme.

What can best be used to persuade the public can be assigned to Schiller's old categories of emotion and aesthetics: "It is through beauty that the sensuous person is made to think." Friedrich Schiller expressed it so plainly and it is so reluctantly heard in quite a lot of culture and science production departments – not to mention those concerned with politics.

If in addition to beauty and emotion there is a really intelligible, simple text that makes an effort to explain matters calmly, the viewer is almost magically absorbed. Beauty, emotional variety and clarity are the clearly recognisable merits of those outstanding BBC documentations that we show in our *Universum* series on Tuesday and my colleagues at the Bayerischer Rundfunk in the main evening programm on Saturdays. Here both stations have managed to create a habit-forming effec which has resulted in the most important thing of all you can achieve in our job in the development of brand goods.

Irrespective of whether it is a daily news broadcast or an invariable programm at weekly intervals: Once the idea of quality has been established, it is accepted with gratitude by the public, which does not go in for 'channel surfing' as much as is always supposed. All our Infratest findings prove, by the way, that this information public, i.e. the consumers of news, culture and science, is made up of extremely regular customers.

Thus in our Teletest we also compile our so-called 'Loyalty Index', which gives the figure that indicates how much of a broadcast is taken advantage of. The higher the Loyalty Index, the longer the average time the viewer watched a broadcast. In the case of our daily news broadcast *Wissen Aktuell*, for which one has to deliberately switch from a popular broadcast on events in the federal states to the first channel, we have a Loyalty Index of 98% in the winter season and an audience rating of about 8%. That is a reliable, regular audience with whom it is possible to build up a genuine programme relationship to be cultivated in the appropriate way.

The hope for the future of our cultural and educational programmes is to be seen in all these merely implicitly mentioned directions. While the era of the public service operators as electronic solo entertainers moves towards its end, there arises on the other hand the chance of turning one's mind back to the intrinsic values for which our broadcasting stations were actually created.

This, of course, does not mean resignation, but increased effort – for the qualities of the above-mentioned kind are neither cheap nor to be acquired in a fast and ingratiating way. We must never fall for the poor excuse that with *this* public we no longer stand a chance. Firstly, *the* public no longer exists, but only a sum of different minorities which very often overlap, and, secondly, we must also abandon the idea that we have to reach everyone.

Although all that is a truism, it has not yet got around in some areas, especially at the public television stations. Similar to another principle the great John Ford coined in the matter of making films. It is simply: ,,Never bore".

All this does not constitute an argument in favour of an uninhibited expansion of entertainment into the area of culture and education. I only wish that all those on television who are very educationally and culturally-minded would remember the actual strengths of this medium, which are:

– clarity and changing rhythm,
– regularity of the programme offer, and
– consideration for all the experience gathered from the information programmes as a whole.

When culture and education present themselves with clear labels and affectations, they have already lost. But they have also lost when they seek to force something onto the public which it simply does not want.

A further example to demonstrate this: in 1990, the ORF, on the basis of almost 200 programme categories, assessed the so-called programme interest which a representative cross-section of viewers was willing to take in certain broadcasts – at least as it was expressed orally. The data refer to percentage values, and the first three and the last three from this table shall be referred to as they are especially typical, but in some cases also surprising.

Zeit im Bild, our main news broadcast, received top marks for interest with 63%. This was followed by the big Quiz Show with 49%. But it is particularly surprising that the category Science Documentary ('Wissenschaftsdokumentation') gained 48%. The television crime thriller trails behind with 47%.

Two points are worth noting about this: Evidently the need for orientation and knowledge to aid orientation is extremely great – people want to know all about this world. But, secondly, it also has to be stated that the actual audience ratings contradict this theoretical need.

On Friday, for example, the Science Documentary is competing with the big crime series, and the easy-going science programme is left trailing by the crime film, which attracts two to three times as many viewers. So there is a great difference between the answer and actual behaviour.

Even so, one should not allow oneself to be greatly influenced by this. For on Tuesdays, our classical *Universum* day, when great subjects are dealt with such as geography and the history of culture, animal documentations, cosmology and archaeology or enthnography, we do not beat the crime films, it is true, − there are none on that day to compete with − but at least we beat the competition from the entertainment programmes with the greatest of ease.

It seems to me that here is emerging what recently was borne out to some extent by the print media: namely that the public as a whole does change. Only last week it was disclosed that the management of the Springer publishing house is considering modifying its policy with regard to the newspaper *Bild:* evidently the readers were becoming rather more highbrow and gradually the education explosion of the last few decades was beginning to be felt. In Hamburg they cannot find any other explanation for the losses in circulation of as many as 500,000 copies in the first quarter of this year.

This trend does not surprise me, and it is corroborated by the sustained results of our *Universum* series on Tuesday which are extremely satisfactory both with regard to the audience rating and the marks it is given. Here, too, the high loyalty coefficient for this series among the consumers has to be pointed out. In the case of entertainment there is the notorious 'entertainment slalom' − one switches to the most exciting quiz, to the best film, to the hardest crime thriller. But you stay with orientation programmes once you have become familiar with them.

The three sorts of programmes that bring up the rear in the survey quoted above must still be mentioned. There is hardly any demand for all three of them on television, and those interviewed do not even feel obliged to make out to the interviewer that they are better than they actually behave. The three at the bottom of the table are: Readings, modern operas and orchestral concerts of modern music. (I exclude the one at the very bottom, the programme for guest-workers, because it only concerns a completely different minority.)

What can be concluded from all this? Firstly: the most important thing when working in the mass media is to know your job. If all those who do not understand how to do it were excluded from the production of educational and cultural programmes the situation would be much better.

Secondly, I am convinced that in the case of the great duel between public and commercial broadcasting it is not a matter of staging a cultural apocalypse, which is allegedly inevitable anyway, but that there are also such things as saturation points for the spread of stupidity and banality. As everywhere in the affluent society, it is not merely the demand that counts in the area of television either, but also the supply, which creates new needs.

44

The public cannot wish for something it does not yet know. If you create reliably repeated quality information programmes which are journalistically first-class productions then you undoubtedly have good chances on the market. But we must note, too, – or certain producers of cultural programmes must do so – that not everything can be conveyed by the mass medium.

Anyone wanting to encode even further an already extremely complex civilisation by the form and contents of his messages is, I am convinced, a square peg in a round hole in the mass medium – and in the end he even cheats the public, depriving it of the achievement of someone who imparts culture and knowledge, for which he is paid as an artist or producer.

We should all honestly consider how we can really help a more or less interested public to understand and enjoy the world. That is our big chance. In other words, one should try to *love* the public – the 'enemy' as we sometimes call it in our professional jargon – even if it is difficult at times. There is, you see, no other recipe for success.

Chapter 2:
Public Service Broadcasting and the Market Situation

Léa Martel

Culture, Education and Training: New Challenges for Public Service Broadcasting

The situation

Public service television stations have been feeling the effects of the serious shocks caused by the storm of deregulation sweeping over the audio-visual world in Europe.

Purely commercial stations are running away with our audiences. The response made to this has consequences for the attitude of public service television stations towards their mandate, which is to inform, educate and entertain the public.

The best viewing figures of practically all stations are obtained by those programmes offering entertainment: sitcoms and other serials or 'soaps', sports reports and variety shows. News bulletins and topical programmes run up excellent scores at moments of great political activity or other important events.

But culture? And education? At the first stage, educational programmes, and cultural programmes in general, saw themselves relegated to the periphery in the majority of programme schedules, with the result that viewing figures were so disastrous that only the worst was to be feared for the future.

After this first period of panic, the European audio-visual landscape now seems to me to be developing in several directions, with a new balance becoming apparent between national and international channels with regard to subject matter and in other ways.

The mandate

In the good old days of national monopolies, the mandate to be fulfilled by public service radio and television did not cause much worry to those responsible for programmes . At the moment, it is setting us challenges. As in fact the licence fee forms our principal source of revenue, the obligation we have to provide a pattern of programmes attractive to different segments of society – which in plain language means that minority audiences cannot be excluded – very often results in low viewing figures. This could make the political authorities withdraw from us our present form of financing. But if we ignore the different segments of society, the reason for our existence as public service television would disappear!

So what is to be done? The financial threats and the unrestrained competition we are facing have stimulated the creativity of the life forces in our old organisations – which have all been around for more than 50 years – in the face of the dynamism of the young commercial channels. New styles of programme have been created, individualism and the 'art for art's sake' attitude have given way – still timidly – to a more outgoing spirit, resulting in a growing number of international coproductions.

At first, some organisations did away with their educational departments (DR), while others reduced their staffs and/or broadcasting times (RTBF, BRTN). On the other hand, educational broadcasts have also been offered supplementary transmission time (NOT) or have even been created, as in Spain, where the new education department of the TVE will commence broadcasting programmes on October 1, 1992. In Ireland the school television programmes that had been discontinued have reappeared!

The response

Instead of remaining on the defensive, those responsible have launched the counter-offensive. The cultural and educational programme has undergone a rejuvenation course and it is doing rather well on it. I will give you a brief idea of a multimedia series produced by the BRTN in autumn 1990. This was a television serial titled *Noordstraat 17* – a kind of 'soap' in ten 20-minute episodes dealing with the lives of a working-class family: father, mother, two children, a dog and a grandmother.

This series was specially produced as part of International Literacy Year. The incidents in the life of this family, in which numerous Flemish families recognised themselves, met with appreciable success from the first transmission on October 24 to the last, on December 26, 1990, these being broadcast on the first channel t 6.40 pm. The average viewing figures at 6.4% (335,000 viewers) corresponded o a market share of 26.4% and to an approval rating of 78%. During the period concerned the average figure achieved by the first channel (as a whole) was only 5.7%.

The educational 'soap' thus achieved better figures than the channel in general. It must be remembered that since 1989 the Dutch-speaking part of Belgium has been confronted with the unexpected spectacular success of a commercial channel (VTM, which has the monopoly of advertising revenue) and that public service television was thrown completely onto the defensive. The figures quoted prove that educational programmes do *not necessarily* result in a decline in audiences. On the contrary. The brief excerpt shown at this conference did not permit an adequate assessment of the educational value of this multimedia project. So where does its value lie?

The aim of the multimedia project was to familiarise a target audience of adults having a low level of education with the basic knowledge necessary for the individual to function well in society. An essential driving element with an important multiplier effect seemed to us to lie in the fact that it was a televised series which was expected to reach a wide audience. This aim has been attained, if the position allocated within the programme schedule and the viewing figures obtained are taken into consideration. Moreover, when it was re-broadcast in 1991 and 1992 on the second channel, which is targeted at a more specific audience than the first channel, the success was confirmed.

These television programmes were complemented and extended in a radio series specially intended for experts in basic adult education, additional information being made available by teletext and by video cassettes provided for the use of adult education centres.

The combination of these media, which lend themselves to both independent and joint use, has proved its effectiveness (if this point still has to be proved).

The example I gave of the educational series was only intended to demonstrate that education on television does not have to be synonymous with boring programmes.

Another example for our response to the new situation is an 8-part series of educational video clips that was intended to draw the public's attention to the problem of domestic and industrial waste *(Wie slim is, sorteert)*. The subjects shown in the clips were treated in depth in a series of 7 documentary programmes, and these were supplemented by a book.

The fact that new ways are being sought does not mean that 'instructional' programmes intending real learning processes have been abandoned − far from it. And, what is perhaps astonishing, this is a kind of programme that is doing well and, moreover, becoming more international.

Learning through television programmes is a well-known topic in Munich, where 30 years ago the Bayerischer Rundfunk started its *Telekolleg*. This still remains a model of its kind after so many years, and it must not be forgotten that the *Telekolleg* preceded the *Open University* in Great Britain.

Other more recent initiatives in numerous countries are to be found in a different context. Television has become the best kind of partner whenever a relatively large number of people need to be instructed or retrained in a relatively short period of time and at competitive cost.

I will give you a concrete example of another BRTN experiment that took place between September 1989 and January 1992. This was a large-scale project introducing teachers in Flanders to computers and computing *(Een computer ook in jouw klas)*. Two television series, one comprising seven and one nine programmes, familiarised Flemish teachers with the principles of informatics and taught them how to use the new information technologies in the different school disciplines. Four institutions took part in the project: the Education Department of BRTN and three departments of the Ministry of Education, in particular the service for correspondence courses, the educational media centre, which distributed the software and video cassettes of the television programmes, and the general teaching inspectorate, which organised practical training sessions.

This initiative aroused great enthusiasm but because of budgetary restrictions only 20,000 teachers were in the first instance able to benefit from the infrastructure that accompanied the television programmes. The video cassette of the transmissions continues to be actively used by teachers, and a new series is envisaged.[1]

I have already emphasised the interest that exists in the use of television as an instructional medium when groups of significant size require rapid instruction at competitive cost. There are other advantages: teaching is on a uniform level, it is accessible to all those interested – thus not only to the target audience. The multiplier effect is therefore not negligible. Moreover, the broadcasting of the courses created a certain amount of publicity around the event. This is an aspect very often neglected by those responsible for public service television.

Promotion

If there is a technique that is perfectly mastered by the commercial TV stations, it is that of programme promotion. Is it that our past as monopoly-holding organisations still has an effect on us in this respect? In fact, I have the impression

---

[1] An extract was shown from a programme which informs teachers how the computer can be integrated into courses for handicapped children.

hat the cultural departments in general and education in particular err on the side
of too much discretion. It is not enough to make good products, this must also
be made known.

This is what is done by the star presenter and producer of the BRTN magazine
Consumer Education. It is a programme transmitted every week. The producer
addresses himself directly to his audience, he takes part as a guest in a large number
of popular programmes, he is endlessly interviewed by the printed press and is a
great hit in terms of viewing figures. He produces an excellent programme but
without his promotional efforts he would certainly not figure so often in the top
ten of the 'hit parade' of the ratings.

The trump cards

Coming out of the shade — this is one of the challenges that those responsible for
programmes will have to answer. Taking stock reveals that there is no lack of trump
cards in our hand:

The rapid developments in society are creating enormous needs in the field of
training and retraining. This is equally true in the field of both private and working
life.

According to recent studies by the EC Commission in the 12 member states, more
than 85 million Europeans will have to be trained or retrained every year if we
wish to avoid being overtaken either by technological developments or by the great
industrial powers such as the United States and Japan, as well as by rapidly growing
economies of 'newly industrialised countries' such as South Korea.

The role that television can play here is a double one: on the one hand, that of
providing information about the need for instruction and about what training
possiblities are available, and, on the other hand, that of itself providing the training
programme.

The big corporations are increasingly getting away from the methods of traditional
training courses in favour of more flexible methods and the concept of distance
learning. Their advantages are numerous and well known: it is no longer the student
who has to move to receive instruction but the reverse. A traditional course takes
place in a well-determined period of time. Distance learning meets the needs of
the student. If it includes television (and thus video cassettes), the student can make
use of it to fit in with his own schedule and abilities.

Teaching by correspondence courses combined with television (and inevitably video)
has acquired a new dimension and is promised a good future. This is all the more
so as other complementary media are being added to the range. The interactive

compact disc has appeared on the market and constitutes a high-quality educational tool. Interactive television, which has been in existence for quite a long time in other continents, can work in our countries. All that needs to be done is to take the initiative. And what more than educational programmes could profit from it? This leads me to another trump card — a term I prefer to use instead of 'challenge'.

I am in fact convinced that we can transform these so-called challenges or even threats into trump cards. The educational departments are the only ones able to deal with *all* subjects since they are expected to provide their audiences with the keys, the instruments, enabling them to enjoy a better life and to defend their interests in our society.

Moreover, they must adopt the form and the speech best suited to their different target audiences. No kind of programme is therefore taboo for them. The excerpts I have shown from television serials, clips and documentaries have proved this. I could have also shown you variety programmes of great educational value. Because it has not yet been transmitted, I cannot show you an extract from our first interactive programme, which, with the casual appearance of a game but at a cultural level that is still interesting, in fact forms an initiation into education in the image media. For practical reasons, I am limited to the recent productions of my own organisation. If I had also drawn on the productions of my colleagues in other countries, you would have seen that the range of European educational productions is still infinitely wide and varied.

This simple enumeration of possiblities demonstrates, I hope, that educational television can also function as the laboratory in which tomorrow's television is being prepared. This is a valuable trump card, which is particularly dear to me. Television must not limit itself to serving as a vehicle for culture — it has a role at least as important to play as an instrument in its creation.

Viewing figures

One more word on those notorious audience ratings, which keep producers and presenters awake at night. It is rather rare for a strictly educational programme to be at the top of the 'hit parade'. And that is the way it should be. In contrast to general interest programmes, an educational programme on principle pursues a precise aim. It carefully chooses the subject, the form and the spin-off of a production to suit the target audience. It is in fact 'made to measure'.

The viewing figures should therefore be interpreted taking into account not the potential general public but the target public that is being aimed at. If the programme is addressed to a potential audience of 500,000 viewers, it is evident that there is no point in complaining that more viewers have not been reached. An audience f 300,000 people would itself constitute a very good market share. The *quality* f the audience makes up for the *quantity*.

n my opinion, the only problems concerning viewing figures are:

. Have we succeeded in reaching a representative fraction of the target audience?
. What is the potential minimum to be taken into consideration with regard to production and television transmission?

'elevision being a mass media and, moreover, extremely expensive, the potential udience and the audience-cost relationship must be carefully taken into onsideration. A correction to this policy could be made if the added value that elevision can give to the treatment of a subject exceeds that of all other usable nedia.

Coproductions and the European dimension

'elevision production costs, which have a tendency to overtake the increases due o the rate of inflation, as well as the almost general decline in the budgets available, ave caused television stations to look for diverse forms of association. We work nore and more in close collaboration with external bodies, with regard to finance, ontents or spin-offs. This may give rise to problems of editorial responsiblity but t also has the advantage of providing a better perception of the target audience.

The same trend can be seen at an international level. And at this level, the European 3roadcasting Union (EBU) has played and still plays a major role. The EBU offers ts members a privileged meeting place and a forum for discussion of all programme ategories. The Eurovision Song Contest and the traditional transmission of the New Year's Day Concert from Vienna would not have achieved the success they ave without the EBU.

The work carried out at the meetings of those responsible for programmes is not nown to the general public but it is there that numerous coproductions and other hings are prepared. In the last two years alone, about forty educational oproductions have come into being, and thanks to them it has been possible for he same pictures to be viewed not simply by a national but by a European audience, ncluding those in what is referred to as 'Eastern' Europe.

At the beginning of July 1992, during the General Assembly of the EBU at Oslo, he radio and television stations of Eastern Europe joined the EBU, which now orms a union of public service radio and television stations taking in 43 European ountries. This represents an enormous potential for exchanges and coproductions.

However, it is not so obvious that an educational production can be easily exported, ince it often owes its existence to regional or even local educational needs and characteristics. And let us not forget either the lingustic handicaps. Fortunately the range of subjects is sufficiently great for these obstacles to be overcome. Ou Finnish colleagues from YLE, for example, are now producing a course i commercial English in collaboration with other stations; from autumn next yea it will be shown practically all over Europe.

Another example is *Tales of Europe*, a series of 10 programmes presenting te European fairy tales, produced – using an exchange system – by six schoo television departments: NOT, YLE, RTSR, SR/UR, BBC and BRTN. The ain was to familiarise 7 to 9-year-old children with the fables of other Europea countries. A book published in all the languages concerned produced by NOT supplements the programmes.

A recent initiative in the field of vocational training seems to be particularl interesting. *Euro-Clic*, which was suggested by the BR, involves half a doze television stations: ARD/BR, RAI, BBC, DRS, FR3 and MTV. Every month al the partners send each other a reportage (free of rights) on a subject relating t vocational training and the job market. Each participant decides independently wha use is to be made of the productions supplied.[2] The production of programme dealing with vocational training was considerably stimulated by the creation of th CEDEFOP Prize in 1988 – at the instigation of the European Community – fo the best programmes produced in this field.

I would like to emphasise the importance of the European dimension in the majorit of our coproductions. It is also present in BRTN's series *Language Training*, th Belgian counterpart of the Bavarian *Euro-Clic*. Just a few words to set the scene Next to a swimming pool in Brussels some language teachers sitting around differen conversation tables are offering to anyone interested the opportunity to perfec his or her knowledge of a chosen language, completely without charge. Peopl coming from very different horizons are meeting here every week and improve thei command of a language in a pleasant way.

To sum up, I have been asked to talk about the challenges facing cultural an educational television stations in the new European environment dominated b competition and budgetary difficulties. If there are challenges – and there ar numerous and serious ones – nothing is preventing us from transforming then into trump cards. That is what I wanted to show. This is also the policy of th EBU's Working Party for Educational Programmes, of which I have the pleasur to be the President.

---

[2] The *Euro-Clic* sequence shown at the conference was produced by DRS and relates to the trainin of foreign hospital staff in a Swiss hospital at Thun; the story concerns a young Austrian nurs being trained in Switzerland.

Brian Wright

BBC Education and the New Broadcasting Environment

My colleague Jean Nunn and I will try to outline how BBC Education is responding to new environments and new challenges. It is a time of great change in the United Kingdom and, in both education and broadcasting, developments have been radical and rapid. In education, for example, all our schoolchildren are following a common national curriculum which, for the first time, includes science as a compulsory subject. There is increased emphasis on raising standards particularly in reading and writing and basic numeracy, and vocational training is more and more seen as central to the future economic well-being of our country.

In the world of broadcasting changes have come thick and fast. For example, there has been a move towards independent production, a new copyright law enabling schools and colleges to use all radio and television output for educational purposes and the emergence of an array of new technologies including satellites, interactive video and CDI. Most broadcasting organisations, not least the BBC, are reorganising themselves to make best use of their resources, both human and financial.

Before telling you how BBC Education is responding to these changes, however, I wish to provide a very brief background to two things about BBC Education: Firstly, how is BBC Education organised? And secondly: What is educational television? What does it look like? What is its range? What is it trying to do?

How is BBC Education organised?

As Figure 1 shows, there are a number of departments supervised by the Controller, Educational Broadcasting. These are the four production departments for School Radio and School Television, for Continuing Education Radio and Continuing Education and Training Television, and there are two support departments: Educational Broadcasting Services (EBS), headed by myself, and Educational Development and Information (EDI), headed and described later by Jean Nunn. Located outside of the BBC, but belonging organisationally to BBC Education, there is the Open University Production Centre in Milton Keynes responsible for the production of radio and television courses for the Open University's distance education scheme. We are currently in the process of drawing all these departments, together with our publishing activities, into a single integrated multi-media structure.[1]

Figure 1: Organisation of BBC Education

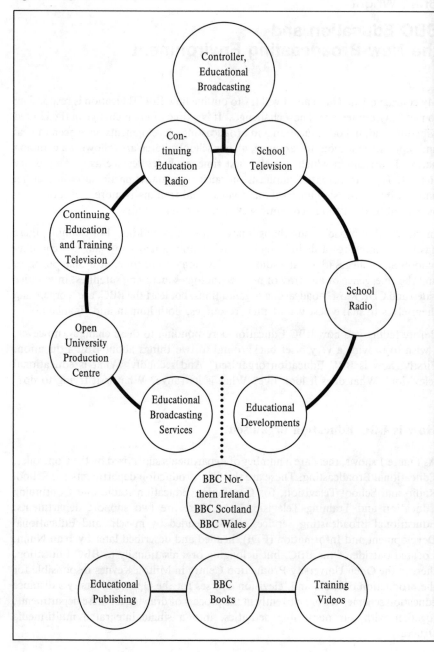

The main tasks of Educational Broadcasting Services are:

- to maintain close contacts with audiences in school or colleges or at home;
- to keep abreast of educational changes and ensure that educational programmes reflect these changes;
- to set priorities because there are many needs but only limited resources to meet them;
- to formulate policies which lead to programmes which are closely targeted to audiences' needs.

EBS achieves all these aims through its team of Education Officers, all of whom are experts in their fields and who act as the bridge between the BBC and the educational world. Roughly speaking, their job is, through constant contact with audiences and by analysing curriculum developments, to ensure that programmes fit schools' needs.[2]

What is educational broadcasting?

It is very difficult to give a flavour of educational broadcasting in a brief outline, since educational broadcasting is as rich and varied as all of broadcasting. It employs all the broadcasting techniques and genres – drama, documentary, animation, studio presentation, etc. Inevitably, the following is bound to be an over-simplification.

Educational broadcasts fall into two categories: on the one hand, there are those which are intended to be used by teachers and learners in schools and educational institutions; on the other, those which are for individuals viewing in their own homes.

School television broadcasts have three defining characteristics:

- they are carefully researched and produced to fit the schools' curriculum (this is where the Education Officers that I mentioned come in);
- they (almost always) assume that the teacher will mediate and extend the pupils' viewing experience;
- they are supported by back-up literature which lets the teacher know the aims and content of the programmes and makes suggestions about how the programme can be followed up.

---

[1] S. Part II: Background Information; Appendix to BBC Education, p. 237.
[2] A more detailed description of the manifold tasks and functions of Education Officers has been given by my colleague Julie Cogill in *"Aspects of School Television in Europe"*, ed. by Manfred Meyer; München: Saur 1992; pp. 201 – 07.

Adult or Continuing Education Television programmes are more difficult to categorise. They vary from

- programmes which form part of a course intended to help people acquire a knowledge or a skill, for example, learning a foreign language;
- programmes which encourage social action or change by helping people to improve the quality of their lives or their environment through health education, child accident prevention or being more environmentally-aware;
- programmes which provide vocational education and on-the-job training; to
- programmes which simply help people acquire or deepen an interest in, for example, gardening, cookery, literature or whatever.

However, nothing is better at giving you a flavour of broadcasting than broadcasting itself. So, let me conclude this part of our presentation by replaying you three brief extracts from very different programmes, each of which illustrates an aspect of educational television.

The first extract is from *Search out Science*, a series specifically designed for primary teachers who are required to teach science to 9 to 11-year-olds without themselves having much background in or knowledge of science. The series aims to encourage practical science involving exploration, investigation and problem-solving, and it employs a variety of teaching styles.

The extract shown came from a programme called *Sounding Out* which explored some of the properties of sound. It is demonstrated how loudspeakers can, by making air vibrate, blow out a candle.

One should notice that the presenter was a woman: in our programmes we always try to counteract stereotypes – e.g. that a scientist is a man in a white coat – and we try, too, always to reflect the increasingly multicultural nature of our society.

The second extract illustrates school television at its most adventurous and innovative. It is from a series on Roman history *(History File: The Romans)* that is intended for 11 to 12-year-olds. By using different types of evidence, the programmes try to build up a picture of what life of an ordinary Roman might have been like.

The extract replayed illustrated how, through the use of a variety of new technologies, a museum of virtual reality is created: The viewer is put in the position of a visitor, a girl called Melanie, to the 'Historical Interface Museum', where she is whisked back to Roman times as if she were a contemporary observer. By questioning the 'Curator' and by using the controls on her glove, she can call up all kinds of evidence: buildings, artefacts, texts, experts, reconstructions of different kinds. She uses these to pursue a different enquiry in each programme and so encounters the limitations, as well as possibilities, of the evidence available.

The extract is of interest, too, in that it appeals greatly to young people who are used to computer and video games and fast moving images with lots of different kinds of information being conveyed simultaneously on the screen.

Finally, an extract from a series for adults. *Play it Safe* was a series of short programmes which focused on child accident prevention. They were transmitted at peak-viewing times on Sunday evenings and were presented by a well-known television celebrity.

The programmes aimed to provide parents, child minders and health education professionals with advice on how to avoid or prevent accidents. A wide variety of topics was covered including accidents in the home, cycle safety and water safety. The extract shown vividly reconstructed an all too common accident, namely a young child falling downstairs.

The series is of additional interest in that it represents a type of activity BBC Education increasingly undertakes – that is there is a national campaign where we join with other partners to encourage people to acquire new skills or learn strategies to cope with issues such as literacy and numeracy, child accident prevention, returning to work or whatever.

Jean Nunn

Extending and Supporting the Educational Use of Broadcasts

My colleague Brian Wright has shown some examples of our educational programmes, the structures through which they are made and the audiences for whom they are designed.

I will refer to the theme of BBC Education and its markets by addressing the ways in which we extend and support the educational use of broadcasting. This falls into two elements:

– First and foremost we can extend the use of the broadcasts by promoting them well to all the various groups that we are targeting – if teachers, trainers, carers, people at home do not know about what we have to offer, we cannot fulfil our public service role to meet their educational or social needs.
– Secondly, we use a variety of strategies for extending and supporting the educational use of broadcasts by publishing, and this is the main theme of this presentation.

Figure 1 shows the range of materials that are published by the BBC and the departments involved in those publications.

Figure 1: Publishing Departments

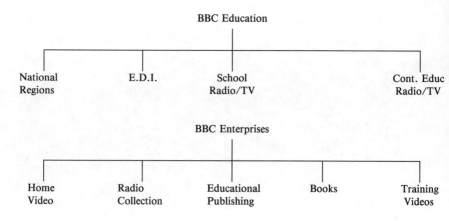

Figure 2: The broadcast-centred 'universe'

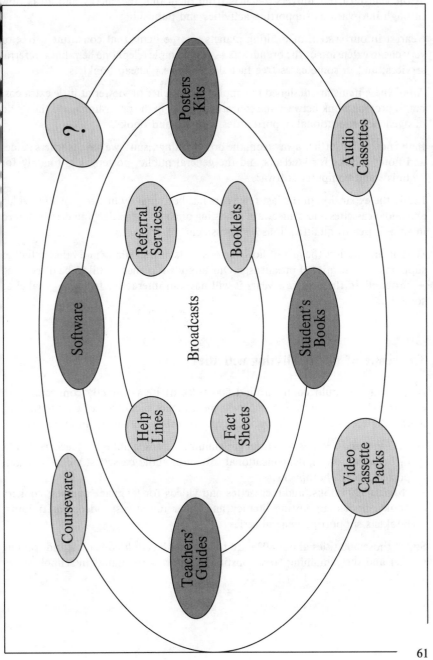

Let me give you an overview of what is involved. You can think of the broadcasts as the centre of our universe – it is from them that the energy and ideas flow through into various supporting activities and publishing.

Nearest in our system of orbiting planets are the items that constitute a free or very cheap extension of the broadcasts – for example telephone help-lines, referral services, and in some cases free fact sheets or very cheap booklets.

All of these items are designed to support the listener or viewer at little extra cost but to provide a link between the educational ideas in the programme and the world of agencies, educational opportunities, courses and books.

In the next orbit further away from the broadcasting „sun" we have teachers guides and notes, books for students and the general public, posters, kits (mainly for schools), and computer software.

Lastly the expansion in the last few years has been mainly in our providing video and audio cassettes and courseware consisting of complete packs of materials, linked in some cases to qualifications or assessment.

So that summarises the mix of how various sorts of publishing and other activities support our educational broadcasts. Our unknown planet is still to be discovered – probably in the next few years it will have an interactive technology label of some kind.

The scope of our publishing activities

At present we could count around 800 titles of items directly connected with educational broadcasts or targeted at the more obvious schools, college and training markets. Here is a list of the various types of media for the main target groups:

- *Children and Schools:* 470 titles per annum, including notes for teachers, books or booklets for pupils, educational software, audio cassettes, video cassettes, posters, kits, photopacks.
- *Adults:* 330 books, audio cassettes and videos for language courses; cookery books, books supporting literacy and other initiatives; videos for training; booklets supporting general series

So, of those 800 titles about 40% are for use by the adult education and training market and the remaining 60% constitute resources for pupils in school.

Figure 3: Published titles: Breakdown by market

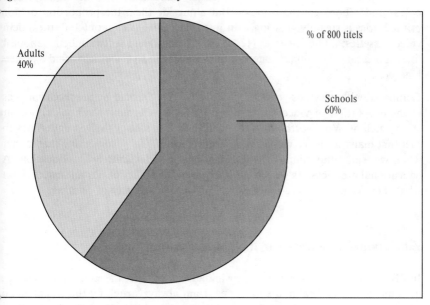

Looked at in terms of the media used we get the following picture:

Figure 4: Published titles: Breakdown by medium

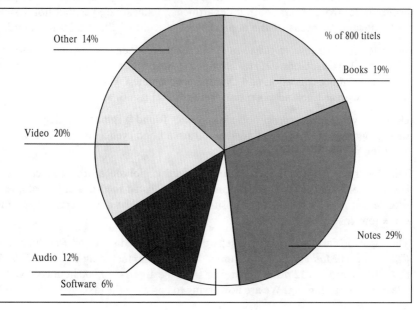

Almost half of those titles are printed materials – with slightly mor⸱ notes/guides/booklets than books. But alongside them the proportion of non printed titles is steadily growing with just under 20% (i.e. about 160 titles) bein⸱ video cassettes, audio cassettes (12%) close behind, and software being about 4⸱ titles at present. The "other" category makes up the last 14% which includes posters⸱ kits, etc..

Compared with previous years the major difference would be the recent increas⸱ in the proportion of video and audio titles. A look around the book shops an⸱ stores such as Woolworth's or the local library or school shelves underlines th⸱ fact that many of us see videos as a natural part of life – something that is ther⸱ when we want entertainment, information or – increasingly – education. A⸱ educational broadcasters we have to face up to the ability of our audiences to bu⸱ what they want elsewhere if we fail to provide it one way or another.

Educational resources for the general output

In BBC Education we now have a new initiative to enhance the educational potentia⸱ of some of our general audience series. I am always struck by the comments o⸱ Americans about our television service in the United Kingdom. To them a lot o⸱ general programming is 'educational', whereas for us a dramatisation of, say Dickens' *Bleak House* or a documentary series like *Life on Earth* are qualit⸱ programmes from general output departments; 'educative', yes, but not designe⸱ with educational needs of the audience at the front of the producers' minds.

We often tend to reserve the term 'Educational Broadcasting' for the output o⸱ educational broadcasting departments – like the departments for school televisio⸱ or for continuing education and training programmes. Yet it would be foolish t⸱ deny the worthwhile and potentially educational use of general series.

Until last year, however, schools and colleges found it impossible, legally, to us⸱ such programmes. And we all tended to turn a blind eye to the fact that they did Now the position is different.

The Copyright Act and the setting up of the Educational Recording Agency in th⸱ UK have enabled licensed educational institutions to record and use almost a⸱ broadcasts. And we have reacted positively to the opportunity offered by providin⸱ some low cost booklets.

The topics so far have been diverse; we have supported series on *Rembrandt* an⸱ *Churchill*, on *Madness* or poetry and a dozen others, including *Trials of Life*. W⸱ have chosen around 12 projects per year from the approx. 10,000 hours of availabl⸱ television programming. We are now trying to correlate the take-up of the booklet⸱

with factors such as transmission times, presentation announcements, price, programme audiences, length of series.

At present we are still exploring how to identify the potentially successful projects and clarifying the best ways of reaching this new market for educational support.

But now let me return to publishing alongside our more tightly defined Educational Series.

Publishing and support activities

Let me give you an example of how one broadcast project might be linked with a variety of published materials and local support activities. I refer to the series *Play It Safe* shown in connection with Brian Wright's presentation.

Figure 5: *Play it Safe* – Project components

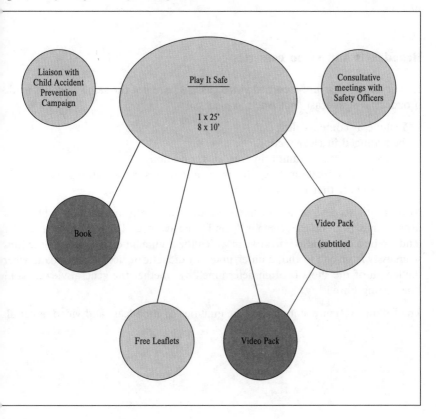

The project originated as a 25-minute documentary followed by a series of 8 ten minute programmes shown at peak times. In order to ensure that this had th maximum effect, the programmes were supported in the following ways:

- free leaflets containing simple information about child safety;
- a book offering more comprehensive guidance on the practical, social an domestic issues;
- a video for use by trainers working with health, educational or community group (because of the importance of the topic and the availability of sponsorship ther was also a signed and subtitled version of that video for those with impaire hearing); and lastly,
- the materials and programmes linked in with a nationally running *Child Acciden Prevention* campaign, and with the work of local safety officers.

So, material originated for the broadcasts has been given a longer life in the hand of local trainers by being made available on video. To do that required additiona production effort to convert the broadcasts into a resource that will stand the tes of time.

Broadcasts and video cassettes

It is my belief that pre-recorded video cassettes are not the same as down-loaded broadcasts — at least, not often. Video can

- include a 'contents' list;
- be arranged in clear sections;
- contain summary frames, instructions, questions;
- cover items in 'real time', e.g. the procedure for testing something and analysing the results if that is appropriate.

None of these devices would likely be used naturally as part of a broadcast programme; print on the screen is by and large avoided. The broadcast equivalent tends to be a continuous narrative in which the argument of the programme flows seamlessly from end to end, uninterrupted by didactic devices and print and where the length of the shots is often determined by whether the general viewer would "be getting bored".

The following figure summarises the qualities of broadcast and video materials.

Figure 6: Broadcasts vs video cassettes

Broadcast	Video
– Large, simultaneous audience	– Small, repeated use
– Continuous narrative	– Potentially interactive
– Transmission slots	– Length determined by content
– Free	– Priced

Broadcasts have the advantage of being able to reach large audiences, all at the same time. They handle continuous narrative or action well, but have to be tailored to the length of the transmission slots. But once the licence fee is paid they are free to the viewers.

In contrast, specially produced video cassettes for educational use will mainly be used with small audiences; an audience of 50 or more people requires some pretty sophisticated technology like a video projector. Video cassettes can be used repeatedly, and they have the potential for being more interactive: they can be stopped, looked at again, "interrogated", and length can be determined by the content. But it usually costs money to buy pre-recorded videos designed for use in education and training.

At BBC Education we try to offer the best of both worlds – a way of stimulating, motivating, educating and training the broadcast viewer. And then, some of the broadcasts are given an 'after life' as quality video resources which can sustain the impact and use of the programmes and offer a way of putting together the book, booklets and other materials supporting the user.

To sum up, I have sought to provide an insight into our work on four levels:

- a picture of the ways in which publishing extends the life and usefulness of our broadcasts to educational markets;
- a glimpse at our publishing of educational support for general output;
- a snapshot of how the various media can support a project, e.g. the *Play It Safe* project;
- examples of how video can provide a slightly different "long-life" version of our original broadcasts.

All this additional activity means new challenges for our marketing colleagues. One of them, Robert Seatter from BBC Education, will talk about the approaches and solutions he has adopted in the next contribution.

Robert Seatter

BBC Education: The Role of Marketing

In my presentation I should like to review educational marketing, and mo
particularly how to galvanise it in a context that is fluid, changing and changeabl
where too many demands are being made on the educator or facilitator and whe
everything is on offer for the learner – a situation that may confuse rather th;
clarify.

What is the marketing response in this climate? We shall look at some strategi
that are available to us, such as on-air promotion, direct mailing, press wor]
advertising, and exhibitions and then home in on one specific campaign.

On-air promotion

On-air promotion is an obvious strategy, but one that is easily overlooked. Tl
promotions department embarks on a plethora of catalogues, leaflets and ad
forgetting that one of the most potent means at its disposal is the company's ov
airwaves.

The use ranges from straight presentation links or slides promoting related resourc
to a much more general promotion.

BBC Education devised a short television 'ad' promoting its output under the stra
line *'Educational programming at its best'*. This was also linked into an advertisin;
print and exhibition campaign.

Other more general on-air marketing comes with the creation of a comment foru»
or magazine programme, where viewers can comment on the output, hopefull
favourably some of the time, at least! . Informal promotion takes place, and
sense of involvement in the audience. This is the case with a series titled *Questio»
and Answers*, where viewers – both young and old, individually or in classroo»
set-ups – sent in their comments on BBC Education programmes.

Finally, with radio and television the BBC has two media, and can use both t
cross-promote their mutual wares, i.e. common thematic areas of programmin
can be cross-referred.

On-air promotion can be very effective, provided one can guarantee getting a tim
slot when one's target audience can be reached.

Direct mail

Direct mail is the commonest form of promotion. All BBC Education's programming is underpinned by a lot of print activity some of which is conceived to be mailed directly, such as Annual Programme booklets, wall charts, etc..

However, as in most educational marketing, budgets are very slim, so it is essential that documentation is prioritised to make sure money is allocated on a correct scale of priorities.

For example, in our schools promotion, we have moved away from producing lots and lots of pieces of promotional literature to the creation of key reference documents which have a longer shelf-life, and become a recognised part of an annual cycle, e.g. the *Annual Programme for Primary and Middle Schools* or the *Annual Programme for Secondary Schools and Colleges.*

Changes in the layout of these advance information booklets sent to schools are the result of a lot of research into how teachers use the document, and what to them was the key information. Thus, the access is made much clearer via colour coding, the document is structured from the users' point of view and not the BBC's, as we know from supporting comments from teachers and the education press.

The Annual Programmes also have their own promotion campaigns − via trails and ads, defining them as key events in the school calendar.

Getting the document right is important, but also its distribution. The *Annual Programme for Primary Schools*, for example, is a clear document going to a focussed clientele. Adult education in the UK is much less clear, and routing promotional literature, e.g. *The Resources for Learning and Training Booklet*, is much more of a circuitous labyrinth.

One-to-one response from teachers in colleges and training centres was positive; but there was continual comment that the catalogue was not reaching them. So we embarked on a major research project, which looked at the specific handling and circulation issues in a spread of colleges. It came down to the question of who put what in which pigeon-hole, and the creation of new databases with individual targets for each college. This is the level of detail necessary to get the targeting right.

Another useful strategy for improving direct mail focus is through networking with linked organisations, many of whom, we have found, are only too happy to collaborate with broadcasters.

This has given us access to advantageous positioning in the market place. Our parents' series *Help Your Child with Reading*, for example, was profiled in a widespread chain of children's toy shops through donated display space. Our new

disability series *Disabled Lives* had poster sites offered at reduced rates in Londo
tube and bus shelters.

Approx. 75% of our marketing activity is direct mail, which often tends to be th
most cost-effective way of reaching our audience. However, the message and targ
must both be very precise. It must also, wherever possible, be measurable, e.g
through reply-back devices such as coupons, telephone lines, etc.. It is only throug
these devices that we can know if our message is penetrating or not.

Press and advertising activity

For the popular press, our marketing strategy is a fairly standard one, seeking pres
coverage via human interest stories or via personality features. However, for th
education press, there are a few rather specific activities we have developed.

For example, we have commissioned general research around specific series, to rais
its general profile, and give the series more impact (e.g. research on reading c
maths).

We also commission, in advance of the series and transmission, specific educationa
articles from our Education Offices or series consultants, which are then offere
directly to the educational press that is often hungry for text.

Finally, we do of course orchestrate advertising campaigns in key journals an
magazines. Less and less do these tend to be general in orientation; rather the
are making a focussed specific claim, and underwriting it by a clear offer whic
can be measured via a coupon or call-back. The advertising for the *Annuc
Programme for Primary Schools*, for example, ultimately promoted a tangib
product rather than a list of broad claims, although there are claims there withi
the copy.

Educational exhibitions

Exhibitions are another victim of constraints on teachers' time and money. Ther
are a vast number of them, so once again, it is essential that they are prioritise
year on year − according to the department's relevant output and to key nationa
needs.

Having decided to take an exhibition stand, we then seek at every opportunity t
maximise our presence, by giving the space a clear focus. It is pointless trying tc
sell all our wares on one small stall: there must be a clear sales claim or messag
for each exhibition. This is supported by a prominent use of the BBC logo, on

f our most valuable assets. The latter is also important for a strategy of longer-erm awareness, so that when the series or specific resource is forgotten, the BBC presence still registers.

Along with this go focussed catalogues or leaflets, seminars or workshops within the conference context, and specific activities to draw visitors to the stand.

Let me illustrate these points with details of what we did at the recent Association of Science Conference:

We had one combined BBC stand, linking together a variety of different internal departments; nine in all. In this way, we created much more joint impact − rather than having a proliferation of individual exhibition points, which was the case in the past. However, the design allowed a number of different entry routes, so customers could access what they deemed most relevant to them. Each part was labelled separately, but linked by overarching BBC headers and BBC banners hung above for clear visibility.

All the information was united in one comprehensive catalogue, so there was no likelihood that visitors could indulge in the shopping bag tendency of picking up a sack of different leaflets and reading none of them.

There were two incentives to come to the stand: a short presentation of our new series for parents wishing to help their children with science, accompanied by drinks, and a televisation of a BBC debate on the role of science in education. Questions for the latter were requested in advance, which brought people to the stand, as well as involving them in the creation of a broadcast, enabling them to see the BBC as a key player in science education in Britain.

Monitoring of the effectiveness of exhibitions is difficult for a public service broadcaster. We can measure the impact by the number of catalogues handed out, the number of specific order forms returned, but also by qualitative feedback from customers and specific research points.

The Second Chance campaign

Having talked about some very general strategies, I should now like to examine a specific campaign, and see how those elements were orchestrated together. The campaign was for *Second Chance*, a joint radio/television initiative to encourage adults to go back to learning and training. It was important therefore to get to both the person in the street, and the facilitator who would ultimately be delivering that training, or learning.

Marketing to the facilitator

The components to reach the highest possible number of facilitators included:

- a vast trawl to all persons involved in the training market:

  - personalised letters were sent 10 months in advance to 25,000 contacts in Further Education colleges, Adult Education Institutes etc.; the list was tested and cleaned after first mailing, and involved list research and purchase;

- the dialogue was maintained with the second mailing:

  - 45,000 copies of a large A3 poster were mailed, with a letter and an order form for a booklet;

- contact was developed:

  - a booklet offering advice on different routes/options,
  - containing all sorts of contact numbers;

- support by focussed press activity:

  - Educational press launch was organised one month prior to transmission;

- specialist articles on Second Chance, written by in-house Education Officers and sent to the education/training press;

- presentation/feedback process to develop involvement:

  - a promotion event was organised 6 months in advance to inform key people in education and training;

- seminars on national scale:

  - in 10 centres around UK seminars were held showing clips from the programmes, galvanising interest and involvement; one or two became even more involved and piloted material with learners, which was a good way to involve teachers, get quality feedback and also set up an effective marketing network.

One could say that the whole action was developed collaboratively, not imposed.

Finally, a high level of awareness was created in the educational market by linking into the *Adult Learners' Week*, a national initiative already happening. Linking *Second Chance* and *Adult Learners' Week* was mutually beneficial for both organisations: BBC benefited from tapping into grass roots training networks, rather than imposing on them; while *Adult Learners' Week* gained media profile and kudos, as well as improved reach.

Marketing to the end user

With regard to the user, the campaign was marked by the following features:
- high visibility:
  A3 poster, placed in colleges, libraries, public forums, with telephone numbers and booklet;
- immediate offer:
  booklet, promoted directly to end user as well;
- specific tabloid/magazine coverage:
  long-lead periodicals targeted and offered human interest stories and personality interviews for features;
- press launch:
  organised one month before transmission, including photo opportunities with celebrities;
- local grass roots access:
  a range of local community activities as a result of links with *Adult Learner's Week*, e.g. colleges/library exhibitions, open days, local ads;
- high visibility on air:
  on-air ads, in the form of short promotional clips;
- radio trail:
  trail made for local radio and sent round to stations;
- immediate action encouraged:
  helpline set up to instigate immediate action after series
  (it worked on a call-back system: callers left their request which was researched by team of experts, then the caller was given specific local advice).

As a result of the campaign to both groups there was a high awareness and a high commitment from both educational facilitators and end users. This was proven by the following facts:

- good take-up of booklet: 350,000 were sent out;
- very high take-up of helpline:
  56,933 calls in 7 days − a record response;
- high press visibility: over 600 articles appeared;
- high viewing figures for programmes of this type:
  at the times shown, 31% had seen one or more programmes (based on research carried out with a panel of over 3,000 viewers);
- increased enrolments from colleges:
  although difficult to quantify, 83% of colleges felt the initiative was worth repeating.

Against this must obviously be set the high costs of mounting such a campaign, which could only have been achieved with financial support from two government departments.

73

Olga Kuplowska

TVOntario's Educational Programming:
The Working Model

Introduction

Judith Tobin and I wish to describe the work we do at TVOntario. We extend our heartfelt thanks and appreciation to Manfred Meyer, who invited us, and to the host organisations, IZI and BLM, who made all of this possible.

TVOntario is a regional, a provincial educational broadcaster which was created and is funded to serve first and foremost the learning needs of the people of Ontario. We are licensed to broadcast only in Ontario, although we know that our signal does stray beyond the borders of Ontario.

At the same time, our programmes are sold around the world; we have international co-production partners; and we engage in various other national and international activities that traditionally have been the domain of national public broadcasters or large private networks.

It is this weaving and interweaving of the local and the global that has enabled us to produce high quality programming, appreciated at home and around the world.

My colleague Judith Tobin will elaborate on the various markets we serve and reach and on our international activities. My intention is to provide an overview of the working model we have been working with over the years and that has helped us produce for local, national and international audiences without sacrificing our educational and cultural mandate.

TVOntario's working model

In fact, you will find many similarities with the ideas and ways of working that were outlined by our BBC colleagues. I will be highlighting five points that I feel are among the more essential ones.

1. Diversity of offerings – diversity of needs served

While TVOntario was born from within the provincial Ministry of Education, from the very beginning, its creators targeted all Ontarians as the intended public, as the potential viewers and users of the network.

Consequently, from the very beginning, different streams of programmes were produced, co-produced, and acquired:

- programmes for preschoolers;
- programmes for use with students in classrooms;
- programmes that supported college and university courses;
- programmes for those who wished to learn at home in a less formal way (e.g. languages, personal finances, politics);
- programmes that helped the viewer understand the world a little better, and so on.

Today, 22 years later, we are still programming for all Ontarians and diversifying our offerings even more. Judith Tobin will describe our most recent venture in diversification in her contribution to this book.

Extensive diversification can be a marketer's nightmare, and certainly in our early years there were those who felt this was more of a weakness than a strength, that we would be better off by focussing on 1 or 2 publics, addressing only 1 or 2 needs. The visionaries persevered, however.

Learning was perceived as

- *life-long* – reason to target all ages;
- *experienced in various ways* by different groups of people:
  - reason to use different formats, various genres of programmes, different approaches;
- *occurring in different contexts:*
  - reason to deliver and facilitate the use of programmes in various places.

Furthermore, it was recognised early on that, for most people, television was seen primarily as an entertainment medium besides a source of news, and so we learned to adapt successful ,,entertainment" formats and styles for educational purposes. You will see some examples of this in the clips I will screen at the end of my presentation.[1]

2. The role of research at TVOntario

A second critical aspect of our model is the role of research. Research is an integral part of life at TVOntario. This means that research is used by all levels of the organisation (corporate/executive, programmers, producers) and researchers become involved at various stages of programme planning, development, production and delivery.

---

[1] Brief clips were shown from the following five award-winning programmes: *Book Mice* and *Picoli et Lirabo*, targeted at young children, with a particular focus on developing reading skills; *Take a Look* and *Concepts in Math* from programmes that were designed to support school curriculum, each using very appealing and innovative ways of explaining science and math concepts; *The Science of Architecture* from a programme targeted at "home-learners", i.e. viewers who want to learn from the comforts of their homes.

For example, extensive planning research on Franco-Ontarian youth led to the creation of a separate Youth Programming Sector on our French network and helped shape its overall directions. Formative evaluation was used extensively to target and design the programmes. And in the coming year, research will be examining the impact of this sector's programming on Franco-Ontarian youth after 18 months of activity.

To help TVOntario re-orient and re-position its Science, Public Affairs, Arts and Schools programming, major research studies have been launched for each area. The information and analysis being provided is both quantitative and qualitative and is being culled from a wide spectrum of sources. For example, in one of the science studies, we interviewed some 30 to 40 knowledgeable and high profile individuals who work in science – either as practising scientists, as science journalists or writers, as producers or hosts of science TV programmes, etc. – to gather their views about science on television. This report is being used by the different programming units to challenge their own thinking on science programming, to stimulate new ideas, and ultimately, to develop new programme plans.

Research is also used to help design programmes, to schedule the programming block, and to determine the effectiveness and success of programmes.

Throughout all of these research endeavours, the client – be it the corporate executive or the producer – is closely involved and helps to shape the research objectives, as much as researchers help to shape programming objectives.

This synergetic working relationship between researcher and client evolved over the years and today; while there continue to be ups and downs, research enjoys a certain presence and respect at TVOntario.

3. Involving the markets in programme development

In developing programmes and services, we work very closely with the public for whom the programme is intended. In other words, programme content and format is not decided solely in the mind of a producer or programmer.

For example, when we programme for the schools, we may do any or all of the following:

– consult with teacher advisory committees;
– visit schools to observe certain practices;
– consult with student panels;
– conduct formal research studies with teachers and students.

The same holds true when we programme for other audience groups. For example, in testing the pilot for a new English as a Second Language series, we communicated in Chinese, Italian and Polish in order to get feedback from immigrants whose command of English was insufficient to respond in English.

In another case, we actively sought out science fiction fans and comic-book readers to help us evaluate and improve a new series that was aimed mostly at this sector of the population; and there are many other similar examples.

4. The composition or make-up of the project team

Another distinguishing factor is the role and influence of educators and pedagogues in developing a programme concept, in identifying a target audience, and in determining learning objectives. These people are usually full and active members of the project team, with a very strong voice about the series content and its treatment.

In addition to this core group, other specialists or content experts may be hired to review the scripts to ensure the content is accurate and that the approach is appropriate for the intended audience.

It should be noted that many of our producers were formerly educators or have strong backgrounds in education and so continue to bring that perspective to programme development.

Even in cases where a programme idea is submitted by an independent producer, by someone outside TVOntario, an educator or pedagogue may be assigned to this project to ensure that the 'learning' objectives are safeguarded and developed appropriately.

5. Learning system concept

Finally, we see our television programmes as but one component − albeit a major one − of a larger learning system, as one moment in the continuum of a viewer's learning experience. Thus

− we produce teacher and student workbooks, viewer's guidebooks, computer software to support and enhance the video component;
− we provide interactive links with the viewer through computer conferencing, telephone tutorials, and other types of phone-ins;
− we invite further participation and involvement by having the viewer send in video-mail, drawings, or regular correspondence, to which we respond;
− we recommend to the viewer − on-air or through our literature − other courses and activities such as books to read or films to see, that a viewer may wish to undertake to build on what was seen, learned, and enjoyed in the TVOntario programme.

All of this is done to enhance the value and the quality of the programme viewed by making it much more meaningful to the viewer.

There are, of course, other factors that have helped to position TVOntario where it is today. But the five I have listed are perhaps the more critical ones and the ones which in the course of time have almost become transparent — we do them out of force of habit.

Judith Tobin

TVOntario's Educational Programming: Reaching a Market of Millions

Olga Kuplowska has described how we at TVOntario reach our market by talking and collaborating with our audience before and during the development of our programmes. I will focus on the markets that we reach — both in Ontario and around the world. I will also describe how TVOntario is responding to the new situations in our market place by developing new products in ways that involve partnerships and cooperation.

The two networks and their audience

There are two networks at TVOntario — one that broadcasts in French and the other in English. The English language network at TVOntario is distributed by satellite and over 200 low-power transmitters to cable systems and homes, allowing us to reach over 97% of the nine million people living in Ontario. Our French network is more dependent on cable systems and reaches 75% of the population.

We have an audience of approximately two million a week. Featured in this group are young children, over 50% of whom watch TVOntario every week.

The use of our programmes in schools has been steadily increasing, but these viewers are not included in our audience figures. Research done in 1989 – 1990 shows that 75% of teachers in English language schools, including over 85% of senior science teachers had used TVOntario materials, and 74% of teachers in French junior and about 50% of teachers in French senior schools had made use of TVOntario productions during one single semester or three-month period. As the full French language network has only been broadcasting for six years, we are very proud of these results.

We are finding more and more that the use in schools is by video cassette recorder rather than by watching off-air during broadcast hours. Teachers enjoy the flexibility that video allows and we have supported this adaptation by providing extensive training for teachers in how best to use video in classrooms.

Considering this use of video rather than the broadcast signal, the need to use the daytime hours for programming directly related to the curriculum has diminished. As a result, we are developing up to 12 hours a week of programming that directly addresses the teachers and administrators and their concerns about curriculum changes, school management, teaching methods, and issues like violence and racism in schools. We employ whatever is available that addresses appropriate topics for professional training and support to Ontario teachers – a combination of live talk and telephone shows, interviews, panels, conferences, etc..

Focus on vocational education and training

The Canadian work force is also in need of extensive training and upgrading of skills and competencies. TVOntario knows that television can provide some of this training quickly and provide access for all Ontarians. In cooperation with employers, training associations, professional groups, and others we are developing skills training for broadcast. We define skills as literacy, numeracy, technological skills, workplace management, communication, and legislation as well as the skills of integrating our multicultural workplaces more effectively.

The broadcast material that we develop must be part of the ongoing training initiatives of the partner, have some form of learner support system in place – whether print materials, or tutors, or computer – and must be recognised in some way through a credit or certification.

We provide the instructional design expertise that allows the appropriate use of television and other technologies and the partner has responsibility for the administrative support. We are working with unions, police forces, teachers, voluntary sector, and many other groups in the development of materials that will provide targeted and credited skills training.

These are some of the ways that we are responding within Ontario, but our audience of millions also resides outside our province and we are working at reaching them as well.

International connections

TVOntario already has a number of successes in this area. We are the largest foreign supplier of programming to the U.S. educational television market and we have sold our product in over 80 countries world-wide. These countries include all of Europe, and countries in Asia, Africa, South America, and throughout the South Pacific. The reason that people buy from us and continue to buy from us, according to our sales representatives, is the quality of the project – whether it is for schools, young children, or adult viewing. They find that we can be engaging and entertaining at the same time and that much of our material can be used in different cultural settings.

Another of the reasons that our programming is successful internationally is that we develop it internationally. This is another part of the new reality: the need for partnerships and co-productions, the blend of our local and the global that was described by the Canadian communications guru, Marshall McLuhan.

TVOntario has long been active in international co-productions as we began to work with NHK, the Japanese public broadcaster, over 10 years ago. This relationship has allowed us access to some wonderful footage and science programming that we have adapted to our Ontario market as well as to an international audience.

These co-productions work in various ways: TVOntario and NHK may shoot together, or TVOntario may provide the North American footage while the Japanese, with their bigger budgets and incredible equipment, shoot all over the world; then, taking the same footage, TVOntario and NHK may create two quite different programmes.[1]

The *Scienceview* consortium

Another style of collaboration is a group called *Scienceview* that TVOntario created with the Japanese. In this consortium, there are now broadcasters from Australia, France, Germany, Britain, New Zealand, Sweden, and the USA involved. Participants agree on a theme, then each of them produces a programme or a part of a programme and they exchange these segments. Thus, for the price of producing one 8-minute segment, the participants can have one or two 30-minute programmes.

In these days of rising costs and falling budgets, *Scienceview* is seen as a very effective way of stretching the budget for programming. It is also remarkably successful as a consortium, as over 70% of the suggested proposals are acted on and the members are responsible for 70% of science production in the world. An example of a co-production, which involved non-*Scienceview* members as well, was *Our Beautiful Planet*, a two-hour, live broadcast that included Germany, Taiwan, Sweden, Thailand, Japan, Canada, and others.

Our French language channel works in the same way with the *Communauté des Télévisions francophones* to mount cooperative projects that fill the needs of French language audiences internationally. TVOntario is working towards that development of special agreements with broadcasters in Spain, Korea, Sweden, France, the United States, and other countries that will allow us to combine our expertise and our

---

As examples of this international collaboration, excerpts from the following programme were shown: a school programme that was re-edited from adult programming; *Nature Watch*, a coproduction with NHK; *Space Journal*, a co-production with Penn State University and NASA in the USA; *Global Family*, another NHK co-production.

programme needs in co-productions and co-ventures. We continue to seek appropriate partners with special skills for our productions in order to better serve our Ontario audiences. Whether through the sales of our actual programmes or through the integration of our offerings in the programmes of other national broadcasters — these are all ways by which our programming reaches people all over the world.

But TVOntario also takes a global view in the sense of its role in the world as a public broadcaster. In many countries public broadcasting as a concept and a service is under fire, with threats to its budgets and its mandate. Even where it is strong it is facing competition from new services — by cable or satellite — that are supplying educational, documentary, high quality cultural and many of the other types of programming that have been associated with public broadcasting.

Public Broadcasters International

Once again, working in collaboration with NHK, TVOntario hosted a conference of public broadcast executives from around the world. Held in Toronto in November 1991, the purpose of *Public Broadcasters International* was to find common ground for mutual support and activity among the 21 major public broadcast organisations who were invited to attend.[2]

After 2 days of deliberations, the chief executive officers and the senior programmer issued a joint statement of the mission and purpose of public broadcasting and their determination to work together to ensure its continued existence. The second gathering was held in Brussels in 1992 where the focus was on outlining the actual projects and actions that will be undertaken.

In this way, TVOntario is trying to play a vital part in guaranteeing that the millions of viewers of public television all over the world and those in countries in which public broadcasting is developing will continue to profit from the kind of programming that public broadcasters can provide.

---

[2] Documentation on Public Broadcasters International is available on request from TVOntario, Div. of International Affairs, 2180 Yonge Street, Box 200, Station Q; Toronto, Ontario M4T 2T1 Tel.: +416-484 2654, Fax: +416-484 7771.

Chapter 3:
Strategies for Increasing the Acceptance and Effectiveness of Educational Programmes

Christopher Jones

Strategies for Increasing the Acceptance and Effectiveness of School Television

We have been asked to talk about strategies for increasing the *acceptance* and *effectiveness* of educational broadcasting, two keywords that are very useful to us. I shall start with an overview, taking for granted that the reader is familiar with the description of the ITC's functions and current educational arrangements.[1] They are changing rapidly and have been updated only to the end of 1992. The problems of maintaining the quality and innovative achievements are not a matter for this occasion.

In the following contribution, David Lee describes the professional network of support by education officers and the ways in which close liaison is sustained with schools. Also directly complementary to this theme, Paul Martin from Central Independent Television reports about specific support activities for science and maths programmes in which he has been directly involved as producer later in this book.[2]

S. this volume, Part II: Background information, pp. 242–248.
S. this volume, pp. 106–114.

Acceptance

First let us look at what 'acceptance' might mean. One could in our case sit bac
and say: "The figures show the service is sufficiently widely accepted to be total
justified".

Figure 1: Levels of Equipment
(Base: all schools, 1990; in brackets average per school)

	Primary schools		Secondary schools	
Colour TV receivers	99%	(1.7)	99%	(7.7)
Video-recorders	93%	(1.0)	99%	(7.5)
Computers	97%	(4.0)	99%	(36.0)

Figure 2: TV Use in UK Schools and by Teachers

	Primary schools		Secondary schools	
	ITV	BBC	ITV	BBC
Schools using any series:	86%	95%	88%	89%
Median take-up (each series)	18%	29%	28%	24%
Teachers who were 'frequent' users of school TV programmes (once a week or more often)	71%		44%	
Average number of days per month when teachers use school TV	6.7		4.5	

These figures, and the ones shown in the BBC presentation, make quite clear tha
we do not have the problem experienced in many other countries − virtually a
our schools use school television and most of them use quite a lot of it. If ther
are problems they lie in whether teachers can get hold of school television at th
time they need it, assuming they wish to use it.

In 1989/1990, we carried out a major research project that sought to establish ho
well school television was accepted, how often it was used, and what it was regarde
by teachers as being effective for.

One of our aims was to check out by a different research method what we alread
have a fairly clear picture of, through the joint Survey of Listening and Viewin
we have with the BBC. Part of the research was published in 1991 as the boo
Television in Schools.[3]

---

[3] Moss, Robin; Jones, Christopher; Gunter, Barrie: *Television in Schools*. ITC Monographs
London: John Libbey 1991. For some aspects not fully covered in this book see also Jones
Christopher: What do teachers expect from school television? In: M. Meyer (Ed.) *Aspects o
School Television in Europe. A Documentation*. München: Saur 1992; pp. 462−476.

84

This is the picture of the sources of television and video used in this sample of all schools in the UK, both primary and secondary:

Figure 3: TV/Video usage in schools by source
(Base: all respondents; n = 969)

| | Broadcasts/videos | |
	made for schools (%)	other material (%)
Tapes recorded at school	40.1	3.3
Tapes recorded at home	14.6	9.0
Viewed live	15.5	0.6
Bought from ITV/BBC	3.7	–
Bought elsewhere	4.4	–
Tapes borrowed (free)	4.2	0.6
Tapes hired	1.0	0.5
other	0.3	0.6

From our data we also know that there is a considerable amount of 'off air' viewing especially in primary schools, despite the availability of video recorders in virtually all schools. The majority of programmes are recorded in schools, but there is a considerable amount that is recorded at home and used in school. On closer examination this is not, as one might expect, mainly programmes recorded from the general output.

We know that these figures reflect arrangements made by teachers with 'other people' (probably within the family) to make recordings at home, because inside the school it is too complicated. So there are a number of teachers who are making the effort from their own resources to compensate for problems that the school cannot readily solve.

Next we look at the frequency of use of television and video in school taken from a sample of 969 teachers:

Figure 4: Use of TV and Video in Schools (Frequency)

	Total	Primary	Secondary
Every day	2	2	1
3 – 4 times a week	14	17	11
Once/twice a week	42	52	32
Once a fortnight	12	8	16

You find the more common frequency of use is about once or twice a week; 58% of teachers use TV at least weekly, 'once a fortnight' is found statistically less often. There are no 'non-users' in this table. We characterised those who used television once or twice a week or more often as 'frequent' users, and those who used it once a fortnight or less as 'infrequent' users.

ITV Schools is one of two school television services in Britain, the other one being BBC School Television – creative rivals even if occasionally co-operative. Our television service is free, i.e. neither the schools nor the government pay any money to ITV Schools for the programme service provided. Support publications are marketed to schools, who choose to purchase or not at their discretion.

Being a free television service it is taken by around nine in ten schools in the United Kingdom. On our side of the two school television services, about 1.5 million published artefacts are bought each year to support the more extensive use of the television programmes – from a simple booklet to a complex package in several media.

Effectiveness

The second keyword in our theme is 'effectiveness'. In Britain, the 1990 Broadcasting Act established a mandate for school television for the first time in UK law. This would come into force 35 years after the start of school television in Britain, and in the new circumstances we are happy to have it.

Part of the mandate required programmes to be broadcast "to meet the needs of schools" – not, as we point out, if ironically, to meet the needs of publishers or the needs of producers. Another part of the mandate was to provide *support publications* to ensure the 'effective use' of the broadcasts. So the legal wording to which we must respond is already very close to the second keyword in our theme.

But 'acceptance' is a prerequisite for 'effective use'. One cannot use what one does not understand, or what one does not know about, and no-one can be compelled in school to turn on the television. The obvious question to ask is – acceptance by whom? The pupil? The teacher? The subject department head, or the school director of studies? The inspectors and advisers both local and national? The parents of the pupils? The managers or governors of the schools? Is it now the curriculum bureaucracies? The government department for education? The politicians?

The 90% penetration figure which we enjoy between ourselves and the BBC was not achieved by a sudden marketing campaign. In 1972, on our side of the school television service, penetration in secondary schools was around 30%. Over the last 20 years there has been a steady growth in secondary schools up to the current

90% – from a minor contribution to education towards being a central resource for schools.

Clearly this development has been much helped by video-recorders, but then why buy video-recorders unless the product to be recorded is regarded as desirable? So the history of gaining acceptance certainly goes back all those 20 years.

In those days the concept of visual literacy was new. Teachers could still regard television as undermining progress towards print literacy, which by consensus was the only true key to open the doors of culture. Television was also seen as a medium of 'performance', related to the theatre or music-hall, and extending to the well-illustrated lecture. That is a sketch of the situation twenty years ago from which we have worked forward to the current much more varied situation.

From the research mentioned earlier I derive three key elements that could be a policy tripod in a strategy to ensure acceptance and effectiveness. These are:

- Authenticity, by which I mean a set of qualities which assure the user of the relevance and value of the programmes;
- Liaison with the users in schools, the planners of the curriculum and the producers – a vital dimension in the process of establishing authenticity. (This is David Lee's subject in the following chapter and should be read alongside what I have to say here.)
- Awareness, which reflects the extent to which teachers are informed about both the programmes and the support materials and services offered to them.

Authenticity

Television is certainly the dominant medium in our society, but it is not necessarily the appropriate medium for every kind of teaching that is needed. To be recognised and accepted as an educational medium, it has to fulfil certain prerequisites that are subsumed here under the notion of authenticity.

Authenticity is most likely to be achieved in the eyes of the users when

- the teaching points are devised and *designed by recognised national experts;*
- the aims of the programmes are *approved by a trustworthy body;*
- the programmes *match the curriculum* framework, or at least the known needs of teachers;
- the programmes *add to the learning experience*, particularly by doing what a visual medium is good at doing;
- the designs of programmes match pupils' attention span and develop from their latent interests;
- the programmes seen in schools *match the quality* of better programmes seen

in the general output of television (if our programmes appeared to youngsters to be a cheap service they would certainly be rejected).

Awareness

Considering the ITV and BBC services taken together, there are in the order of 1700 school television programmes offered in one year; or about 3000 programmes broadcast and potentially video-recorded over the past 5 years. We repeat new programmes in the following year, so that library of 3000 programmes continues to roll on, and it grows even larger if older material is retained. What one teacher needs may be just one programme, even just one sequence.

If I were to use the analogy of *books*, throughout the analogy let us try to think just how it might apply in using *television*. Publishers have a more limited output each year; librarians select and build up libraries; a library has a unified cataloguing system; main reference libraries aim to be encyclopaedic, and employ expert staff to help searchers. However, are there *television* equivalents for what is now in place for *print*?

At the same time as access to books is being organised at a higher policy level, individual readers buy books. They either shelve them neatly or put them in disorderly piles. Perhaps they scan a few pages and forget them; some books they read avidly, and with some they struggle with more complex writing or ideas and absorb, lose heart or misunderstand them. Their choice of reading may come from a newspaper review, from the recommendation of a friend or even a teacher, from an eye-catching display in a bookshop, or, during a tedious wait, from a railway station bookstall.

How much does the same sort of thing happen with individual television viewing?

Books are 'accepted' in schools, but choices more often than not are haphazard; *at school* a pupil gets some form of direction, maybe even a ration of personal help. Television viewing *at home* is equally haphazard, but at school the pupil also needs and expects the teacher to make choices and direct the viewing. In this sense television is less accepted than books.

Our research showed that 60% of teachers who are described as 'lighter users' (i.e. those who used television less than once a week) wanted to use television *more* than they did. They outlined a series of problems that inhibited greater use of television .

Only one of these problems could be eased by the originators of the broadcasts. That was the problem of *awareness*, both of programmes and of the support materials and services that go with them.

Information services, old and new

Advance information in print

The ITV Schools service has an efficient free advance information service that starts with an annual programme catalogue, very similar to that of the BBC. We each change the layout of the catalogue from time to time as we think of a better idea or presenting information. But the fundamental idea is the same – about six months ahead of the school year teachers should have a reasonable opportunity to see what's on and to decide if they want to buy any of the support materials.

Each term there is a wall-poster sent to schools. The BBC does the same; theirs is a little more complicated, as it has to include information on radio programmes as well as television programmes. Received in advance of each term, the wall-poster timetables are the most up-to-date information that schools can receive in print. There is, however, another method that does not use print.

The KEY database

For five years now the IBA/ITC has developed a database service to allow a school microcomputer to be used to search intelligently for information on programmes and support materials. It uses the KEY data-handling system.[4]

KEY is now probably the most generally available data retrieval system in our schools. We started off with the BBC-B computer, which was the micro that revolutionised the availability of information technology in British schools. Today we provide a service for every popular computer used in schools.

There is now an advanced version KEY PLUS, with a very wide range of extended facilities. In school it is used on Archimedes computers that are already available in 64% of secondary schools, and 36% of primary schools in the UK.

There has been relatively little interest in British schools in the range of IBM-compatible PCs, which are thought to be too slow and to have a clumsy operating interface. As in many other European countries schools have taken on IBM-compatible PCs, an IBM-PC version of KEY PLUS was launched, using MS-Windows 3. We have therefore added a version of our Schools TV information datafiles for this system, too.

There is more detail on the genesis and development of the KEY system in my article 'Keeping track with KEY – A database for school television programmes and support media'. In: M. Meyer (Ed.): *Aspects of School Television in Europe. A Documentation.* München: Saur 1992; pp. 221 – 226.

Our intention has been to develop a unified core database that can be adapte through specific software to serve a growing variety of tasks. We are using th nuclear KEY file, assembled at a simple level to be usable on the lowest level c commonly available microcomputers, and we can then develop it for differen machines, and use it for all sorts of different purposes.

In our own office the KEY filing system is used to keep all our own records an to use the files for various office purposes, including the catalogue of our vide library.

Perhaps the most important function is that, having assembled what i fundamentally our own office database in a form without complication, we mak disc copies of some of our files available to any school user who wants it. Of cours to get the data onto one school-sized disc requires us to make *subsets*, for eac term and for each of the four national regions of the UK, or as an option for primar schools that may only have the minimum level equipment. But those with mor advanced equipment, for instance in libraries or teachers' centres, are using exactl the same database as we are using in the office, updated to the day their particula copy was made.

Weekly information on teletext

The KEY datafile is also used to provide information which is broadcast on *teletex* On the Channel Four teletext service one can see a continuous carousel of all th programmes that are on the air that week for secondary schools and primar schools.[5]

Interactive video disc

Hypothetically, we could aim to have our programme informaton catalogue in th form of a CD-ROM or *interactive video disc*, which I think has enormous potenti: for the future. There has already been a pilot example, where short video excerp from series and the index lists by subject and age-range were combined by softwa to control an interactive video cassette tape.

Searchable fields

What is it that schools receive now when we copy a disc for them? We can tak a brief look at just one record: each series has of course a title, some series hav units within them, and all programmes have an individual title. The days c

---

[5] Here the audience was able to see a demonstration of the Channel 4 teletext shown in the U that week. From January 1993 they could be found on pages 391 and 392.

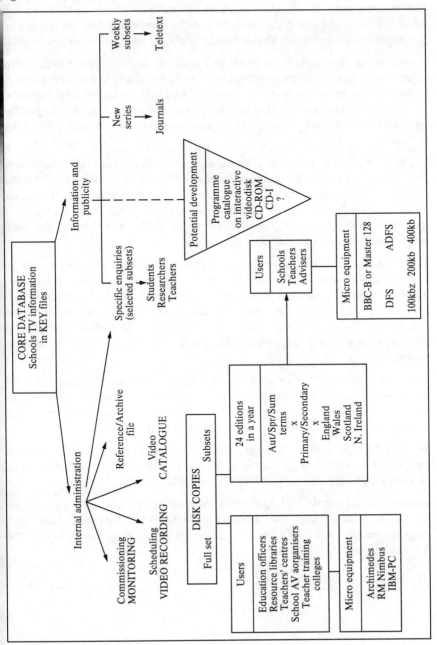

broadcast are shown; it is noted if the programme is not available in one of the four national regions. A teacher can make an intelligent search for the two main subject fields — the foundation subjects (i.e. the compulsory subjects defined by the National Curriculum for England and Wales) and the cross-curricular themes.

As well as the curriculum in England and Wales we have two more curricula to serve — with quite different philosophies — in Scotland and in Northern Ireland, so there have to be two more sets using the preferred terminology for those curricula. Then comes a short description of each programme — perhaps the most important part, and this is in fact the only information medium in which such a summary is found.

Teachers' booklets tend to be published quite a long way ahead of the transmission, they often have to describe an unmade programme or simply state the intended objectives. When programmes enter the cycle of repeats the booklet usually contains a full synopsis, but at a length unsuitable for an easy-to-use database. So when the producers supply us with these short descriptions it is a vital link in the chain of information, and one that does not exist in print.

There are of course fields other than the subject areas on which searching can be carried out — the *age-level*, or the *key stage* for which the programme is designed, whether the programme is new or repeated, which was the producing company etc.. Searching can be in a more generalised way, e.g. what programmes are on the air this week, the whole range of what is available, say, in English or Maths, or to generate a list of new programmes which a school technician should be asked to record.

There are also other files available apart from the programme descriptions. All the *support materials* for a school year are given, i.e. everything available in print and other media. There is a special file for the software linked to programmes, with something like 230 software items to support the ITV Schools service.

We look retrospectively at the programmes for the last two terms, so that a whole year's picture is available on one disc. New in the latest edition is the catalogue of *videos* that may now be purchased by schools.

We also include the Welsh language school television programmes produced by BBC Wales. This is because it is the fourth channel in Wales that provides the Welsh language programming, and the BBC programmes are integrated into the ITV Schools timetable for Wales.

Support services

I hope it has now become explicit that our school television service is not just about the production of good programmes. The services summarised in the following checklist (Fig. 6) are provided to support the television programmes.

Figure 6: Support Services

Support Services

* Information services
* Publications
* Links with publishers
    Print
    Posters
    Audio-visuals (tapes/slides)
    Data
    Software

The advance information already described is a major part of the operation − the annual catalogue, wall-posters with the timetable of broadcasts, pupils materials. For many years it has been taken for granted that there is a teachers' booklet to go with every series or unit of programmes. But it goes much further than that.

Each year, 1.5 million published artefacts are bought to support the more extensive use of the television programmes − from the teacher's booklet which many would regard as essential, to the sophisticated software that can create a form of interactivity with the broadcasts.

At the minimum level the good teacher will rely on the teacher's booklet, an easily used guide to the intended value of the programme. Experience has produced some consensus as to the essential content of the teachers' booklet.

To illustrate the manifold links with publishers outside the broadcasting organisation, let me describe what was planned to support the Yorkshire TV's dramatised social history series *How we used to live* − as an example of a rather sophisticated level of support.[6]

---

[6] Cf. M. Scarborough's article "How we used to live" − A case study in History and Community Education; in M.Meyer. op.cit, pp. 386 − 391

Figure 7: Essential Content

Essential Content in any Teachers' Booklet
* programme synopsis * aims * key teaching points * key words * suggestions for follow-up/activity * linked concepts in other programmes * related support materials * bibliography and references

A simple teachers' booklet, in slim A4-format, contains the basic information. Another publisher has produced a picture book that goes with the series, using both archive pictures and photographs and also some dramatised scenes from the programme where no original of suitable quality can be found. Another organisation has produced a quite hefty pack, which is mainly a collection of A4 worksheets which schools can photocopy. Also with it is an audiotape of popular songs from the period.

I would like to show two contrasting examples of programme support that go well beyond print support. One is through linked software, and the second through counselling and referral.

Software

Software can provide both direct and indirect support for programmes. Most of our Information Technology (IT) programmes have very extensive software backing to them.

A good example is the series *I.T. Across the Curriculum*, which in the Annual Programme lays claim to being "a new approach to active learning in the secondary school classroom". The series consists of ten packages, each of which comprises a twenty-minute video that interfaces with a major piece of computer software, a data disc relating to events shown on the video and, of course, a teachers' guide with exercises and background notes.

In the programme *Life and death of a river*, for instance, evidence is provided in the film, and data from the real River Goyt is provided in print and in the software.

Stage by stage students are guided in the video towards a point at which a decision has to be taken, and they are invited to join in the decision-making activity. When they reach a *decision point*, they are asked to break off and set about the problem the video has revealed, using the data provided on disc and in print form and the

94

oftware to process that data. They have a decision of economic and social politics o make by the end of the programme. The exercises on the way are real science exercises that have already been carried out by authentic professionals.

As the series title suggests, the series is not all about environmental science but uses several quite different social contexts for IT applications. The essential point of each programme is that the students should be handed real data about a real life situation, and then attempt to come to grips with possible hypotheses and answers.

While scientific education is more obviously ready to be supported by interactive styles, there are other kinds of support that are quite different in nature.

Counselling and referral

My second example draws on adult and community education, in which the concept of *social action* is vital. In the current ITV contracts, at the end of their lifespan by December 1992, each company was required − from 1982 onwards − to appoint a community education officer, whose job it was to establish links with community organisations and provide the opportunity to support a variety of programming, both local and national.

A Small Dance was a full-length drama broadcast in June 1992 in the peak evening output. It was supported by an immediate phone-in service and back-up print material − each in turn refers on to appropriate social support agencies.

The story that leads to the excerpt that I am going to show reads as follows: Donna, a teenage girl brought up in a bleak and isolated farm, becomes pregnant. She hides it from her parents − fearing particularly the attitude of her father. The baby is born in a farm outhouse. Donna abandons the baby at a petrol station on the main road. Soon it becomes the scandal of the neighbourhood, but until this point Donna has remained silent and unconcerned . . .

(Donna at home, a small farm cottage. Watching TV. Mother returns.)

Mother:	Did you remember EastEnders? . . . Rewind it.
Donna:	It's done.
Mother:	Looks like the poor little bugger's going to die then.
Donna:	What?
Mother:	That babe, poor thing.
Donna:	What's wrong with it?
Mother:	The police was back. Incubator it's in now.
	(Donna runs out) Donna?

(Phone box outside the garage)

Woman Telephone Operator: Directory enquiries . . . what name please?

Donna: The hospital . . .
Operator: Which hospital?
Donna: I don't know which one.. it's in King's Lynn. The place babies go in incubators.
Operator: I'll give you the number of the King's Lynn General. 7.. 8..
Donna: Hang on! 7 8 0.. 9 6 3 OK.

(The hospital number is engaged. Donna dials 999.)

Man Telephone Operator: Which service do you require? Fire, police or ambulance?

Donna: They've got my baby in the hospital.
Operator: Is it the ambulance service you want. . . . . Is it about the abandoned baby? Hold the line please.

Woman on the telephone: Hallo. Thank you for calling us. Would you like to tell us your name?

Donna: No.
Woman: You were asking about the abandoned baby. Hallo, are you still there?
Donna: How is she?
Woman: Can you tell us why you're asking please?
Donna: Is she dying?

(In a police car)

Policewoman: Are you warm enough, love?
Donna: Is she dying?
Policewoman: I haven't heard anything about her being ill, but we might not . . .
Donna: Will he have to know? . . . my Dad? Yeah . . . I just want to see her.

(The end of part three in a four-part broadcast)

For Donna this was the 'decision point', where she can be drawn back into taking responsibility for her baby, and can begin to respond positively to the help available.

The support pack had two elements: one was a special edition of a teenage magazine titled *Girl Talk*, the second a folder of advice to youth leaders and organisers of community education groups.

In the week when the 90-minute drama was broadcast, a series of five 10-minute social action programmes in the early evening, called *Help!* took up different linked

96

hemes, for example the quality of sex education in schools; a second an extended nterview with a young and isolated mother.

n July 1992 the UK government announced a target for reducing the number of eenage pregnancies. At the same time a group of MPs have tabled critical questions n Parliament about the offensiveness (to them) of the support materials for this ery programme.

he audience for *A small dance* was 11.1 million. It took a 49% share of the elevision audience on the four UK channels that evening. The appreciation index vas 87 in general, and 90 among the 16 to 24-year-old age-sector. There were 300 mmediate telephoned responses to the help-line. Extensive support and follow-up aaterial for the series had been developped by the Mental Health Media Council.[7]

his has been an example of structured community education support on a single ssue. It also illustrates that effectiveness and acceptability may mean different things t different levels of society. The educationalist, whether in school or in the wider ommunity, relies on the best advice for effectiveness. Television, in a structured ontext, has become recognised as one of the most valuable assets available to public ducation.

Those interested in this material should turn to Sylvia Hines, Director of the Mental Health Media Council (MHMC), 380 Harrow Road, London W9 2HU; UK.

David Lee

A Professional Network of Support: Education Officers and Effective Liaison[1]

Any organisation whose function is the design, development and promotion of product needs a constant stream of market information allied to efficient system of trialling and evaluation. Broadcasting is no exception. Over the years it ha initiated various forms of consultation and research into audience response in th quest for better programming. Nowhere is that spirit of enquiry better exemplifie than in educational broadcasting. The reasons for that are clear.

Educational broadcasting is not just a form of communication but a utilisabl resource which meets specific needs of teachers and learners. Its function is to b translated into concrete activity, and its linkages with various multi-media suppor materials such as computer software, targeted print, realia, tapes or slides, exten and deepen the programmes' options and concerns. For that reason, suppor materials and their visual analogues need to be part of a coherent packag responding at every level to a wide range of audience requirements. To succeec educational broadcasting needs to be not only good of its kind but relevant to range of specific demands such as those of:

- national or regional curricula;
- set texts and other prescribed syllabus and examination schemes;
- curriculum development projects.

In the entire process of educational programme planning and production, at lea five separate agencies collaborate in providing the educational output:

- the committee(s);
- the producers;
- series advisers;
- the educational audiences and the wider community (teachers, pupils, parent resource providers);
- the field force of liaison officers.

---

[1] This is the reproduction of a talk at MediaNet '92 based on a series of overhead transparencie Readers with specific interest in the scope of liaison work with independent broadcasters in tl UK, including its historical dimension within the duopoly of public service broadcasting, a referred to my article 'Ears to the ground. Independent Television's liaison activities with tl school audience' in M. Meyer (Ed.) *Aspects of School Television in Europe. A Documentatio* München: Saur 1992; pp. 167–195.

:fore I outline the main functions and directions of our current field liaison and
e essential thrust of the work of our Education Officers, let me comment on some
these agencies.

he committee

1e committee has usually either an advisory or an executive function. It is a *think
nk* which provides a collective mentality renewable in short or long term. Its
nction is to develop and formulate policy, to vet programme proposals and to
t agendas for development. Its members are the 'theorists' of the system
sponsible for the overall balance and shape of the output.

committee can vary enormously in composition, size and nature. Whatever its
ape, its role and function are those of a group of experts representing a wide
ansect of educational experience and advice. Membership may be through some
rm of election, designation or even by invitation. It was, for instance, at one
ne, normal procedure for interested agencies, such as the former H.M.
spectorate, teachers' unions, and subject specialist organisations, to nominate
:legates to various national advisory committees such as the Educational
oadcasting Councils of the BBC.

n the other hand, members may be invitees selected by the host organisation on
e basis of individual reputation and known contribution to education. This was
ore commonly the case with the committees of the Independent Television
ommission (ITC) or those of the former Independent Broadcasting Authority
BA). Once appointed, such members were likely to serve for at least two years
ough their term of office was often renewable at times of change and crisis.

'rump' of more experienced members could always be relied on to provide the
ntinuity and stability necessary for ongoing policy development. Some effort was
ways made to strike a rough balance between male and female, old and young,
tional and local representation, regional diversity and ethnic minority groups,
eoreticians and practitioners. There was, inevitably, a bias towards curriculum
velopment and intermeshing links with other committees and agencies in order
provide an element of networking and a means of tapping ancillary sources of
formation.

ich committees may enjoy either statutory or discretionary status. They may be
ee-standing or be integrated into a regional advisory network. In order to conduct
business properly there would frequently be a basic requirement for such a body
meet some 3 – 4 times a year when it could proceed to define custom and practice
rough the usual manner of formally presented papers and minuted decisions. The
sultant case lore would come, in time, to embody a number of precedents necessary
r dictating future development.

Such central committees may also carry on associated or subsidiary business throug cooption, special ad-hoc groups or sub-committees. One particular example of th was formerly found in the IBA 'satellite panels' containing experts and practitione from various phrases (PreSchool/Middle/Secondary) whose chairs would repo to the IBA's Educational Advisory Council. However, this practice was late discontinued when the burden of administration proved too great. There is no a much smaller Schools Advisory Committee which is serviced by ITC.

The producers

Educational programmes were originally conceived and produced by experts i television rather than in education. That was fine all the while those programme represented very broad concepts of enlightenment and enrichment. However, ɛ the remit of such programmes became ever more specific and related to externall determined frameworks for the curriculum, the demand for educational specialis grew.

The establishment of such a cadre of producers with educational background an expertise had long been a desideratum of the governing body of Independe Television companies. As new franchise periods occurred and various forms c mandatory national curricula appeared, the desire became transformed into contractual requirement for the producing companies. The reasons behind suc a policy are self-evident.

a) In a dispersed and federal system it was necessary to build up stable 'centre of excellence' in which companies specialised in certain types of programmir and built on their achievement.

b) The specialist education producer shares with his audience(s) the same theoretic context of background knowledge and of current educational thought an development.

c) The specialist producer can conduct a dialogue between both parties based o shared assumptions and a common language.

d) The producer's ability to match audience requirements shows a capacity t translate a shared vision or philosophy into practical and relevant resource

e) The specialist producer is also able to draw on a wider network of advice an information than the generalist. He or she knows 'ways through the system

f) The specialist producer is also able to commission materials from first-han knowledge and experience. The right criteria for selection and development a brought into play. In the long and fallible chain of transmission of ideas th ability to define and to interpret is crucial.

It is, of course, vital to the role of specialist producers that there should be continui and stability in the provision of a production base as well as a guaranteed marke

lealthy budgets, defined and protected air-time and long-term planning are essential
) the enterprise.

he producer, however talented, cannot always be a polymath. Where then does
ie larger dimension of expert advice and orientation come from?

move now to the series adviser whose conceptual grasp and first-hand knowledge
f curriculum development and classroom practice is essential to the success of
ie series.

he series adviser

he concept of a series adviser who would collaborate with the programme
:searcher and oversee the production of back-up materials is long-standing. The
erson concerned is usually a curriculum developer or a practising teacher who
as established a reputation for innovation and for excellence within the subject
rea. He or she may be drawn from an individual school or in-service centre, a
ational curriculum agency or development project, national or local inspectorates
r subject-specialist associations. He or she is vital in defining

- the right concepts and messages;
- effective illustrations of classroom practice;
- contacts and programme outreach (such as programme-related activities,
  bibliographies for further reading, computer software and other forms of
  back-up);
- feedback into the system;
- new perspectives and directions in new subjects as well as in old ones.

hough series advisers may be individuals or small teams, sometimes the staff of
complete project (as in Health or Humanities) may become associated with series
evelopment thus developing forms of interaction and shared identity. One of the
ost noteworthy of these large-scale advisory processes occurred when the complete
esign and Technology panel of HM Inspectorate provided advice and evaluation
r the pilot series *Craft, Design and Technology*, which was an area they wished
) see developed with greater coherence in schools. Similar in-depth associations
ave occurred between the producers of in-service programmes and the staff of
ie National Curriculum Council or with consortia of local education authorities.
he process is, however, both complex and time-consuming and needs to be very
utly managed.

The educational audiences

The educational audiences – these are the customers whose take-up and quantifie use of programme materials is known or whose needs can be deduced and defined However, evidence about the quality of their use is sparse and disparate. This usuall results from the fact that programme users are dispersed or remotely situated an therefore difficult to access. Their involvement in their work may also allow ther little time for dialogue or response. The main methods of establishing contacts wit them is usually through letters, report cards, telephone calls, school visits an structured INSET meetings. Their responses need *investigation:* What do they thin of the resource? How do they use it? What adaptations were necessary? Whic follow-up was most or least successful?

If one tries to explain the interrelationship of these agencies, the following diagrar of an Information Loop might be useful:

Figure 1: Information Loop

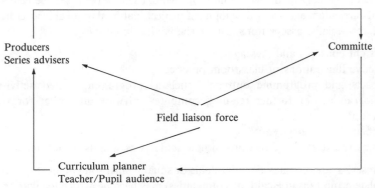

Hence the importance of liaison and its central function in this consultative proce becomes evident by the way in which it binds all these disparate elements togethe through systematic contact and the creation of networks of respondents and c regular interchanges of information.

Liaison and educational broadcasting

What is 'liaison' in the context of educational broadcasting? In the definition c 'liaison' it is essential to bear in mind the fundamental distinction between th following:

– *series-related liaison*, e.g. the research/promotion of a particular subject or approaches;
– general *field liaison*, when the whole system activity is aimed at identifying or responding to trends, issues, priorities, projects and curriculum change.

The plurality of systems in use suggest a multiplicity of interpretation deriving from the nature, structure, remit and budgets of the directing authority. First, it is therefore probably easier to briefly mention some of the features, tasks, functions or activities common to most national educational broadcasting operations before going on to a description of the differing tasks and functions as derived from the location of a Liaison Officer.

Principally, the work of a Liaison Officer may include a broad spectrum of activity encompassing the following:

– being the eyes and ears of the producers;
– sifting, processing (i.e.analysis/interpretation) of data;
– finding out (intelligence gathering);
– identifying trends;
– building up a mosaic of information;
– making known, communicating the results;
– getting involved in the following dimensions of fieldwork:
  Outreach – Promotion – Feedback – Corroboration – Action Research.

In which areas is 'liaison' applied? I have compiled two checklists which refer to the differing tasks and functions as they can be derived from the location of a Liaison Officer, i.e. whether he is affiliated to the headquarter of a federal system like ITV in the UK or working with a regional independent company.

The work of an ITC headquarters Education Officer

The following checklist gives some insight into the work of an Education Officer located in the headquarters of the IBA/ITC up until 1993:

– Appraisal and auditing of national and local liaison needs between
  – Agencies
  – Educational audiences
  – School broadcasting services;
– Creation and development of links and interactive networks for information, promotion and planning;
– Assessment of national and regional education policies and priorities:
  – Dialogue with experts and opinion leaders
  – Links with national curriculum planning agencies, (e.g. the National Curriculum Council, the Curriculum Council for Wales, the Scottish Consultative Committee on the Curriculum, and the Northern Ireland Curriculum Council);

- Intelligence gathering, i.e. analysis, interpretation and collation of data: the transformation into hard evidence and scenarios for development;
- Representation at national conferences/committees in addition to maintaining links with nationally and internationally sponsored projects;
- Servicing a shared programme of field liaison (with BBC and others);
- Work in connection with implementing overall national curriculum reform especially in school-based or school-focused in-service education for teachers (INSET);
- Providing a clearing house of relevant information for the rest of the system (courses, conferences, meetings, internal briefings) and feedback on audience reaction.

The work of an ITV regional Education Officer

Looking at the tasks and functions of the EOs working at a regional level, we find some similarities, but also some differences. In principle, his or her work is directed at two levels within the cooperative network. These are:

- for the employing production company;
- for the whole system.

Work for the employing production company

This includes:

- Market research prior to and during production;
- Development of Local Education Authority advisory networks for programme producers;
- Ensuring producer contacts with school;
- Editing and trialling programme support materials;
- Monitoring programmes;
- Carrying out post-production research and follow-up meetings.

- Co-operative arrangements with BBC Education:
    - commissioning and coordinating research;
    - co-operation in connection with teacher training projects (e.g. Media Literacy, Audiovisual Training, Video Libraries, integration of media into whole school policies and classroom practice).

Effective liaison work in a national network

It must be borne in mind that all these various activities would of course not contribute towards a common goal if there were no set of minimum requirements in terms of coordination and agreement. The following list may serve to provide he various rules-of-thumb for effective liaison within a federal system but at national level:

1. Comparability of function within Education Officers' job descriptions – hybridism does not work.
2. A common code of practice:
   Central discussion of specific tasks and responsibilities, agreement on objectives.
3. Dynamic field work – Proactive rather than reactive strategies: Search! Find! Fix! Strike!
4. Interactive networks with respondent groups, outreach organisations, multipliers, practitioners.
5. Teamwork and partnerships – collaborative projects with federal outlook.
6. Systematic recording: feedback/reporting/collation; central databases.
7. Adequate support (e.g. secretarial, technical, administrative, transport).
8. Respect for regional identity.
9. Whole system operations generated by dispersed and federal networks.
10. A degree of central coordination, communication and control, based on agreed norms and methodology.

Perhaps in conclusion one might quote from an article written by Elizabeth Hunter-Grundin in the *Times Educational Supplement* in 1986:

"The critical question is whether the broadcasters will plan the future in their own studio world – or whether they will involve themselves in a much broader kind of educational development . . .

In order to 'do much better', broadcasters and other educators will need to engage in ongoing collaborative planning and innovative development: looking at a variety of issues: aims, priorities, curriculum development, learning experiences, evaluation to name but a few – things they have not so far tackled *together*".

To achieve that outcome we must first will the means to accomplish it.

Paul Martin

Support Activities for Science and Mathematics Programmes

Central Independent Television is a private company, licensed to operate in the central area of the United Kingdom, in the Midlands, and gains revenue from the sale of advertising time and – to a smaller extent – through programme sales. It operates under a public service licence, part of which requires an educational output for schools and colleges, which has continued for some thirty-five years. That service can be recognised in a number of related contexts, e.g. the broadcasting context, the educational context, and the political and technological contexts.

Broadcasting contexts

The independent television system in the UK, comprising some sixteen private commercially funded companies, currently operates on a public services basis.[1] This means that we make programmes of breadth and depth that would be unnecessary if we were simply concerned with delivering viewers to advertisers.

A part of that commitment is represented by the activities of the Education Department at Central Television in Birmingham. Until the end of 1992, Central Television contributed programmes and other materials to the national ITV Schools service in association with four other major companies, i.e. Granada TV in Manchester, Yorkshire TV in Leeds, and Thames TV in London. Central was responsible for the preparation of about twelve hours of new programmes a year and spent about £ 1.8 million a year on those productions. At times, we have provided a similar support for adult education.

Currently, the service for schools continues for twenty-eight weeks in a school year, transmitting between 9.30 a.m. and midday throughout the week using the transmitters of Channel 4. Approximately 60% of those broadcasts are repeat transmissions.

The new franchise period, starting in January 1993, changes the ways in which ITV Schools is to be organised but does not remove the obligation to provide such a service within the independent system. Central Television, as a shareholder in the

---

[1] See the description of the independent broadcasting system in Part II: Background Information; pp. 242 – 248.

newly formed Educational Television Company, will provide programmes to Channel 4 which now takes responsibility for the service to schools.

Educational contexts

The ITV Schools service is independent of the education service generally, both nationally and locally. Until the end of 1992 the Independent Television Commission, (formerly the IBA), remains constitutionally responsible for the contents, quality and scheduling of programmes, but this power to regulate and control changes as from 1993.

In developing educational materials, the producing companies have relied and will continue to rely on the advice and support of curriculum and other experts, contracted to the companies for particular series of programmes.

The newly introduced and still evolving National Curriculum in England and Wales will have a significant effect on the ways in which television is employed to support the work of teachers and pupils, particularly in light of the parallel initiatives in pupil assessment. Part of the drive for a National Curriculum has been to make the Education service more publicly accountable through reports to parents and by being more open about its achievements. Thus, parents are encouraged to be more aware of what is going on in schools and make a greater contribution to those activities.

Political and technological contexts

Following the 1990 Broadcasting Act, there has been an erosion in the public service ethos, although paradoxically in the UK the new broadcasting regulations have established schools broadcasting as an obligation, as opposed to the more general obligation for an educational service.

However, the changes in requirements have significant and important implications for those education departments that remain within the Channel 3 companies. Whilst the work of programme production is guaranteed for three years, the volume of production is cut by one half to allow the use of independent programme makers. There will be pressures to lower the costs of production, bringing these more in line with costs in the independent sector.

Although we are a broadcasting operation, virtually all the use of our programmes in secondary schools is through 'time shifting', which means that programmes are recorded and used at a more suitable time for that school. Typically, secondary schools would have up to seven or so video recorders. Every primary school has at least one video recorder, some more. Recent figures suggest that about 60% of primary schools record programmes and use them at a time that is more convenient to them. This is a rapidly rising figure.

Re-organisation in the broadcasting industry and the availability of satellite channels make it possible that some alternative way of distributing schools programmes will develop including perhaps a specialist satellite channel that will be used for all educational broadcasting. Under the new arrangements, Channel 4 will transmit a certain part of the schools output at night to remotely operating recorders in schools to be down-loaded there.

New technologies, bringing together the powers of the video image and computer data and graphics, will have a considerable influence on learning, both at school and at home. The power of systems such as CDI and CD-ROM lies in their potential, as yet mainly unrealised, to support the needs of individuals in ways impossible with linear video. Well-crafted materials should allow users control over the information held in the system and offer an opportunity to follow individual paths in a genuinely interactive manner.

Undoubtedly the technological changes that are taking place around us colour what we do, and will have a significant influence on our activities in the near future.

Programme output

The purposes of schools broadcasting over the last thirty years is typified by a slow evolutionary adaptation to school audience needs, punctuated by occasional quantum jumps.

I should like to show you a brief selection of sequences taken from programmes that we have made over the last twenty years to illustrate what I am describing.[2] I have presented those clips of programmes as examples of how, over the years, our perceptions of teachers' needs have changed, and how the service that we offer to schools is dependent on a continuing dialogue between ourselves and schools, to find out what it is they want, and how we can be useful to them in what we present. As a consequence, our programmes are results of rigorous planning and advice-taking sessions.

Television for schools developed for political purposes, not as a consequence of demands by teachers. There remains an uncertainty about the powers of the medium, and how these are best employed within education.

---

[2] The sequences shown here were taken from *Primary Mathematics* (1964); *Figure it Out* (1972); *Leapfrog* (1978); *Videomaths* (1988), and *Science − Start Here!* (1989)

The abilities to take a pupil audience out of the classroom – maybe to the farm down the road, or the factory just the other side of town, or to other sides of the world – are well understood. Television can open the doors of the classroom and bring in things that are not easily available otherwise.

The powers of television also arise from an ability to juxtapose images, to create meaning by the ways that pictures and sounds are assembled. Moreover, this juxtaposition of television images can work powerfully on the emotions. Effective television works on both our cognitive and affective understandings.

Educational broadcasting operates within a relatively well-defined context, in that the majority of the audience is known to be in school, pupils working under the direction and control of an adult professional. In areas of the curriculum which themselves were evolving, and perhaps not well understood by teachers, television has been used to replace the teacher, providing the agenda around which classwork could be constructed. Television forms the focus of activity and 'follow-up work' is pushed to the peripheries. Many of our earlier mathematics and science programmes have had this sort of style and purpose.

Perhaps the need for those instructional programmes lessened, or television producers became more imaginative. But, for whatever reason, in many cases schools programmes have adopted other styles. In science and mathematics, for example, we started to develop a strand of programmes that took the model of children's programming, programmes that often used magazine formats, were fairly fast moving, and used humour. One of my colleagues described this as a 'cafeteria' approach to broadcasting. Other educational series have tried similar collections of items, tied together under a particular theme. Pupils took and explored those ideas that appealed to them, leaving the balance for others.

Nowadays we are concerned with offering a flexible resource for use by teachers. We hope to use the powers of television, the images of television, the strengths of television, to enthuse and engage children, to encourage them to activity.

We know that the problem with television as a teacher is that it has no sense of what pupils' individual needs might be at any time. We bear in mind that children in the classroom are working together with a professional who knows the needs and weaknesses of the children in that audience.

Currently, we are concerned increasingly with the powers of the television image to convey what can be seen as important ideas in maths and science, for pupils to interpret and to explore at their own levels of understanding.[3] We are convinced

---

[3] Comprehensive and critical accounts of Science (pp. 282 – 294) and Mathematics (pp. 311 – 321) broadcasting by ATV Network/Central Independent Television can be found in Manfred Meyer (Ed.) *Aspects of School Television in Europe. A Documentation.* München: K. G. Saur 1992.

that television can be seen both as a resource for teachers, and as a support for pupils' learning.

In support of learning

Television can be very powerful, it can move its audiences both to tears and to action. But in the educational context, those ideas need to be worked on by pupils, to be incorporated into existing ways of understanding, to be made personal. In making ideas personal, pupils can be supported by a range of imagery and through varied activity, presented on a variety of media, including print, sound tapes, slides and computer disc.

We would describe our programmes as planned to support the *learning* of children. I deliberately say to support the *learning* of children, and not the *teaching* of children, because I think that there are very important distinctions to be made between those two concepts – a distinction that is important to us.

Teaching is what a teacher does. It involves an adult reflecting on things which he or she knows, bringing them together in a structured way where the links between ideas are obvious and familiar, and presenting them to children with that map in the back of his or her mind. That logical map we call a curriculum.

If we think about learning, and reflect on our own behaviour as learners when we are faced with ideas which are novel, we come to realise that learning – unlike teaching – is not a well-defined activity which moves us unambiguously from place to place. On the contrary, learning is fragile, unpredictable and prone to regression. It is not a logical process, it is a haphazard, random process. Sometimes we know things, sometimes we think we know things, sometimes we know we know things. What learning is about, is the rehearsing of a new idea and the fitting it into the mind to make sense with those things that we already think we know.

Educational broadcasting for schools should be concerned with offering resources to both pupils and teachers that supports children in that uncertain process where they move from some slight confidence with certain ideas to a greater and richer confidence in what they are doing.

Programme enhancement

Since the early days of educational broadcasting, producers working with professional advice and support have looked to enhance the television programmes by a range of other materials that make those programmes more effective in their support of class-based learning. Enhancement is what we build around our television offerings that makes them more useful to teachers and pupils in schools.

When I think about programme enhancement I look under these headings – books for teachers, support through professional associations, books for children and computer software. A number of those elements come as a result of constructive joint ventures with commercial publishing houses rather than through our own immediate expertise.

I remember coming to a conference here in Munich some years ago in which we spent several happy afternoons talking about what I would call the educational technology approach to broadcasting. We had long and interesting conversations about the ways in which different media might be integrated – video with print, print with sound tapes, and so on, as if somehow our offerings could be assembled into a neat, logical jigsaw.

Within my Company we have moved on from that sort of view, and for various reasons. The most obvious reason is that we are incapable of preparing many of those things by ourselves. We do not have a publishing division, nor do we have a radio section.

Secondly, curriculum materials are often the product of a particular person or a particular group of people at a particular time. They serve the needs of those people wonderfully, but they rarely exactly match the needs of the much larger number of people who are going to put those materials into practice. One cannot devise closely integrated packages that will also be flexible enough to reflect the diversity in schools.

Thirdly, although there might be some intellectual reward in trying to create a tightly integrated package of materials, in fact this does not reflect the way the children learn, become more able and more confident with what they are doing. We have reason to believe that children learn through experiencing the same ideas in different forms at different times and in different places.

When we enhance our programmes, what we are hoping to do is to offer the opportunity to youngsters to experience, in the context of the classroom, some of the activities that have been suggested through the watching of certain things on television.

Maybe this will be a direct copy of what was seen, because the experience of actually doing it yourself is so very significantly different from the experience of watching other people doing it. Perhaps those classroom activities will *relate* to the television activity rather than copy it directly.

In connection with Central's programme output, the first thing perhaps I should talk about is the range of books that we produce, as part of an umbrella of support activity that we build round television programmes. We conceive this as a way of taking television from the centre of attention to put it back to the peripheries, as just another resource. This would leave the needs of young people, as learners at the centre, with their own teachers best able to mediate those things to make their learning more effective.

Every programme we produce is supported by a comprehensive guide for teachers, sixty or seventy pages thick. It usually includes information for teachers, telling them what is in a programme, what are the general purposes, what are the particular purposes, how it fits into the National Curriculum. Then there are suggestions for activity with children – suggestions for long-term work, for investigation, for short-term work, or suggestions for things you might like to do immediately.

Many of my colleagues have suggested how dependent we are on the advice of people – teachers, advisers, inspectors, experts in all fields, in ensuring that what we do is appropriate.

Not only do we rely on professional support and help in producing programmes but, as a part of the enhancement of our programmes, we also cooperate with a range of professional associations developing curriculum material of their own. Teachers and pupils benefit from the enhanced value of such packages, and from any synergies that might arise.

The choice of media is never a truly open one. Central Television, for instance, has expertise in video production, an ability at some forms of printing, but no radio experience.

Since we do not have within our own organisation the ability for colour printing, we rely on joint ventures with educational publishers and specialist organisations in order to produce sophisticated colourful material that is attractive to children and so to enhance the print side of our activity. These science books are available in bookshops, but schools can also buy them as part of a package with the video programmes that we produce and broadcast. The books complement and add another dimension to the subject.

One particular example is the project *Science and Technology in Society (SATIS)*, a project sponsored by the Association for Science Education (ASE), a professional association in the United Kingdom to encourage the teaching and learning of science.

Under the title *Science – Start Here!* we produced a series of fourteen science programmes for children of 8 years and over, the ASE produced print materials. The programmes were broadcast, but video copies were also made available to schools as part of packages that contained the video tapes, the pupils' booklets and a sound cassette produced by the BBC.

Another example the publication *What's your reaction?* Here the Royal Society of Chemistry produced a comprehensive book to support primary science. We produced a series of videos that were broadcast as part of our INSET series

Programmes for Primary Teachers; the series is also available in a package for teachers. The two together are more useful to teachers than the individual elements. Lastly, we prepare packages containing computer software using the skills of software companies. We do not have the expertise in our Department for software programming, but we have the ability to make joint ventures with software houses to produce packages of software that provide another element to enhance our television programmes.

An example is *Video Maths*, a maths series for primary schools. Apart from the usual pupils' and teachers' booklets we have prepared a package of computer disks with a guide containing descriptions of the programmes and cards for children to use directly if they so wish.

I should say that we are not in the business of making huge, expensive materials; we do plan and commission attractive but discrete pieces of software over which children have control and which they can use as part of their learning.

The marketing mix – beneficial for all

In summary, ITV Schools is distributed as a free service of programmes, through broadcasting, supported by the sale of publications. Contact with schools is maintained through television or by an extensive mailing operation.

Through associations with professional bodies and curriculum development projects Central gains considerable benefit in the planning and subsequent exploitation of educational materials. This includes extra marginal revenue from royalty arrangements and through the direct sale of packages with videos.

By the sharing of writers and advisers, we are able to focus our materials in order to support particular areas and activities within the curriculum. Conversely, print and software publishers have an advantage from their association with broadcast television.

Examples already mentioned include work to complement the *Science and Technology in Society* project of the Association for Science Education, and in connection with the Royal Society of Chemistry. Those Associations gain through the development of potentially expensive video materials, at no cost to them; Central gains through a proper targeting of its audience, and from the support professional organisations give in promotion, particularly the organising of in-service activity for teachers. Both parties benefit through the sale of video-based packages.

Outlook

The ways in which we support pupils and teachers in schools within the United Kingdom has evolved over thirty years. Current thinking politically, technologically and pedagogically makes significant change inevitable. The future of our activities will crucially depend on an understanding of the needs of teachers and pupils and our ability to satisfy these through productions of quality.

The National Curriculum offers a unifying framework for such work, although paradoxically, curriculum development and support may look towards more flexible ways of satisfying individual needs.

Packages of materials and the new evolving technologies would be ways of meeting these conflicting demands. Joint ventures with publishers and other specialists benefit both the producers and users of materials.

The pressure to involve parents more actively in the educational process, and the need for continuing education and training through adult life, in association with new technologies, will open to broadcasters a range of activity for the use of their skills outside broadcasting.

Rolf Horneij

Learning Foreign Languages by Television: The Role of Back-up Material

have been requested to talk about the importance of back-up material, a theme that I gained some knowledge about during my experience as an educational broadcaster. This time the subject has been confined to language teaching by television – a theme particularly dear to me. As Head of the Programme Department for Foreign Languages I am in the fortunate position of being able to combine television with almost all conceivable 'back-ups'. 'Accompanying material', 'auxiliary material' or 'support material' – they have been called many names, these little things that make television a viable didactic tool.

work for the Swedish Educational Broadcasting Company *Utbildningsradion* (UR), which is a broadcasting company within the Swedish Radio Group. It is a public service organisation financed by licence fees; 5% of the total budget is dedicated to educational programming.[1]

The way the company is organised gives us an idea of the educational policy that we believe in. There are three operative units, producing either programmes for schools, or courses for adult education, or courses for language teaching to be used either in schools or by adult learners.

Each unit has access to all media: television, radio, print, teletext, and that is an important factor. We can combine the media, create multi-media projects, and we do so in most cases, particularly in language teaching. Many other broadcasters in Europe cannot combine the broadcast media radio and television as easily as we can due to organisational matters: TV and radio are separate houses.

venture to say that, in language teaching over the air, radio is the best medium. Radio and language teaching are congenial. Of course television is stronger, has more impact, whereas a radio programme has difficulty in reaching its intended listener. Alternatively, radio is not as exposed to the public ear as television is to the public eye. A dilemma, a paradox? – It need not be. One medium can back up the other, and that is what I intend to demonstrate in the following, also as a strategy for the future. I will now give you a glimpse of a Swedish experience of language teaching by television and related media.

For some information on UR, see Part II, pp. 224–226.

115

I have chosen one project that will hopefully convince us all that television – a powerful as it may seem – cannot function by itself as an effective didactic tool *Pozjalujsta* is the name of the course. The word is Russian and means 'please' This course was an enormous success when it was launched in the autumn of 1991. It had good press coverage and – what is most important – many students. The book accompanying the course was near the top of the list of the best-selling books of the month of September. There must have been an explanation for this which was inherent in the material. The historic coincidence is evident. Time for analysis!

Our policy is to provide opportunities for adults – late in life – to learn a foreign language, and there are always at least two courses on the air, both on radio and on television, in the languages that the younger generations can learn at school. Following English, German, French, Spanish, Italian it was now Russian's turn. We see as our target student a man or a woman in the middle of life, working, with children, maybe with aging parents to look after – with very little spare time, and to a large extent with no previous study practice.

Being licence-fee payers, people are of course entitled even to something as exclusive as a course in Russian. In fact, it is not as exclusive as it may seem. With the advent of the *'perestroijka'*, Swedes cruised in large numbers over the Baltic Sea to St Petersbourg. Motivation to learn Russian was at hand. We decided to produce a course with a broad appeal, open and with a pace suitable to people with limited access to spare time.

In order to dedramatise the idea of the complexity of the Russian alphabet, we decided at an early stage to split the course into two parts, the first part being an overture presenting the Russian alphabet together with a phrase-book. We accepted the sad idea that many students would be content with only that first part. The 33 Russian letters were presented in six television programmes, and these first programmes also introduced the two main characters for the whole course: A Russian singer called Jelena, and – as her pupil – Täppas, a known figure in Sweden and a TV personality. They were chosen because of their public appeal in the hope to stimulate the viewers to continue and take the whole course.

The programmes were broadcast at next to peak-time, with what was a comparatively large audience for an educational programme. It seemed so easy to learn the letters. But, alas, it was also easy to forget them. So we provided a back-up in the form of a booklet with explanations and exercises, and an audio-cassette for the pronunciation.

Audio-cassette and booklet were as a matter of fact sufficient to achieve the learning goal. A motivated student could do without television. That was the nature of the relationship between television and its so-called back-up material. I think this deserves our attention. I am not inferring that we can do without television. We must appear on it, as that is where the audience and the market place is.

As to the main course, it so happened that the Finnish television had produced a multi-media course in Russian with parts of it filmed in the Soviet Union. Scripted parts were performed by Russian actors. These scenes were the nucleus, with various exercises in radio and television grouped around them. Within the framework of the Nordvision Treaty we acquired the Russian scenes without having to pay for them, and we used them as a raw material and adapted them for a Swedish context, which means that explanations of grammatical matters were given in Swedish and, linguistically, Russian was contrasted to Swedish.

We created a pedagogical situation on the screen: A living-room, a video-cassette player, the Russian singer Jelena and the publicly known, humorous personality Täppas. She teaches him Russian and his role is that of the interested and very 'average' learner. Her teaching material is the video player, and they look at the scenes from the Soviet Union. It is a story about a Finn going by train to Moscow. The television audience is invited to share the learning process with Jelena and Täppas.

The programmes were said to have had great entertainment value, more specifically didactic entertainment. It has been a deliberate ambition to give each medium a very specific role, taking into account its characteristics. The principle is that each new chapter in the course book is introduced by a television programme where the two programme leaders look at the filmed story, comment on it, explain linguistic items and finally view the whole story again. Graphics are used extensively.

The mastering of a language is not only an insight, a knowledge. It is a skill. To obtain a skill one has to practise. We have found that television does not lend itself to inviting the audience to be active in the sense of producing phrases or pronouncing words aloud for example. Television has to be backed up by other means, and this is where radio and language learning prove to be congenial, provided that you are alone with your radio in your room.

The way the ideal learner is supposed to act goes from

– firstly – watching television to
– secondly – listening to the radio, with the book in his or her hand.

On each chapter in the book there is one television programme and four radio programmes. The television dialogue is the nucleus; it presents the language that is studied, and thus it is also printed in the book and recorded for use in the radio programmes.

The radio programmes do not just continue where the television programmes finish. They introduce the new text in their own way, proper to the possibilities offered by radio. Reactions from the audience told us that two successive presentations of the same text were not too much.

Each lesson is presented in one 30-minute television programme and four 20-minute radio programmes broadcast during two weeks. Presuming we as broadcasters have been successful in reaching the learner, we may conclude that he or she undoubtedly has many opportunities to acquire a certain command of Russian.

It is difficult to say which medium backs up the others. In this project design all media are necessary. It may be expressed as follows: They are all back-ups − they all back up the learner in his desire to learn Russian, in our case. Radio and the course-book are totally integrated. At times the programmes are incomprehensible without the printed page.

It is possible to study on your own with a book, television and radio. The back-up activities may be extended, however. We inform the audience about the possibility of joining a study circle and thus receiving support from a teacher and fellow students. The audio-visual centres scattered around the country are entitled to record our programmes and distribute them on tape to schools, adult education associations as well as libraries.

If you as a learner choose to join a study circle you may not want to listen to and watch the programmes when you can listen to them and watch them at home. What you want in a group is the text − the scenes. To satisfy that need we provide the audio-visual centres with special versions of the programmes where the 'teaching' elements are cut out.

The classical Teacher's Guide is of course included in the package. We organise week-end courses together with adult education centres where our main function is to recruit the participants with the help of our media. A distance education school provides the possibility to get an upper secondary school certificate in Russian.

I would like to mention one last back-up possibility which, however, is not used in the Russian course because we cannot yet produce Russian letters − and that is teletext. But in the other language courses we use some pages of the teletext service that is broadcast by my company for word lists and various exercises using the possibility of hidden text. For instance, the student receiving teletext is asked to produce the corresponding nouns to the verbs written on the screen.

Even teletext can be used as a didactic tool in other ways. It can be used to back up a television programme. We broadcast documentaries in foreign languages for educational purposes where the only back-up is a word-list on teletext.

Having watched television alone, the viewer or learner will have gained an impression of what it is like to learn Russian; he or she will have felt joy at coming so close to understanding some of this strange language, or will have gained an insight and a certain knowledge. However, he or she will not have developed any skill. A skill presupposes practice, and, in my view, a wisely conceived television programme leaves this to other media, to radio, print, group studies, etc.

have worked with educational broadcasting, including the teaching of foreign anguages, for nearly 20 years. When I started, Swedish Television was in sole ontrol, i.e. it was a monopoly. That is no longer the case for now we are competing vith many other broadcasters on a battlefield. On battlefields one needs a strategy. 'rom my experience the best strategy is to link programming with other activities, ›e it radio in conjunction with television, the publishing of printed material, the ›rganisation of study groups.

'or a successful educational programme the ultimate goal is activity at the receiving nd. Mere viewing is not sufficient. The command of a foreign language is a skill, .nd obtaining a new skill presupposes training and practice. A network of ›ossibilities aiming at helping the viewer to be active is essential, and this is what listinguishes an educational programme from general output programming. That s the quality factor in an educational programme − and our contribution to the hriving, aggressive media landscape.

Henk Jakobsen

Promoting and Marketing School Television Programmes in the Netherlands

Intensive direct mail campaigns

For over 25 years, virtually all Dutch television programmes for schools have been accompanied by written material in the form of books for pupils, teachers' manuals, posters, slides, and sometimes audio cassettes with songs. The *Nederlandse Onderwijs Televisie* (NOT) believes in this multi-media approach, and the educational system is glad to make use of it. There is a high level of satisfaction, both with the television programmes and with the accompanying material.

Every year NOT supplies schools with approximately one million books; the total annual turnover of the publishing company is about 4 million guilders. Despite the many problems in the field of education in the Netherlands, including cuts and the introduction of a new budgeting system, the turnover of our publishing company's products has remained at more or less the same level. With a view to increasing the average viewing figures and selling the related written material, NOT carries out a communication programme every year, in the form of an intense direct mail campaign.

Means of communication used by NOT

The school television guide

This television guide contains all the information about both programmes and the related materials. On the basis of this information, the teachers can determine which television projects they wish to use in their classes. The guide is published four times a year and distributed regularly in four waves:

1. the autumn edition sent to all schools always at first by the end of May;
2. the autumn edition sent to all schools again a second time in August;
3. the spring edition always sent at the end of November;
4. the spring edition sent to all schools again in the first week of January.

Posters with the broadcasting times

There is a poster with the broadcasting times that goes out with every guide, mainly used for planning video recordings, as well as an order list. Virtually all schools hang the poster on the wall, and when it has been decided in which projects the school will participate, the order list is filled in and returned to the NOT. These mailings are sent free or charge. The NOT has its own address file which contains the addresses of all the schools in the Netherlands. Business companies and institutions can also advertise in the school television guide.

Interim mailings as a reminder

For primary schools, interim mailings are sent out as a reminder. The great advantage of these direct mail campaigns is the fact that the response can be measured. On the basis of the orders sent in as order lists or by telephone orders, it soon becomes clear which projects are doing well and which are not. In a thematic promotional campaign it is much more difficult and expensive to measure the response. Furthermore, it takes much longer to plan and produce a thematic campaign. The artwork must be completed in time, foolproof arrangements must be made with the media, such as television and magazines.

As NOT organises every direct mail campaign itself, which includes developing the ideas and producing the texts, we are able to try and improve the viewing figures and the turnover just before the start of the planned broadcasts. In this respect, the Public Relations Department of NOT is enormously flexible. Sometimes an interim mailing results in a gigantic response. A few years ago, a mailing about a series on the life and work of the painter Vincent van Gogh resulted in a 100% increase of expected sales. Thus an interim mailing can have a significant effect on the ultimate turnover.

Becoming increasingly important: the telephone

Members of the teaching profession do not only send letters to order materials. On the contrary, there is an increasing tendency to order materials over the phone. The PR department is strongly encouraging this trend and the school television guide reminds readers of the telephone number of the sales department at every opportunity. It is clearly printed on every page. The telephone number is also clearly shown on order lists and posters, and at the end of every broadcast the number is always shown on the screen.

Over a quarter of all the orders are taken by telephone, and it looks as though this trend will continue in the next few years. On very busy days, for example, immediately after the holidays, employees in the sales department have taken as many as 400 calls in a single day.

Mailings to private addresses of teachers

Communicating with teachers in secondary education is quite a different matter. It is true that secondary schools always receive the school TV guides, posters and order lists, but NOT considers that it is very important, in addition, to send information about the current school television programmes directly to subject teachers. These mailings are carried out very simply; they usually consist of a letter with an order card. Nevertheless, the mailings reach a very wide readership. In summer 1992, for example, the mailing list for geography teachers contained 5,430 addresses, the one for history teachers 4,714 addresses, and the one for teachers in physics 6,876 addresses.

The PR department produces all the texts of these mailshots itself. Obviously this also applies to the production supervision, planning etc.. The addresses are purchased externally. The pre-postal processing and printing is carried out by a graphic agency. The external purchase of addresses and postal costs mean that this strategy is reasonably expensive. Nevertheless, the viewing figures in secondary education remain fairly high, and NOT believes that this result is partly due to the intense mailing strategy to the private addresses of various subject teachers.

New trend: sponsorship

Dutch broadcasters in general, i.e. not only a small organisation such as NOT, will be faced in the 1990s with reduced budgets. Because of the arrival of the commercial channel RTL-4 with an expected viewing density of 25%, a significant proportion of the advertising income is disappearing from the public broadcasters to RTL-4.

In addition, the Minister of Public Health and Culture is not very interested in increasing television licences, the source of income which also finances Dutch school television. Therefore the NOT is increasingly introducing sponsored school television projects. For example, last spring the NOT launched a series on crime prevention entitled *Criminality* with the financial support of the Ministry of Justice. The available funds were spent not only on the production of television programmes, but also on direct mail. Every teacher of social sciences was sent free of charge a sample copy, a letter and an order card to his or her private address. The result: 25,000 booklets were sold within 4 weeks.

Name advertising: TV commercials and outside advertising on buses

Of the entire communication strategy, NOT spends the largest part of the budget on direct marketing activities in the form of school television guides, interim folders and mailings to teachers. As stated above, this results in a response that can be measured. This is necessary because the NOT posts the written material accompanying the school television programmes *directly* to the schools.

Obviously, advertising its name is another essential activity for the company. However, there is no structural budget available for this. During the autumn of 1991, NOT produced an expensive television commercial, but this was a great exception. The commercial, which was regularly shown in September, presents a colourful television set with human eyes driving into a school.

The campaign was supported with large stickers on city buses in large towns such as Amsterdam, Rotterdam, The Hague and Utrecht. In addition, the NOT advertised regularly in several national newspapers. Evaluative research has shown that the TV commercial scored the highest in terms of *what was remembered*. It became also clear that the general public is not very familiar with the name of the NOT. This is quite logical, as NOT broadcasts its programmes only during school hours. Nevertheless, we will continue to try and find other ways of making the name of the NOT more widely known to the general public, for example, by broadcasting a new educational magazine entitled *School Matters* in the early evening.

In addition, recently the NOT has been participating in the national schools' football competition, in which nearly all Dutch primary school children are taking part. By means of an attractive style of reporting on the tournaments, broadcast during and outside school hours, and NOT advertising boards during the finals, the public was also confronted with the name of NOT.

Summary

Intensive direct mail activities are and always will be the spearhead of our communication policy. Direct mail provides us with a response which can be measured (viewing figures and sales results). Successful direct mailing requires permanent attention and professional supervision. The project leader must be familiar with all the ins and outs in the field of direct marketing.

There is a great deal of flexibility in internal planning, production of text, and production supervision. A well-structured database can provide interesting possibilities for sectoral communication. For example, the NOT can send separate mailings to the group of non-orderers and can make a special offer to this sector. With the use of reply cards identifiable by a special code, it will soon become clear whether this strategy is worthwhile. The telephone is becoming increasingly important. The technical possibilities for processing replies are growing daily. Voice response systems (talking computers) and orders by modem or Teletext are fascinating developments in the fields of information technology.

Yoshiyuki Fukushima

Activities in Support of Educational Programmes in Japan

Introduction

With the start of the satellite broadcasting age, transmissions in HDTV − or Hi Vision as we call it − have now been started in Japan for around 8 hours a day NHK, the Japan Broadcasting Corporation, has quickly responded to this new trend by producing new educational programmes for HDTV. We are keenly aware of the need to explore new possibilities for education, making full use of the latest media, for today's children who will shape the 21st century. On the basis of this concept, NHK has been encouraging all its stations across Japan to produce high quality educational programmes.

Basic facts about NHK's educational programmes

NHK is Japan's only public broadcaster, with a history of well over half a century and it is financed mainly by receiving fees. On its nation-wide networks, NHK currently operates two satellite TV channels, two terrestrial TV channels, and three radio services. One of the two terrestrial TV channels is used by NHK's general programme output, which broadcasts mainly news and entertainment programmes for the general audience, and the other channel is devoted to educational television with programmes related to education of various sorts. Having a channel exclusively for educational purposes, which started 30 years ago, is a major feature of NHK

Educational television is broadcast daily for a total of 18 hours, from six in the morning until twelve midnight. Its programmes are full of variety. They can be broadly classified as follows:

- programmes for schools
- programmes for preschool children
- programmes for children and teenagers, to be viewed at home
- programmes for life-long education, sub-divided into
  - general culture courses
  - courses on hobbies
  - welfare-oriented programmes for the elderly
  - language courses

124

A recent survey shows that more than 30 % of the Japanese watch NHK's Educational TV at least once a week. In other words, one out of every three Japanese watches this channel regularly. This figure is expected to further increase in the future.

Comments on the categories of educational programmes

Programmes for schools are the core of NHK's educational programmes. In Japan, the compulsory education system requires children to attend primary and junior high schools for a total of 9 years, from the ages of 6 to 15. More than 95 % of those who have graduated from junior high school then proceed to attend senior high school.

NHK prepares systematic programming for use in primary and junior high schools, which is broadcast daily from 9:00 to 13:00. The programmes cover practically all the subjects taught at school, including music, Japanese language, natural science, social science and ethics. In addition, programmes outside the school curriculum or related to new educational trends are also presented, such as those on environmental issues.

All the programmes are strictly in accordance with the standards of school curricula set by Japan's Ministry of Education, and they take full advantage of the audio-visual characteristics of television broadcasting.

Today, 95 % of the primary schools across Japan use NHK's school programmes in their classrooms. The programmes are all produced by the NHK staff, but when it comes to drawing up programming policy and planning, the staff consult with school teachers, educational researchers and other people concerned. They also discuss the contents of the programmes.

So-called lifelong learning has become very popular in Japan today, which is rapidly becoming an aging society. With the life expectancy for Japanese men reaching 76.1 years and that for Japanese women 82.1 years, people are becoming more concerned about how to enjoy their lives after retirement.

For this reason, a growing number of Japanese are taking interest in lifelong education, and their demand for related educational programmes on television and radio is on the rise. As NHK's educational programmes meet this demand in their function as a useful source of educational and cultural information, they are frequently watched by adult learners.

For general viewers, there are cultural programmes featuring lectures by well-known authorities. These programmes enjoy a good audience response because of their high quality, comparable to that of university lectures.

There are also welfare-oriented programmes, which teach sign language for the hearing impaired in addition to basic knowledge about social welfare and nursing care techniques. Other programmes show senior citizens enjoying life by keeping busy in various activities.

Furthermore, programmes for young mothers and children at home, including cartoons and children's cooking lessons, are broadcast every evening. The ratings of some of these programmes exceed six percent of the audience − one percent corresponding to one million viewers in Japan.

Learning foreign languages is regarded by many Japanese as a sure way to improve international understanding. In response, NHK broadcasts ten language courses, with the main emphasis on English. There are also Japanese language courses for foreign residents in Japan.

Table 1: Main Types of Educational Programmes Produced by NHK's Educational Television

	Length and number of programmes per week (including repeats)	
Programmes for schools	1,375 min.	
For primary schools		73
For junior high schools		17
and senior high schools		——
		90
Programmes for pre-school children at home	1,110	66
Programmes for correspondence courses, educational seminars	510	1
General culture courses	250	5
Courses on hobbies	900	2
Welfare-oriented programmes (programmes for the elderly)	190	10
Language courses	900	43

The staff members working on educational programmes study hard to acquire special knowledge regarding the subjects they are assigned to, but they are also willing to seek help from experts and university researchers. They do so by setting up committees or inviting suitable advisers for each programme, so the educational point of view receives the consideration it deserves. After all, the value of educational programmes depends on reliable contents.

Support activities for educational programmes

The aim of educational programmes is not only to convey knowledge to students via broadcasting media but also to provide a variety of services to help strengthen their will to learn by means of supportive activities. I would like to refer to a few of these currently provided by NHK.

Publication of textbooks

Each educational programme I mentioned earlier has a textbook containing a synopsis of each programme, supplementary material and broadcasting schedule so that viewers can prepare themselves before watching the programme and thus understand it better.

Establishment of committees

In the case of programme series, a committee is set up consisting of users, educational experts and production staff to discuss whether the programmes are satisfactory to the viewers, and whether the programme contents are suitable. In addition, symposiums on the use of programmes are held from time to time, and producers may take this opportunity to make suggestions on the educational effectiveness of the programmes.

Wide range of media mix activities

NHK makes full use of high-tech new media in preparing value-added teaching materials. For example, broadcast programmes are repackaged as videotapes or videodisks, to expand the learning environment by allowing multilateral and deeper study.

Recently, what is called the HYPER media learning system, linked with a computer, has been attracting wide attention. NHK launched the development of this learning system two years ago, and it has produced related software, including an environmental feature titled *Man and Forests*. This was produced in Hi-Vision or HDTV, which can give viewers a sense of being on the scene.

The HYPER media learning system allows direct printing of textbooks from the Hi-Vision images, and these images can also be recorded in a laser disk together with many other images. When these are linked with a computer, children are able to engage in interactive study. This multimedia educational system is very well suited to studying environmental issues and other subjects that must be dealt with from various angles; hence it has been arousing considerable interest.

Now that broadcasting in Hi-Vision is under way in Japan, educational programmes on history, environmental science and many other subjects are being produced in Hi-Vision. These will form the core of our pursuit of new possibilities in multi-media education.

Table 2: New educational TV programmes in Hi-Vision
expanding the scope of learning through broadcasting

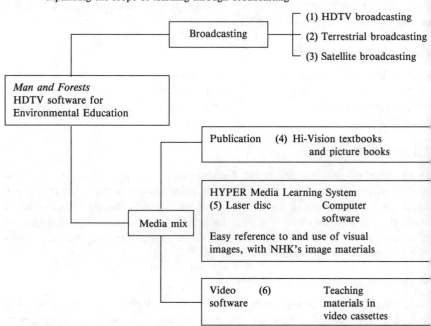

Future prospects of educational broadcasts and supportive activities

Application of multi-media

What we see on the television screen today is not only images from broadcasting studios but also from computers and videodisks. The picture tube is no longer the monopoly of broadcasters. In this multi-media age featuring many technological innovations, we broadcasters are required to develop new ways of using them. Telephone calls and fax, for instance, can now be used in live programmes to answer questions from viewers directly.

Personalisation of study

There has been a growing trend toward the personalisation of studies. In addition to the conventional style of collective viewing of educational programmes and studying together, more and more children take keen interest in personal study which can be done whenever and wherever they like.

For the youngsters who grew up playing with computer games, studying means an interactive relationship with picture screens; they feel this is the natural way to obtain information. Since last year, Japan's primary and junior high schools have seen the introduction of large numbers of computers. Like television in its early days, computers today are regarded as the most up-to-date tool of education.

Mass media were originally targeted at as many people as possible. But in view of the recent trends toward the diversification and personalisation of the learners' needs, mass media must do much to cope with the new situation.

Problems to be solved

NHK is fully aware of the necessity to do its best in the development of high quality educational programmes that reflect the needs of the times. With the progress in this age of images, it is almost certain that they will play the central role in the new media.

In this respect, there are great expectations regarding the vast amounts of visual materials stored at NHK and its know-how in creating visual materials for educational programmes. I believe that the future development of multi-media, with broadcast programmes at its core, will prove highly viable in the educational market, which explains why a data base system for visual materials should be established.

In the evaluation of educational programmes, the criterion should not be the viewing ratings. It is the close feedback circuit between the programme staff and the users that contributes to the development of confidence between them and to the improvement of programme quality. Instead of aiming at immediate results, we should concentrate on how best to use broadcasting media for education, with the goal of creating new value for educational programmes in the long term.

Chapter 4:
Cooperation and Partnership: Media Integration and Shared Responsibility

Hans Paukens

Cooperation with German Broadcasting Organisations: Experience of the Adolf Grimme Institute

have been asked to give a talk on the experiences of the *Adolf Grimme Institute* (AGI) in its cooperation with German broadcasting organisations. For many the question will certainly arise, what the Adolf Grimme Institute is and whose interests represents, for example, in its cooperation with German broadcasting organisations. The Adolf Grimme Institute has always been an agent of German adult education in the Federal Republic of Germany – and cooperation between broadcasting organisations and adult education is the subject of this talk.

The cooperation of German adult education with the broadcasting organisations older than the Adolf Grimme Institute, which was founded in 1973 as a media institute of the German Association of Adult Education Colleges. In 1963 the German Association of Adult Education Colleges donated the *Adolf Grimme Prize*, which was awarded this year for the 28th time. The Adolf Grimme Prize is today one of the most prestigious television prizes, because it is independent. It was and ill is the aim, the intention, of the donor, the German Association of Adult Education Colleges, to generate discussion on the social areas of culture, adult education and television, on the programme, on programme performances and programme quality.

131

One of the tasks of the Institute is to test models of cooperation between televisio and adult education in the area of the systematic integration and combination c teaching media and organisations that we talk about in Germany as *'Medienve bund'*.[1]

Research, counselling, information, training and qualification are the central tasl which could be given to describe the current profile of the Adolf Grimme Institu in a nutshell. The Institute was and still is an organisation which fosters a cooperati relationship to the broadcasting organisations, even though the conditions c cooperation have constantly changed in the last 20 years. Taking three projec as an example, I want to describe and explain the development of the integrate media in the Federal Republic of Germany and thus the cooperation and chang it has undergone.

'Un-Ruhestand' (Restless Retirement; 1980 – 1983)

The integrated media's project *'Un-Ruhestand'* was implemented in the area c social learning and political education between the Second German Televisio (ZDF), a paperback publisher, the Adolf Grimme Institute and the institutes c adult education.[2]

The aims

The multi-media project aimed at providing ideas for conscious and active way of dealing with growing older and wanted to promote the effective representatic of old people's interests.

The instruments

The Second German Television produced seven feature films on the followir subjects:

– The relationship of older to younger people
– Partnership in old age
– How old people live
– The financial situation in old age

---

[1] Articles on different aspects of the 'Medienverbund' and its historical development have be compiled in the workshop report 'Medien – Bildung. Welche Zukunft hat der Medienverbund (Media – education. What future for integrated media systems?). Marl: Adolf-Grimme-Instit 1990.

[2] Cf. Borchert, Manfred; Derichs-Kunstmann, Karin; Hamann, Magret: Un-Ruhestan Reinbek: Rowohlt 1986 (2nd Edition).

- Coming to terms with death
- Women growing older
- Going into retirement
- Elderly people's self-help groups

was intended that the plot should offer an opportunity for identification and provide emotional ideas for discussion in the adult education courses.

paperback – a print of 65,000 copies – was meant to introduce people to the subject by means of examples, illustrations and photos. Material for discussion readers was devised as working material and gave them additional hints on the media and other written matter.

The meetings in further education were intended to make people start talking; they were the place where information could be given, where discussions on the subjects brought up in the films or by the participants took place.

'Un-Ruhestand' was – even though there were a number of smaller and larger problems in implementing it – one of the most successful multi-media projects in the area of social learning. More than 4,000 discussion circles involving well over 40,000 participants took place as part of this project from 1980 to 1982.

The reasons for the success

- The project had a sufficiently long preliminary phase; it was possible to intensively prepare personnel from adult education and to carefully organise the coordination of the constituent parts;
- The discussion leaders had a chance to make use of the individual parts of the multi-media programme according to their requirements and those of the participants, because it was conceived so that it was didactically flexible;
- The interest of those involved was addressed by the subjects of the multi-media programme.

Alphabetisierung' (Literacy campaign; 1984 – 1988)

The aims

Unlike the integrated media project described above, which had a strong didactic component and in which the television films were also planned as instructional material, the aims of the project with the title *Writing and Reading For All* were:

- to use the opportunities offered by radio and television to inform and enlighten the public and the social groups concerned on the problem of functional illiteracy in the industrialised nations; and

133

- to motivate the target group, which meant encouraging adult illiterates to tak part in reading and writing courses at institutes of further education.[3]

The instruments

The TV spots:

The Norddeutscher Rundfunk and the Westdeutscher Rundfunk produced 12 five minute television spots. They were also transmitted in Hesse and Bavaria. Variou TV personalities (e.g. Dagmar Berghoff, Götz George, Eberhard Feik, Will Millowitsch and others) gave basic information on the causes, extent and distribution of illiteracy, the conditions under which it arises and possible ways of effectivel combating it. Prominent people from television were chosen to increase the intende effectiveness of the spots and also to bolster the credibility of the information, which at first seemed implausible to the great majority of viewers.

In addition, those affected presented their individual problem area. This was mean to strengthen motivation and appeal and to encourage people to take advantag of appropriate learning courses in Adult Education Colleges and other adul education institutes.

In a final service section the TV personalities pointed out the courses offered in further education and gave a telephone number under which illiterate viewers, thei friends and acquaintances could obtain information and advice.

Telephone counselling:

The telephone counselling centres were as a rule located at the regional offices o the Adult Education Colleges. Their purpose was to give information on appropriat courses available. It could be felt in the case of most of the callers, the telephon counsellors reported, how difficult those concerned found the first call. Ofter partners, acquaintances or relatives would call on their behalf. Some callers only wanted brief information on courses offered in their area; others, after a short time were describing their situation and problems with great urgency.

Material for local and regional public relations:

In addition to the mass media radio and television, material was developed by the Adolf Grimme Institute for local public relations. Not only data and facts but also interviews and conversations with German illiterates on the causes and background were printed and prepared for the local press.

---

[3] Cf. Horn, Wolfgang; Paukens, Hans (Ed.): Alphabetisierung, Schriftsprache, Medien. (Literacy, written language, media.) Ismaning 1985.

n this prospectus the integrated media did not mean didactically conceiving teaching and learning courses aiming at making the learning and teaching process more effective; it was, rather, a matter of using the media-specific opportunities offered by radio and television to point out a problem and ways of solving it.

Integrated media was understood as a campaign. This was developed to produce learning conditions for educationally and socially disadvantaged people which encourage autonomy, self-esteem and the ability to act on one's own authority.

The success

The television spots – broadcast in the Third Programmes – were seen by 2% – 15% of the viewers. Altogether the television spots reached more than 13 million viewers. Over 5,000 potential participants rang up the telephone counselling centres. In the service area of the Norddeutscher Rundfunk (Schleswig-Holstein, Hamburg, Bremen, Berlin and Lower Saxony) the number of participants doubled, for example. Here the cooperation between the broadcasting organisations and adult education was also successful. Thus from the first considerations, producing a self-learning concept and a television reading and writing course was not pursued, and the idea of using spots was jointly developed.

The reasons for the success are to be found, in my opinion, in the mutual acceptance on the part of the participants. The adult education representatives realised the efficiency of television, just as the producers in the broadcasting organisations concentrated on their strengths by not backing a course concept for people unused to learning and recognised that teaching competence should come from the adult education institutes.

One of the features common to both projects I have presented is that they had a long period of preparation:

In the first case, in order to work out a joint concept, to agree on joint aims and to comprehensively inform those involved who worked at the adult education institutes. In the second case, also to agree on a joint concept, to clear up any reservations the literacy course leaders had about television – since television is for many one of the principal culprits for functional illiteracy – and in order to develop the appropriate infrastructure in terms of learning opportunities in adult education.

Both projects were supported by the authorities, by the Federal Ministry for Education and Science in Bonn, so that the Adolf Grimme Institute was able not only to provide the necessary coordination and work out the appropriate written material but also to hold the information and counselling meetings for the adult education workers.

'Eine Welt für Alle' (A World for All; 1991 – 1992)

It was under this title in April, May and June of this year, that the ARD, i.e. the First German Television, realised one of the main items of its programme on the complex of subjects surrounding the environment and development. The external reason was the Earth Conference in Rio de Janiero in June. But this main item was not realised in the Federal Republic of Germany alone; 52 broadcasting organisations throughout the world participated.

An internationally produced programme package, which was also transmitted in the countries of the participating broadcasting organisations and in addition was supplemented by productions in the individual countries, was meant to draw attention to the problems of the environment and development.

Apart from the broadcasting organisations more than 35 non-governmental organisations that are engaged in development cooperation and environmental protection were and are involved in the project, and through the Adolf Grimme Institute German adult education was incorporated into this project, because we believe that such an event as the Earth Conference in Rio and such a major item of the programme should not just remain a political and media event but also become an educational event.

The instruments

So the public service broadcasting organisations produced a large number of television programmes. The internationally produced programme package consisted of:

- six stories from developing countries (*'Innenansichten'* – inside views), i.e. two television plays and four documentaries by authors and directors from the Third World produced by the BBC, which examined the connection between the environment and development from the viewpoint of the South;
- a series of four programmes under the title *'Die Farbe der Zukunft – Familien proben den Umweltschutz'* (The colour of the Future – Families try out environmental protection), showing families in industrial nations, concentrated on the question of what each individual can do in everyday life if he or she assumes his or her joint responsibility for the environment and for the people in the One World seriously;
- the series *'One World Art – Artists for One World'* portrays 12 artists from all over the world that were asked to create a work of art entitled *'One World for All'*.

For all these productions copyright was cleared for use in educational work. The broadcasts could be recorded when they were transmitted and be screened publicly at meetings. Such an arrangement is rare in the Federal Republic.

The media package

The Adolf Grimme Institute took it upon itself to compile a media package out of these television productions and to make it available to the adult education institutes. This media package contains not only the television productions on four video cassettes but also a handbook listing and reviewing further films, videos, slides, instructional material and literature on the subject of the environment and development.

Currently a reader with texts on the subject is being produced, and folders for each of the video cassettes with the television programmes containing background material, references to the literature and suggestions for their use in adult education work.

Meetings

In the autumn 1992 the Adolf Grimme Institute was putting on a large number of meetings to introduce the media package as well as workshops to test new pedagogical and conceptual approaches to bring the subject of environment and development interrelationship into adult education.

The last example represents a model of cooperation in which the partners have a relatively large degree of independence; there was no adjustment of the constituent parts – for example, television programme and print material – to each other before production started, and the joint planning and coordination effort was minimal, remaining limited to what was absolutely necessary. The specific competence of those involved was meant to come to fruition, thus making use of synergistic effects.

The examples of cooperation between adult education and broadcasting organisations reveal a development whose end cannot yet be foreseen. Many will regret and lament this development and even accuse the public service broadcasting corporations of not keeping to their remit.

In conclusion I want to briefly outline this development in a few theses and also describe the necessary steps which have been taken at the Adolf Grimme Institute.

1. The broadcasting organisation as a cultural enterprise

The broadcasting organisation is becoming more and more, both nationally and internationally, a cultural enterprise, and programme decisions are becoming increasingly entrepreneurial decisions. The public service broadcasting corporations are, as a result of the private competition they have received, faced with the task of maintaining and defending their shares of the market.

Audience ratings are therefore at present the most important criterion for decision-making. Programmes with a mass appeal (sport, feature films, series etc.) are ousting programmes for smaller sections of the audience. The programme time and the budgets for education and culture in the programme are being reduced. Educational and cultural programmes still − and I say 'still' quite deliberately because I am convinced that in some time this will change − play no part in giving the television channels a distinctive image.

2. Television as an entertainment medium

Quite apart from the change in the programme policies of public service broadcasting corporations, the public is exhibiting an entertainment-orientated behaviour in its use of television which is becoming increasingly distinct. Why do people watch television? Very few of them to get educated. 88 per cent of the audience − according to a poll of the viewers − do not associate television, at any rate functionally, with the term 'education'.

Television does not have the image of an institution which is connected with education and culture. If one also consults the data of the ARD and ZDF Study on culture and the media[4], this shows that only about 13 per cent of the population make intensive use of the cultural programmes offered by television. And they are the people who use other cultural opportunities available as well.

This also applies to educational programmes to an even greater extent. In a study accompanying the Dortmund Cable Pilot Project[5] it emerged that " . . . only about 4 per cent of the Dortmund population . . . used special cultural programmes for the explicit purpose of learning". It also says that regular users of educational programmes in Dortmund − 6 per cent at the most − are made up of groups in the population who have especially privileged educational qualifications and who can be described as active in furthering their education.

3. Television education is supplementary education

As far as the programme is concerned, it can be ascertained that concepts of education on television are related clearly and unequivocally to users interested in

[4] Berg, Klaus; Maletzke, Gerhard; Müller-Sachse, K.-H.: *Kultur und Medien. Angebote − Interessen − Verhalten.* Eine Studie der ARD/ZDF-Medienkommission. (Culture and media. Supply − interests − behaviour.) Baden-Baden: Nomos 1991. (Publication Series *Media Perspektiven* Vol. 11
[5] Begleitforschung des Landes Nordrhein-Westfalen zum Kabelpilotprojekt Dortmund. Abschlußbericht, Teil III, Band 19. (Final report of the State of North Rhine-Westphalia on the Dortmund Cable Pilot Project.) Düsseldorf 1989; p. 614.

education, to an audience which arranges and organises its learning opportunities, its integrated media, for itself according to its own individual requirements.

In addition, there is a tendency to depart from the claims of intentional learning and instead to pursue the casual imparting of knowledge for purposes of orientation. Education in the media has the function of supplementing, of individually enhancing knowledge already acquired, but also of supplementing institutionalised, formalised educational processes.

When, however, a clear distinction is no longer made between the educational function and the other functions of television, as a colleague put it, there is the danger of the demand "Education for all" turning into the notion that "Everything is education".

4. From imparting to acquiring knowledge

Much more important and helpful than the permanent lament that the broadcasting organisations no longer take their educational remit seriously seems to me at present to be the attempt to see things from a different angle. Up to now education on television has been based on the premise that imparting knowledge, providing instruction, presenting and structuring are all important. A *pedagogical* teaching/learning situation or communication situation is taken for granted.

We have known for some time from communication research, however, that reception is determined by a large number of factors, whereas acquiring knowledge, i.e. learning from the material presented, is dependent least of all on the intention and structuring of the individual communication contents. It therefore appears important to me to concentrate for a change on the acquisition process of the audience.

It would mean starting with the viewers and thinking about when, where and also how educational processes occur in the case of television, how the viewer acquires knowledge and with which learning strategies this takes place; how, for example, he or she establishes a link between the subjects and contents presented, on the one hand, and his or her life-world and life plans, on the other.[6]

---

6 Cf. Kohli, Martin: Fernsehen und Alltagswelt. Ein Modell des Rezeptionsprozesses. (Television and everyday world. A model of the reception process.) In: Rundfunk und Fernsehen; 25/1977/1; pp. 70 – 85.

5. Making learning individual and flexible

The resources of funds and personnel for implementing large-scale multi-media projects that have been developed in cooperation are no longer available, or the authorities are not so willing to use them for purposes of coordination and organisation in view of the dramatic state of the authorities' budgets.

Nevertheless, an audience that is interested in education and culture avails itself of the still large number of broadcasts available in all sections of the programme for purposes of information and orientation, as it does of the specialised journals, books, computer programmes, CDs, audio and video cassettes, theatres, museums, libraries and adult education centres.

Making education and learning more individual and flexible finds expression in the fact that there is a large ensemble of institutionalised and non-institutionalised educational opportunities to choose from which are put together according to individual interests, budgets, methodological competence, involvement and the degree of commitment. The television programme is used in the same way as literature, the specialist book and the film are used. It seems as if the public no longer requires television that offers instruction, just as it no longer requires the school textbook.

Henny van der Eng
The Multi-media Conception of Teleac

Before describing Teleac, i.e. how we are organised and how we make, broadcast and sell our products, I shall first try to explain in a few words how the Dutch broadcasting system works and the position Teleac occupies within it. It is not possible to explain this in a few lines, as we have a rather complicated system.

The Dutch broadcasting environment

In the Netherlands, we have at present four television channels, one of which is used by the commercial station RTL-4. The remaining three channels are placed by the Dutch Government at the disposal of so-called 'authorised broadcasting companies'. These are companies with a certain number of members. The amount of broadcasting time allocated to each of them depends on the amount of members they have. At the moment, there are eight authorised companies, all having roughly the same amount of transmitting time. We must therefore assume they also have roughly the same number of members.

These companies are supposed to attract members for reasons of their identity. This explains why there is a Catholic broadcasting company in addition to a Protestant, a staunch evangelical, a socialist and a liberal broadcasting company. Some of these companies, however, do not try to win members through their identity, but solely through the programmes they transmit.

To make things even more complicated, the government also grants broadcasting time to organisations with social and/or cultural aims. It is therefore a very complicated system, but it is a system which affords many groups the opportunity to express their opinions. Hence we like to refer to it as a *pluriform* system.

One of the organisations having such a social and cultural aim is Teleac, with about 240 hours of television broadcasting time and about 260 hours of radio broadcasting time per year. Teleac is short for Television Academy. It was set up in 1963, at the time when Saturday as a day off was introduced in Holland. In those days, some people thought that the increase in leisure time would also result in an increase in the demand for education. Television – still relatively new at the time – was considered to be the best medium for this.

As the name suggests, at the outset Teleac was basically a Television Academy. Its educational aims were achieved solely through television programmes. Soon,

141

however, it became clear that television alone was not sufficient. So in addition to television broadcasts, students were provided with course books, audio-tapes, tutorials, homework and radio broadcasts.

This led to a carefully planned multi-media approach, which we have adopted for both the courses we produce ourselves and for those we buy. The multi-media approach can lead to a simple booklet accompanying the radio and television programmes, to a somewhat more substantial book, and even to a package consisting of a book and software, or a book and additional audio-tapes.

Production of Teleac courses

I would like to continue with information about the kinds of courses we produce, the way we produce our courses and the way we are organised.

Teleac has a permanent staff of 110, plus approximately 40 freelancers, which means there is a total of 150 people working in some capacity on the production of multi-media courses, or providing the back-up services for these productions.

Each year, we transmit around 30 courses on the public broadcasting network. About half of these are new and the rest are repeats. We ourselves produce eight out of nine of the new courses. Four out of five are (partly) purchased in other countries; one or two are co-productions with foreign companies.

We always divide the topics of our courses into 5 areas:[1]

1. *Business or Business-oriented Courses*
   Some examples are courses on *Marketing*, *Desk Top Publishing* and *Database Management*. Books and sometimes software are available and a final examination completes the course. Those who pass it receive a certificate of participation.

2. *Languages*
   Apart from a book, language courses always include audio-material. Previously this consisted only of cassettes, but more recently we have also used Compact Discs. The language courses we publish and broadcast are produced for various levels and vary in scope. There are small, simple holiday courses such as *Andiamo*; beginners' courses in Greek and Portuguese; advanced language courses such as French for commerce and work but also extensive courses for Italian, Russian and even Chinese.

---

[1] For those interested in more information on Teleac courses, there is a catalogue available in English with a complete list of titles.

3. *Hobbies and Leisure*
   A few examples under this heading are courses such as *Drawing and Painting, Landscape Drawing and Painting, Calligraphy, Handicrafts, Designing your Own Clothes,* and *Snooker.*
4. *Culture and Science*
   This includes courses on culture, history and natural sciences. Some examples are: *The Middle Ages, The Roman World, From Ouantum to Quark, Cities and their Past, Modern Art* and *Biotechnology.*
5. *Man and Society*
   This includes courses on health and important social issues, such as *Information on Aids, Stop Smoking, Learn how to Sleep, Information on Social Security* and other issues.

The importance of team-work

Teleac courses are produced by teams which comprise a television director, a radio director, an editor/producer for the book and a member who is entrusted with student support. Last but not least, there is a didactician who is also supposed to coordinate the activities of the teams' members. Additional expertise, for instance from scientists, authors, actors, presenters, designers and others is hired by the members of the team.

Once this team is formed and experts are hired, the production of the course starts. Each production is based on a number of set standards and on the information provided in the assignment. This assignment describes first of all the subject of the course, the audience we intend to reach, the course level, the budget available, the number of television and radio lessons and chapters in the book, and the price we will charge our students.

It should be pointed out here that the media I have referred to play different roles in the project. The book provides the student with all the necessary information. Television is used in particular to motivate and to encourage students but can also be employed to demonstrate things impossible to visualise in a book. The radio lessons are usually aimed at giving additional information and – especially in the case of language courses – to provide the student with all kinds of speech and listening exercises.

During the production of the course, the team has to submit regular reports to a committee, which checks whether or not the team is keeping to its assignment. If this is not the case, the team is instructed to make necessary adjustments. In this way a course is slowly but surely put together.

The production period for a complete course, i.e. the radio and television broadcasts and the book, varies from around eight months, for courses of only 4 or 6 lessons, to two years for more complex courses of 16 or more lessons. It ought to be pointed out, however, that the members of these teams seldom work on just one course at a time. Usually they work on two or more projects.

Once the production is completed, the radio and television programmes are transmitted on the public network − currently on Channel 2. The books and other course materials are sold via bookshops or a mail-order system. In this way we sell between 140,000 and 200,000 course packages each year in Holland and Flanders. The population in this area is around 15 million. About 70% of the courses are sold via bookshops and about 30% via mail-order.

The Programme Support Department

Teleac consists of three production departments, i.e. the Radio Department, the Television Department, and the Department responsible for Programme Support headed by me. There are also a number of departments providing services and support to each of the three.

The Programme Support Department consists of the following organisational units:

- the Publishing Office, where the editing and producing of the course material takes place;
- the Audiovisual Office, where pre-recorded videotapes are produced;
- the Marketing and Sales Department, responsible for the sales and sales promotion of our course packages;
- the Student Support Unit, which provides every form of assistance to our students, answering all their questions and organising tests, exams, telephone consulting hours, excursions, workshops, etc.;
- the Telematic Group, responsible for matters such as teletext and videotext.

My department employs about 26 people. Unlike the radio and television department, my department is not financed by public funding. We must therefore obtain the necessary funds from the sale of our course packages. Teleac is a foundation, which in the Netherlands means we are not allowed to make a profit. So we must sell our course material at cost price.

In the Netherlands, everyone who owns a television or a radio set has to pay a licence fee. The broadcasting organisations, and hence Teleac, too, are financed by the money raised from these fees and from advertising revenues, i.e. we receive a certain amount for every hour we broadcast on radio and television. This amount has to be used for producing radio and television programmes.

The video market

In conclusion, I would like to mention a few words on the video market in the Netherlands. Although 60% of Dutch households have a video recorder, the market for pre-recorded video cassettes is limited. People record programmes, films and courses directly from television. In addition, many video-tapes are hired out by video shops and libraries. The result is that very few video-tapes of our programmes are sold. Last year, for example, we sold 35,000 copies of the book *Landscape Drawing and Painting*, but we sold only about 300 copies of the video-tapes of the complete course, i.e. ten episodes of half an hour each. This figure constitutes barely 1% of book sales.

Recently the demand for courses on video has been increasing, however. Companies, schools and institutions use video for in-company training rather than expensive courses, seminars, and so forth. We think however that, in the future, video as a medium for educational purposes will be superseded by the Compact Disc Interactive (CDI). This new medium offers many possibilities for interactive instructions. That is why we have already made a pilot programme on CDI. There are advanced plans to issue two courses on CDI which we have already broadcast. However, we do not expect this system to make a breakthrough in the short term. The machine will be launched in the Netherlands and the rest of Europe in the coming autumn, and it is expected that it will slowly find its way to the consumer in the second half of the nineties.

Finally, I would like to briefly mention one of our ambitious projects, i.e. the series *Music in the Netherlands*, which we transmitted in spring 1991. It dealt with the history of music and the way music was made in the Netherlands from 1100 A.D. to the present day. Each episode is dedicated to a special theme, e.g. The Music of the Court, Street Music, Church Music, and so forth. The course consists of 10 television lessons, 10 radio lessons, a large course book and 5 compact discs. As the course is in Dutch, you probably would not understand much of the book or the television and radio lessons. However, this does not apply to the compact discs. Although the music was made in Holland, everyone can understand it.

I would like to present each of you with the set of 5 compact discs of *Music in the Netherlands*. These compact discs were produced by my department and were part of the course. I hope that you will listen to them with pleasure, that you will then be able to appreciate that a Teleac course is more than just television or radio.

Derek Jones

Commissioning Television Programmes and Back-up Material: The Model of Channel 4.

Channel 4 is approaching its tenth birthday, but it cannot be said any longer tha we are the child of British Television. However, I think it is true to say that Channe 4 is still regarded as the *enfant terrible*, as a rather wayward child by many bot in broadcasting and outside it. Indeed, if you ask most people what they mak of Channel 4, how they would characterise it, how they would identify us, I thin they would say that we were controversial, and it has been shown in research tha this is the way we are still summed up by many.

The major reasons for this can be traced back to how we came on air with a bang – it certainly was a bang in all sorts of ways – in 1982. People – and this i something I believe we have to take notice of – are to some extent worried b a channel which actually deliberately sets out to bring opposing views to the screen They are not altogether comfortable with controversy. I am not sure whether tha is a criticism of us, or whether it is a criticism of them. I believe, however, tha it is rather important that a television channel like ours should retain its reputatio for controversy.

As well as understanding everything that has been said in the last few days abou markets, I think it is very important that we actually keep intact a prophetic edge an ability to make people angry as well as to make people pleased.

Nevertheless, ten years old, we are on the threshold of considerable change. W have had a very privileged ten years. Our colleagues in the old Independen Television in Britain have sold advertising on our channel, and made it possib for us to do many things which – if we were in a total market situation – w would have found more difficult to realise.

In 1993, we will take over the responsibility to sell our own advertising; we wi be responsible for making our own money. There will be a constant tension in th future between what we are and staying afloat, which has always been true in sense. In 1982 there were those in the popular press who thought that we were nc Channel 4, but Channel Bore!

There were those who thought we could not survive, and they had some evidence We were getting such a tiny proportion of people actually watching us. It looke as if we might have to close down simply because there would not be any advertiser who would be willing to actually buy space on a channel which set out in the firs place to be a channel for minorities.

146

think over the years we have discovered a little about what that might mean in terms of markets, or what are now known as segmented markets. One of the big lessons we have learned is that we can keep our respectability with the advertisers by careful targeting and careful marketing and really thinking about different audiences, which is our real purpose in any case.

That gives us hope for the future, but nevertheless I hope it does not mean that we will lose everything of the past. Of course there was a sense in Channel 4 in 1982 trying every kind of new subject which previous broadcasters had not tackled. It was a dangerous strategy, and I think it would be true to say that at times more effort was put into making programmes in keeping with that remit than scheduling them carefully. People felt bombarded with all sorts of new, fresh, different kinds of programmes. Perhaps there were too many of them over too short periods.

Thus we gained considerable experience, but we were always concerned that – however small the audience – we should not lose our prophetic edge whether they would hear or whether they would forbear. I think that still must have a part in the Channel 4's future if we are to be ourselves.

Again, in 1982, we were concerned with minorities, with specialists, with gay people, with black people, with disabled people, the young, the old, the non-Christian religions – all the people who had not had a voice, found one through Channel 4.

Bee-keepers, quilters, minority sports enthusiasts, even the organisers of village flower shows all had a voice on this channel, an educational and educative voice, speaking to people about their passion, their interests, the motives for their lifetime involvement.

We accepted too easily in 1982 that we were not a mass medium. We said quite specifically that we did not expect to compete with the big boys. We were expected to talk to audiences in the plural. We hoped – and that was often said at that time – that most people would watch us some of the time, but we did not expect all the people to watch us all the time, and that people would make a conscious choice to come to Channel 4.

Of course that was a privileged position to be in, and in a sense we were able to do it through the ability of ITV to make money through what we showed on the screen, through advertising. It was also a valuable insight, which we will not lose, because it has helped to influence our future.

On average we now are watched by about 11 per cent of the television audience of Britain. That may change to a certain extent, but this figure will certainly not increase to as much as 25 to 30 per cent of the audience. I do not believe that could ever happen because of the nature of Channel 4.

Another snapshot of 1982 which is especially important for our considerations here We were committed by charter to seven hours a week of educational programmes for adults, but we never had a conventional Education Department. There were commissioning editors for education, but their involvement with their other colleagues in the commissioning college was as important as was the fact that they were identified as having a particular responsibility to fly the flag for education

Thus from the beginning it was believed – and it is still believed – that Channel 4 is itself an educational channel. There are some programmes which are set up and commissioned by education editors with a stated educational purpose. But there are other programmes, commissioned by editors for science, for the arts, for music, for documentaries, for religion, for current affairs, who also can work with the educational editors and with the Support Services Unit which have educative potential.

Despite the fact that the overall economy of the schedule in Channel 4 has changed somewhat and that there are probably more programmes brought in from abroad then they were in the early days, up to 50% of our output could in principle be categorised as having a relevance, a penetration, a spark for people who want to learn.

As you know, we are a publisher of programmes, we are a fosterer of independent film-makers. We of course have worked with ITV and will continue to work with ITV. But we have been known particularly for a plurality of styles, which has been brought about by great multiplicity of independent film companies which came into being, because Channel 4 was in being.

By these means, we were enabled to avoid the overall and rather difficult constraints of what was known as balance. The IBA and ITC, who are responsible for seeing that we obey our charter and maintain our education broadcasting responsibilities, kept us on a fairly long rein and enabled us to attain balance over a number of weeks rather than within a single programme. It was very refreshing to have programmes, which were made by people who had a passionate opinion to share.

We are not only publishers of programmes, we are also publishers – and here is the final snapshot of 1982 – of a very considerable amount of supporting literature, and we are publishers, together with Broadcasting Support Services, of helplines.

We took it for granted in 1982, and we take it for granted now – and this is why it was very interesting to listen to Dr. Paukens' report at this conference – that many programmes, perhaps 50% of all programmes we have ever made, were not complete in themselves.

Whether they were labelled as education or whether they were parts of the general output, they could be made educative by the addition of a helpline, a booklet,

148

something which would take up the stimulus of the programme and enable an individual viewer to develop the new enthusiasm it had aroused, to take it to a stage further, to join a formal class, to read more books, to go and get help. Whatever it was, there was a bridging operation which was essential to the nature of our programming.

Thus, from the beginning, what are known as Support Services were accepted by the Channel, and continue to be well-funded. Amazingly, even in post-Thatcher Britain, there is a department within Channel 4 which is licensed to lose money! They give us a budget, we spend it, we make some money, we spend it and so we get a new budget, and that is because it is important to the Channel to offer this service to viewers. It enables us to act on the view that programmes are not complete in themselves.

I think there are some significant gains from this approach and there have been some significant changes over the past ten years. Some independent film-makers, for example, had a background in educational television, but many had not, and it is interesting to note that many independents now queue up to make educational programmes. So you get a fresh, a journalistic lightness of touch and some documentary skill, which can complement the skills of dyed-in-the-wool educational broadcasters.

An extremely useful formula was devised in the early days, whereby three hours a week of Channel 4 would be commissioned by education editors, and a further four hours would be validated as education through the provision of back-up and through a set of criteria which were applied to the programmes. This continues.

Another very valuable innovation, which I believe is now coming along in the rest of broadcasting as well, is the development of seasons. It is a consequence of the fact that there is a college of commissioning editors, where many can contribute programmes to a single theme, either from the point of view of the arts or sports or politics or education or anything you can name: for example, the *Disabling World Season*, or *Soviet Spring Season* – a major season in which we looked at many aspects of life in the former Soviet Union. And, most recently, there was the Censorship Season, *Banned*, which was accompanied by a publication which acted as a primer on the subject and which was distributed to schools and adult-education centres all over the country. This was a very pertinent thing to do at that particular time because there was serious concern about the interference of the Government in the broadcasting of television programmes on other channels.

Another useful innovation brought about by this approach is that we are no longer imprisoned by the educational series. We talk about strands. A strand was commissioned by different editors, for example, which was concerned with the human heart. Some looked at it from a mythological point of view, some from

149

the physiological, some from a medical point of view, and some simply said what is necessary to look after it: a multi-dimensional approach using different film-makers, different styles, an approach also embodied in the accompanying booklet.

Finally, one major advantage of having education as a forefront word in the Channel is that educational programmes are always, on principle, unlabelled, and they are at prime time. An educational programme may be televised at eight or nine o'clock in the evening or on a Sunday afternoon, also a prime time for watching, i.e. at any time in the output where we know we can gather an audience. We obviously have to compete for time, but there is a readiness to recognise that there is no division between education programmes and the rest of channel output.

There is no doubt that we have changed. The generation of commissioning editors now in place is concerned about our commitment to minorities. It wishes that majorities could actually enter conversation with minorities and make programmes accordingly.

It is also true to say that with 1993 coming up when Channel 4 begins to sell its own advertising, there is a new concern for audiences and scheduling. There certainly is good reason for this concern. We have to find new schedules without losing our soul, and we should take into account the need for audiences of a reasonable size. The good news is that the ITC has confirmed a requirement to Channel 4 to have as many educational programmes as it had before.

My job is in the provision of supporting information and literature and helplines. I would quote an Irishman, Justin Keating, an educational broadcaster with the Irish broadcasting organisation RTE, who over 20 years ago was asked to define an educational television programme. He replied that it was " . . . one half of a conversation between equals", and I think we need to have this sense of equality in our approach to people. The viewers are as important as the makers of television; there is a partnership between them, and we need to look carefully at the receiving end as well as at the creative end and thus, in part, at the Support Services unit.

We provide all sorts of support: literature, helplines, events. It is available, on principle, to the whole Channel, to every single part of the commissioning body.

It is not for educators, not for educational institutions. This is where we differ from other educational broadcasting units. It is first and foremost for the individual viewer, who chooses to send for it, or who chooses to ring us up and says: "I need some help. Can you direct me to the place where I can get it?".

Yesterday we referred about crafty education, some people would call it education by stealth, and I think that is in part what we do. We have built up almost an industry of attaching supporting literature to all sorts of unlikely programmes. Of course the very diversity of the output makes it possible to have a very diverse back-up service, covering some programmes you would not necessarily expect.

My latest example is the back-up literature to the Tour de France, which is currently on Channel 4 seven nights a week for three weeks. I value the opportunity to put into a celebratory booklet not only things about the bikes, the race, the route, but also about the history and geography and culture of provincial France. That seems to me to be a valuable way in which people, who have a primary interest in the race can develop that into a wider interest in France.

You would not immediately think that a series called *The TV Heaven*, which was an archive series about broadcasting over the last 30 years, would merit back-up, but we took the view that this was a marvellous opportunity for individual viewers and media educators to obtain and to use these clips from the 1950s and subsequently, as the basis for media education.

You would not expect necessarily that there could be back-up to the News, but we have done it despite the problems involved. When we can get early information about a series of 15-minute reports on the Channel 4 News, it is possible to develop something very fast which people might need to follow up or which helps them to analyse what they have seen on the news.

Of course we also do back-up in the main stream, for consumer programmes, for health programmes, for arts, for literature, for music, and nothing is forbidden to us. The previous speaker said that everything is education – indeed it is.

I think it is important to say that it is not enough just to characterise this work as back-up or follow-up: it is a fine art. There are a whole lot of partnerships involved in it. You have to penetrate the nature of the programme and discuss with the programme maker how we can go beyond it and develop its ideas. That is not easy, especially when the programme maker is an independent jealous of his own position. But nevertheless, many independents now regard it as prestige to have some back-up.

It is an important task to decide the most appropriate form of back-up, whether it is a newspaper, a fact-sheet, a magazine, an illustrated booklet, or a very high-class illustrated booklet. It is a fine art to judge when it should be priced and when it should be free, whether it should totally reflect the programme or whether it should take you beyond the programme. These things take care, analysis, thought.

Sometimes the programme-makers are the writers, sometimes not. There are dilemmas about the objectivity of programme-makers to write something which is in itself repeating what has been said in the programme, when we want to take it a bit further. So we also use other writers who, in turn, must collaborate closely with programme-makers.

We have now calculated that since 1982 we have produced 1,250 titles, around 3 booklets a week. It is commonly said that if anything moves on Channel 4 there is a booklet attached to it.

There are partnerships between us and commissioning editors, between production companies, writers, compilers and the British Support Services office. There is a partnership between the editors of our literature, the print-producers, the designers and the distributors, and, crucially, there is collaboration between ourselves and Broadcasting Support Services about which I do not need to say too much because Keith Smith is going to speak after me. But I have to say that the extent, the range and the quality of what we have done would not conceivably have been possible without them.

We fail often, we succeed sometimes, we keep trying, we keep experimenting, we are often surprised. We were astonished, for example, when we published a booklet to accompany a series of extremely arcane programmes called *The TV Dante*, which we sold for £4.95. It was broadcast on very hot evenings in August, but we sold over 5,000 copies of a booklet, which included the text of part of the *Purgatorio*, difficult discussions about television graphics, about medieval poetry, and so on.

There is certainly a market for those people who expect more of television than just a reflection of mass taste. Thus, currently we are running a booklet accompanying a programme which was commissioned by the editor for independent film and video called *Talking Liberties*. It consists of interviews with some of the best intellects of Western Europe: Jacques Derrida, Julia Kristeva, Helen Cixious, and others. I am amazed by the fact that over 2,000 of these booklets have been sold.

You keep trying, you sometimes fail. It might have been expected, of course, that the programme which expanded on the Mediterranean diet – and had one announcement only – would get a response rate of 58,000. It could also be expected that a series on organic gardening could get a response of over 90,000.

I think we have to be aware at present, that people are financially worse off and that they are more cautious. They have perhaps seen what we offer as the icing on the cake which they may have to forego, but nevertheless we are holding on to our policy. There is a backlist which we hope to use, and we know that the booklets we have produced can stand alone even if people have not seen the broadcasts.

Finally, the most important partnership that we have – as I indicated – is with the viewers, and I am sure that the important step that we will take in the 90s is to develop what we are now calling learning clubs or learning networks. We are going to complement our provision for individuals, and take account of the fact that people who send for a booklet in a particular area, or even ring a helpline on a particular subject may be presumed to have an interest in it beyond that particular programme.

hey might wish not only to be kept in touch with future programmes but might lso want to know about other activities and other back-up, might want to wish ɔ be saved of the job of sending for it every time by subscribing for a year. Members btain booklets at a discount or in some cases free.

Ve are building on these interests: we have now a gardening club with over 10,000 1embers, building up well, and a science club which after only two announcements ·n air has over fifteen hundred members. A range of activities have been developed 1 collaboration with British university departments of continuing education, ıvolving up to 500 or 600 people initially to discuss a programme called *A Brief listory of Time*, featuring Professor Stephen Hawking.

'here will be more clubs: the next one – it may not surprise you – will be the Aovies Club, and the next one after that will be a real rekindling of the spirit of 982, which will be the Thinkers Club covering people who are interested in religion nd philosophy and parts of the arts and talks and books and so on. I think that ; developing strongly.

'here is a lot to tell. There is ten years' experience of building up our knowledge nd our sense of risk and experiment in this work. It does not become any less ıteresting, it is fascinating. It is a real privilege to do it. It is very nice to have job, which you really enjoy – I enjoy mine.

Keith Smith

Broadcasting Support Services –
A Joint Enterprise

I thank Manfred Meyer for the invitation to speak. As an organisation it is no
very often that we are asked to address international groups of broadcasters, sc
we feel a certain coming-of-age in being asked to give this talk.

I have been requested to focus on Broadcasting Support Services as a joint enterpris
of the BBC and private competitors. I am taking the liberty of changing the titl
slightly and calling it 'Broadcasting Support Services – a Joint Enterprise'. I hesitat
to define the people that we work with as competitors, preferably they ought t
define themselves either as competitors or as colleagues.

My argument will be that in a situation where audiences are fragmenting, audience
are declining, and cash is scarce, there may be an argument for having a join
enterprise outside broadcasting organisations to provide some of the broadcastin
support services. So it is an argument about fragmentation of audiences, declinin
audiences and declining cash, which is something which came up in the earlier part
of this conference.

Services

Broadcasting Support Services (BSS) runs helplines and provides follow-up service
for viewers and listeners on BBC, Channel 4, ITV and other media.

The services we offer include: providing educational booklets, telephone helplines
charity appeals, a National AIDS Helpline, outreach and clubs, dial-and-listens
and telephone conferencing. I should like to take the opportunity to explain som
of these activities.

Educational booklets

Booklets announced on air within or after a programme allow the viewer or listene
to follow up the topic of the programme. We produce 115 such titles a year anc
distribute over 700,000 copies.

Helplines

Every year we run telephone helplines on 100 or more occasions. Each of these telephone helplines is set up for a particular programme in order to offer viewers or listeners personal help, after the programme, on an issue that is of concern to them or is a problem in their life. Thus our helplines cover topics such as drug abuse, divorce, old age, sexual relationships, racial attacks, etc..

Appeals

British broadcasting runs many short programmes and a few long ones each year which invite the public to donate money for charities and good causes. At BSS we provide donation taking services such as 1,000 telephone lines to take down credit card donations. We also provide an appeal administration service which helps to administer the money donated to such large appeals as the *BBC Children In Need Appeal*, which itself has received over £20 million a year in donations in recent years.

National AIDS Helpline

One of our temporary helplines on AIDS was so popular we have opened it as the permanent full-time helpline on AIDS. It supports all forms of media including public health advertisements. Taken together with our temporary helplines, these services receive 960,000 telephone calls each year.

Outreach and clubs

We have fairly recently developed the services we offer to viewers' clubs such as the Channel 4 Science Club, which caters for enthusiasts for science programmes.

Dial-and-listen services

These have not yet been referred to at this conference, so I will include them at this point. I am concerned about some of the conversation here about CD-ROMS and interactive video-disks, in that they are owned by a rather small minority of the audience. A dial-and-listen service is a facility we could use more. It is a simple three-minute recorded telephone message, that viewers and listeners can phone after a programme to obtain additional information.

We find them very effective if they support a television programme on a topic such as panic-attacks; when somebody quickly needs some further information. We have 500 lines open and the caller can hear immediately a short piece of information about how to tackle panic-attacks.

155

Telephone conferencing

We have held one successful series of telephone conferences for women with breast cancer, where we brought them together on the phone after a programme about breast cancer. We hope to use the technology of telephone conferencing more in the future.

History

The BBC founded us in 1975. Three months after they founded us they said we would be better off independent and as a charity and working for other broadcasters.

In 1978, ITV joined in by asking us to perform some services for them, Channel 4 did so in 1982.
In 1985 radio became much more interested in support facilities and it was also the time when we undertook more for appeals such as *Live Aid*.
In 1986 we set up the National AIDS Helpline.
In 1990 we organised support for the *One World* project, and I am pleased to say that
in 1993 we hope to develop our work with the Discovery and Learning Channels.

We are now located in London, Manchester and Cardiff and have 75 full-time equivalent staff. Our annual expenditure is £2.5 million.

Evaluation

A few years ago we conducted a study with a number of British broadcasters. It showed that 9 out of 10 people thought that offering information (e.g. booklets) after programmes is a useful public service.

Other studies of our work show that during the 1980s we developed our skills at producing useful booklets. Over 80% of respondents have found the booklets useful but the proportion finding them very useful has risen from 22% to 54%.

When we asked viewers how they would like us to develop our services they said they would like on-air announcements changed so that

– the address was simple,
– the same address is used every time,
– the address is held on screen for longer,
– the address is given in the programme listings in the press.

When it comes to evaluating helplines these are the features callers most appreciate about media-linked helplines. They can phone

- without anyone knowing
- without giving their name
- at any time
- from their own home
- without feeling silly or shy
- and ask their own question
- and remain in control.

When it comes to a helpline such as our National AIDS Helpline the particular value of the helpline is evident in some of the respondents' statements.

"For people who might be embarrasssed, a faceless voice, someone you'll never know, not inhibiting − it's a marvellous thing."

"You can phone when you want to."

"It's especially helpful for some people. I wouldn't ask a doctor some things, or my family. Some women are just too afraid to say these things − but here, there's nobody with you, you can't see anybody, its a voice at the end of the line."

"You can ask what you want to ask, rather than reading the facts."

'It was easy. You didn't know who you were talking to. If I'd felt silly or embarrassed, I could have put the phone down."

"It's one-to-one, more personal. You can talk about particular areas. That helped."

"A one-to-one basis. On TV, they're telling you. Here, you put the question."

Most recently I heard Michael Grade, the Chief Executive of Channel 4, say that broadcasting gives permission to face up to worries. Here was a worry that people could face up to and, having seen a programme, could phone in immediately. I would argue that running an AIDS helpline is a form of education. It is educating people about how to protect their lives and those of their friends and family.

These are some of the changes that callers said they would be making as a result of a one-to-one conversation on our AIDS telephone helpline: adopting safer sex, thinking more about new relationships, talking more openly.

Derek Jones, Editor Support Services with Channel 4, mentioned a definition of educational broadcasting as a conversation between equals. A helpline is a method whereby that conversation can be two-way.

Europe

These are the countries we have been working with over the last two years:

Austria, Belgium, Bulgaria, Czechoslovakia, Denmark, Finland, France
Germany, Greece, Hungary, Ireland, Italy, Japan, Latvia, Luxembourg
Netherlands, Norway, Poland, Russia, Spain, Sweden, Switzerland, USA.

Our work with other European countries is most encouraging. For example we hav
worked with a number of countries to provide follow-up to the major Europea
collaborative season on development and the environment called *One World*.

For this, together with our UK partners, we offered the manuscript of an education
pack to accompany the programmes. This is currently translated and produced i
17 language versions in 16 countries. We have most recently learnt of its use i
Latvia.

More recently BSS was commissioned to stimulate a co-ordinated drug educatio
week on radio around Europe. With the support of the Commission of the Europea
Communities we found major broadcasters in eight countries who wished to moun
such an initiative. What was special about each of these initiatives is that a dru
helpline was linked to the broadcasts which allowed young people to obtain furthe
information and help.

Benefits of a joint enterprise

Turning now to what I see as the benefits of 'a joint enterprise between competitors'
I can identify a number, most of which are particularly valuable benefits in th
current era of fragmenting audiences.

Economies of scale

As was mentioned above, we run 100 helplines a year on 70 phone lines. Ther
is phone rental to be paid for these lines. There is an economy of scale to be gaine
here by having a variety of broadcasters coming together to use one set of telephon
lines. There are further economies of scale I could refer to.

Concentration of expertise

We can provide a concentration of expertise because we only undertake suppor
work, we do not do anything other than support work.

Singleness of purpose

We have a singleness of purpose. Nobody can be distracted by the needs of programme-making.

Internal career structure

We are large enough to have an internal career structure, which I think is an advantage. It allows people to grow in skills.

Tax concessions

The support agency can be registered as a not-for-profit organisation.

Ability to draw in funds

Of our £2.5 million turnover, £1 million comes from outside broadcasting. So we bring in over £1 million to assist in our work, much of which is a benefit to viewers and listeners. This money comes from the different departments of the British Government, but increasingly from the European Commission and from the Council of Europe. To win these European funds we are very keen to form partnerships with organisations or broadcasters in other European countries, for only then can we all benefit from European funds.

Positioning

Lastly I would say that one of the advantages of a joint enterprise is the positioning that enterprise has. We are not seen as a broadcaster by many of the adult education institutes or by the voluntary organisations we work with. We are seen as being positioned somewhere between them and the broadcasters. So hopefully we provide something of a cultural bridge between sectors.

Conclusion

I hope I have met the request to provide my arguments in favour of the benefits of a joint enterprise. I would not wish to say that it was the only formula nor necessarily always the best formula. Nor would I argue that it should be an exclusive formula. I think that various formulae can exist within various different broadcasting cultures. But I would argue that in any country it is well worth considering establishing a joint enterprise for broadcasting support. If anyone wishes to talk through these options further, we would be very happy to contribute to the discussions.

Rosemary Bristow

Public Attitudes to Back-up Activities

Instead of engaging myself in a tiresome attempt to define the term 'back-up activities', I shall confine myself to saying that I think of *back-up activities* as a range of ways of supporting radio and television broadcasts by giving interested people added information or advice. By *public attitudes* I am referring to the opinions and beliefs of the ordinary British viewer or listener, established through quantitative surveys or through qualitative group discussions. So I am excluding specialist users of educational back-up material such as teachers or Open University students.

In the United Kingdom, Broadcasting Support Services (BSS) runs helplines and provides follow-up in various ways for viewers and listeners on BBC Television and BBC Radio, on Channel 4, ITV and other media. The services are in the areas of health, social welfare, education, the environment and recreation.

I want to concentrate on the attitudes of adults in Britain to two main kinds of back-up:

- printed material (especially free booklets, referral leaflets and information packs), and
- freephone helplines.

I also want to refer to large, coordinated campaigns such as *Second Chance*, described in detail by Robert Seatter elsewhere in this volume[1], that combine broadcasts, back-up literature, helplines, posters and local organisation.

The BBC's Broadcasting Research Department, to which I belong, has been asked to investigate viewers' general attitudes to back-up literature and the opinions of young adult listeners on the value of helplines. Over the last five or six years we have carried out about a dozen pieces of research on listeners' and viewers' evaluation of specific back-up literature that they have requested.[2]

---

[1] Robert Seatter: BBC Education: The Role of Marketing; this volume, pp. 68 – 73.

[2] The literature evaluated in this context ranges from very simple single sheets to glossy, 48-page A4 booklets. They are listed in an appendix to this paper; in some cases, summaries of the findings are available on request from BBC Broadcasting Research Department, Woodlands, 80 Wood Lane, London W12 0TT.

Research on the public's response to specific helpline services was not carried out by our Department but by BSS itself, or by other research organisations in Britain. Two of the helplines were targeted at young adults listening to the BBC's pop music station, Radio 1 and supported broadcasts on drug usage or on serious money problems. These were called *Drug Alert '91* and *Moneyfax '91*. The third helpline, or *Second Chance* in March this year, was the biggest ever mounted in the UK. The following table outlines the questions and the issues dealt with in this paper.

1. Who uses back-up?

– How many people?
– What kinds of people?
– Demographically, are they different in any way from the general population, or from other people in the audience who *don't* use broadcast back-up?
– What about different kinds of back-up? Do these attract different users?

2. What do people think of the back-up service?

– Both generally and specifically?

3. What works?

– What is likely to attract the target audience for back-up in the desired numbers?
– What will satisfy users, meet their expectations, and be of benefit to them?

The use of back-up in Britain

How many people use broadcast back-up?

The most recent overall estimate I have of use of back-up literature or print material is now rather old. It is for February 1988, over four years ago, when one in six adults said that they had sent off for back-up literature following a programme seen on television. A further one in four had thought of doing so but had not got as far as taking down the address, finding the right sized envelope or the right stamps. However, in 1988 over half the adult population had never even considered sending off for any back-up literature, either because of apathy or because they hadn't seen anything of interest to them.

There are a number of reasons for assuming that by now more than one in six adults would say that they have ever used print back-up. Back in 1988, the kinds of material people most often said they had sent for were cookery information or consumer advice. Since then, back-up is available on a much wider range of subjects and it is often targeted either at a wide cross-section of the population or at a range

161

of specific groups, such as parents of young children, people with poor spelling or with emotional difficulties, etc..

The back-up now is often more easily obtained by ringing a helpline rather tha by looking for a stamped addressed envelope to send. Finally, people normall seek back-up for their own personal use rather than for someone else. Since the are usually writing in or phoning in for the first time in their lives, new peopl are being added to the numbers using back-up each time new material is produced

Helplines are less used than print back-up. In February 1992, even considering usin a helpline was limited to about one in twelve adults in Britain. However, that wa before *Second Chance* was launched in March 1992. Almost 57,000 calls were logge within a week of the broadcasts. This event alone involved more than one perso in a thousand in Britain ringing in for the free support booklet or to ask abou adult education opportunities. It seems likely that the February figure of 8% thinking about using a helpline has now increased.

What kinds of people use back-up?

Users are *not* spread evenly throughout the population, and often they are somewha different from the broadcast's audience. Women usually write off for print suppor more than men do; so, too, do middle-class and better educated listeners an viewers. More requests for print support come from people aged 25 – 54 than from those younger or older than this.

However, this pattern varies according to the subject matter of the broadcasts, th target audience and whether the back-up is printed material or a helpline. In th particular pieces of print back-up that we have researched, women usually do writ off for it in greater numbers than men do. However, the kinds of material the concentrate on is stereotypically within the female domain – that is, to do wit children, the family, health, emotions and saving lives. When it came to using th telephone instead of writing, more women than men rang the *Second Chanc* helpline to ask about career information and about returning to adult learnin generally.

The position was reversed when the support was to do with science experiments the environment, drug use or serious debt. In these cases, men wrote in or ran helplines more than women did.

The only areas where gender seemed irrelevant were to do with improving one' spelling or basic communication skills, or pursuing art as a hobby. The art fake Tom Keating on Channel 4 seemed to appeal about equally to men and women if those answering our postal questionnaires are a true guide.

While it is true that middle class and better educated listeners and viewers are mor likely to use back-up regardless of the subject matter, this is especially so wher riting in is required. Our Department has a slogan: 'Letter writing is a middle-ass activity'. Even when audiences for a broadcast are disproportionately working ass, the back-up is more often sent for by middle-class viewers or listeners.

here were two exceptions to this middle-class bias. Firstly, the booklet to go with *Wordpower*, a BBC series on basic communication skills, was requested by all social asses in the same proportions as in the population at large. Perhaps less educated iewers recognised that this booklet might be relevant to them, and therefore useful. econdly, people did not have to write in for the booklet because a helpline was vailable to contact. Working class resistance to putting pen to paper was then vercome.

he other exception to middle-class dominance in the use of back-up was on the *ave a Life* campaign. People were encouraged, through a series of short television rogrammes on BBC-1, to write for a referral leaflet telling them where they could ttend emergency first aid classes in their area. Although the leaflets were requested iore by middle-class than by working-class viewers, the first aid sessions themselves ere attended by a representative cross-section of the public. This was due to idespread posters and local publicity advising people where to go. This ounteracted the selective social class bias in obtaining referral leaflets by post.

ge differences among back-up users

.lthough users tend to be in the 25 – 54 year age bracket, younger people use back-p under certain circumstances; that is,

- if the subject area is appropriate to the young (for example, drug taking, money problems or science experiments for teenagers);
- if the broadcasts are aimed at a young audience, by being on the pop music station, Radio 1, or on television in the early evenings when young viewers are more likely to watch;
- if a helpline is provided.

Vhat do users think of back-up?

his can be broken down into *general* attitudes among the public towards print ipport or helplines and attitudes to *specific* back-up literature or helplines among iose who have used these services.

n July 1987 – 88, public attitudes towards the provision of back-up services were ery favourable. Nine out of ten people who were asked agreed that offering iformation after television programmes was a useful public service, but they were ivided 50:50 as to whether such offers were personally useful to them.

163

In group discussions, people felt that broadcasters *should* be providing back-up firstly because the information is not available elsewhere, but also becaus broadcasters are seen as a source of impartial, unbiased information. Four or fiv years ago, people were pleased with the print back-up they received because the did not expect much. They were often surprised when it even arrived at their home Nowadays, expectations are higher, so disappointment can also be greater.

In coming to these conclusions, people attributed a variety of motives to broadcaste for providing back-up material; they presumed that

- it is an extension of public service broadcasting;
- it is a necessary part of programmes such as cookery or do-it-yourself (DIY
- programme-makers are trying to stimulate interest in similar topics in othe programmes, and perhaps encouraging channel loyalty;
- it is an efficient way of dealing with a large number of individual requests fc information all at the same time;
- it is a guide to how large the audience is for the broadcasts and how much th programmes are enjoyed;
- perhaps programme-makers are acting as government agents in providin information as in AIDS awareness campaigns.

More recently, in 1990, we carried out group discussions among young people age 16 – 34 on their attitudes to helplines. They did not readily think of helplines o information lines as places to go for information. They were generally aware o campaigns with helplines run by BBC Radio 1 but were vague about what thes entailed. They assumed they must be for teenagers because this was the perceive target audience of the station.

No-one in the groups admitted to having used an information line or a helpline Helplines had a rather 'desperate' image, as being a last resort rather than a firs step to getting help or advice.

People did recognise, however, that the telephone has the advantages of being quick convenient and cheap, and appropriate for sensitive issues.

Why don't people use back-up?

Attitudes to print back-up

People who had never thought of sending off for print back-up claimed that th main reason for this was that they had never seen anything of personal interes or relevance to them.

Those who had thought of doing so, but had not got round to it, gave a variet of reasons – principally that they never had a pen handy when announcement ame on screen, that they were too busy or that the address was given too quickly. eople said that they needed encouragement to send off for things immediately, efore they lost interest or laziness set in. The main difference between this group nd those who did write in seemed to be one of personal organisation.

,lthough some of the obstacles to writing off for information are overcome if a elpline is provided, this also has problems:

ome people reject helplines because they feel perfectly capable of making their wn enquiries. On the other hand, other people are less competent at finding out aformation independently, or feel intimidated by using the phone, or think it is oo expensive. Not everyone realises that some helplines are free.

,ack of access to a telephone, or reluctance to use one, are more common in Britain mong the least skilled and least educated sections of the community − the very eople with fewer sources of information open to them and who are least likely o write for information. Other ways are needed to encourage the unskilled to seek nformation or advice.

'eople who *did* send for back-up literature were generally positive about the material hey received, but were not necessarily enthusiastic about it. They tended to be noderately pleased, rather than very pleased. They usually claimed that the booklets vere easy to understand, useful, interesting, informative and attractively presented, ·ven though the material itself varied considerably in quality of production. Iowever, sometimes recipients were disappointed with the material saying that

− they found it too basic;
− no new information was included that they didn't already know;
− they expected more than just summary notes or tips on what to do.

I should like to illustrate this with a few examples. *You in Mind* was a series of ;even 10-minute television programmes on BBC-1 at peak time in 1987 aimed at ;iving general viewers insight into a range of common emotional and psychological ›roblems, and how to overcome them. The free back-up booklet had seven chapters written by mental health professionals.

Though there was high satisfaction with it among those asking for it, four out of ten claimed that the information was not detailed enough. This may be because its middle-class readership is more interested or knowledgeable than the average viewer or that recipients had expected more detail in solving their own personal problems.

Spelling it Out, a 16-page booklet giving spelling tips for adults, was considered clearly laid out and would help people with minor spelling problems. Three quarters said it gave new information. However, one in six were disappointed, feeling that the information was too simple or lacked practical exercises. Some thought it would not help people with serious spelling difficulties, or that it was unsuitable f¢ children. The fact that the booklet was not designed for these groups did not sto some recipients feeling misled or disappointed with the material.

In the same vein, the booklet *Help Your Child with Reading* was criticised by som parents as irrelevant for children with severe reading problems. This free bookle generously funded by the Paul Hamblin Foundation, is colourfully illustrated an aimed at parents of children under 12. It offers advice to parents on *helping* the children with reading rather than *teaching* reading. The booklet was generally ver well received. Parents said that it gave them confidence and understanding on ho to help, and that it showed them new methods.

The last booklet I will cover is that for *Second Chance*, the one designed for th end user – members of the public seeking to return to education rather than th detailed fact-pack for the education facilitators. It was phenomenally successf¢ in that 340,000 publications were distributed very rapidly after the week ¢ broadcasting; 51% of those requesting the booklet by ringing the helpline receive it within 3 days of asking.

Attitudes to the *Second Chance* back-up were assessed by IRB International o¢ behalf of the Department of Employment, the BBC's partners in the campaign

A sample of around 520 people calling the helpline were surveyed within a wee of their call. By then, two thirds had read all or part of the booklet. Over thre quarters claimed that it was good or very good. They liked the clear informatio and good presentation. Many were able to relate to the personal case histories c people returning to education or furthering their careers and they found the materi¢ easy to read.

However, about one in five still felt that it had no information relevant to them that it was too general, or that it did not include a list of colleges or courses an gave too little local or regional information. This complaint about lack of specifi local information has been found for other back-up literature related to the gener¢ public undertaking courses – for example, in emergency first aid or communicatio skills.

Attitudes to helplines

Public attitudes to specific helplines are less well-known than their response to back up literature.

BBC Radio 1 ran a *Drug Alert '91* helpline in 1991 to accompany broadcasts o drug usage. Social and Community Planning Research carried out a small-scal exploratory study on how callers using the helpline evaluated the service. Abou 52 people – almost all young males under 25 – took part in the evaluation study

One caller summed up *Drug Alert '91* as a 'damn good idea' on the grounds that drug-taking is so widespread and there is so little reliable information available to the young.

The advice given was appreciated because callers found it reassuring to learn that other people were experiencing similar problems with drugs as their own. The illegality of hard drugs makes information-seeking a problem. The helpline provided an authoritative source for people who could not go elsewhere for it.

Drug Alert '91 found that almost all the callers were ringing for the first time. A few had tried other sources – including a solicitor, a drug dependency agency, the Samaritans and a doctor. One caller had even rung his vet for advice because his dog had eaten a lump of his cannabis!

Other elements of the *Drug Alert '91* helpline were that the advisers answering the calls were good listeners who didn't preach or appear to be against drug use. The fact that the advisers were knowledgeable and 'street-wise' was crucial. Some callers wanted to talk to ex-users on an equal basis of experience.

Because drug use is such a sensitive area it was important that callers could remain anonymous. The telephone made it easier for some users or potential users to get information than it would have been face-to-face. It was also important that the service was advertised as an information line, rather than a helpline. Some callers had avoided ringing because they had got the impression that the service was for addicts. Reliable information on the effects of the drugs they were using or contemplating was valuable even to habitual drug users. Such people had no intention of giving up and did not regard themselves as addicts or in need of help.

In contrast to the hesitant, secretive nature of a helpline giving advice on drugs was the huge public success of the *Second Chance* campaign. The UK-wide free helpline was staffed by over 1,000 experts on adult education, training and careers. The Department of Employment's evaluative research was limited to 20 – 49-year-olds. The callers got through fairly easily to make their requests – 71% were successful within 3 phone calls. There was also a very efficient response from the advisers. Two out of three enquirers were telephoned back within three days of making their call.

Reaction from those using the helpline was again very positive. Over three quarters found the information or advice they were given was useful. In fact, nearly half (44%) claimed it was very useful to them. The service was praised as being helpful, informative, quick to respond and to provide contact numbers for callers to use. The advisers were seen as polite, friendly and sympathetic and gave people encouragement to find out more about enrolling in courses or undertaking some form of adult training. Finally, people were pleased to be phoned back and that the phone call had not cost them any money.

As with other back-up evaluated – whether print or helpline – a minority wa not satisfied with the advice given on the *Second Chance* helpline. About one ir five had not found the advice helpful. Suggestions for improvements to the helplin included provision of more local or regional information on courses that wer available in the area, more people available to take the calls and more informatior given on the first call without having to wait to be rung back.

Ingredients for successful back-up

Let me finally, in a summarising manner, put together what are the essentia ingredients for broadcast back-up to be successful with people using it.

Back-up literature

For back-up literature to be appreciated by people sending for it, it needs to be

– relevant:
   That is, it must be closely linked to programme content and appropriate tc people's needs. BBC Television showed an early evening series on health callec *Go For It!* watched on average by 5 million adults and children. The informatior pack available as back-up consisted of four separate booklets – one each or diet, fitness, alcohol and smoking. People sending for the booklet were mainly female, middle class and aged 16 – 44 – not representative of the audience. Though they appreciated highly the booklets on healthy eating and how to keep fit, they rejected those on smoking and drinking as irrelevant to them. These were not what they were expecting. However, people sending for the pack who were heavy drinkers or smokers were much more appreciative of these two booklets and were prepared to take note of the advice in them.

– unique:
   It should not be easily available, at least in that form, from other sources;

– timely:
   If it does not arrive within a month of the request, interest in it fades;

– informative:
   Booklets and further addresses are only acceptable if accompanied by something of interest in itself;

– free or appropriately priced:
   The material has to be worthy of the price paid, or of the cost of a stamped addressed envelope. Whether a price should be charged over and above the cost of the envelopes and stamps depended on the production quality of the literature on offer, whom the material was for and the subject matter. Basically, material

should be free if just a fact sheet or a 'flimsy', if aimed at low-income groups and if it contains public information, such as health advice.

Glossy booklets, material aimed at high-income groups and information to do with leisure, nature or charitable causes would be paid for. Some people, however, are wary of sending money if they are unsure of what they would receive in return. People felt that more information should be given on radio or television about the kind of back-up on offer, particularly when a price was being charged.

– appropriately specified:
People found it annoying if they were asked to provide a large envelope for print back-up and all they received was a small leaflet.

Helplines

Helplines work if they are perceived to be free – some people assume that the calls, particularly long distance ones, will be expensive. They do not always realise when a freephone service is being provided.

– It helps if the helpline is seen first as an information supplier and then as an adviser. On the *Drug Alert '91* helpline, a number of the callers rang to ask a factual question about the effects of particular drugs they were taking, or were thinking of taking. Once they realised they were not being judged, they often felt encouraged enough to ask for advice about drug problems they had.

– The phone numbers for helplines need to be widely promoted, and promoted by a reputable source. For example, when Radio 1 ran a *Moneyfax* helpline last year, it needed promotion on air at breakfast when large audiences listen in order to alert people to the existence of the helpline. Radio 1's *Drug Alert '91* attracted callers because the number was often repeated on air at different times of the day, and because the station was trusted. Despite his fear of being traced, one man said he called because "if Radio 1 does it, it must be worthwhile".

– It has to be approximately staffed. It would seem that no matter what efforts are made to have the right number and right kinds of people answering the phones, some callers will not be satisfied. Efforts are made to use people who have had experience of other helplines as well as people with specific areas of knowledge. To the *Moneyfax* helpline on young people's problems with debt, bank employees were used as some of the advisers.
On *Drug Alert '91*, one or two complained that the advisers had no first-hand experience of drug-taking – they wanted to talk to ex-users on an equal basis. And on *Second Chance*, despite over 1,000 experts on hand to take the calls, this was insufficient to cope immediately with the flood that came in.

– The unknown quantity of who will call and how many people will call makes it difficult to know how to staff the lines. However, callers appreciate it if telephone lines are open for long periods of the day and night. Wherever possible, the phone lines will be extended to further days to take excess calls, but this depends on funds being available.

– Finally, helplines need to be confidential and the calls untraceable if the subject matter is of a sensitive nature. Sometimes the only way to ensure anonymity is to ring from a public telephone box.

Campaigns

To succeed in marrying broadcasts with motivating the public to take some specific action, a huge amount of organisation is essential.

– It requires the broadcasts to be widely dispersed in order to reach a large audience representative either of the whole population or of the specific target. The *Save a Life* campaign in emergency first aid succeeded in this because the series was shown four times on the main BBC television channel at different times of day and of the week. In this way it was seen by more than half the population of the country and across all ages, classes and sexes. It was supported by local radio. In the same way, *Second Chance* reached huge television audiences because fifteen 1.5-minute comedy sketches were interspersed like advertisements between very popular, primetime programmes.

– A campaign needs to be seen as having broad public usefulness.

– It should be supported by widespread publicity and local organisation.

– It needs money. For a campaign to succeed it must be both prepared well in advance and well-funded – preferably both privately and by the state.

Appendix: Research reports analysed

1. From BBC Broadcasting Research Department:
   [Address: 80 Wood Lane, London W12 0TT; UK]

Irene Shaw: The Education Roadshow – Fact Pack Survey
(SP8 7/33 8; June 1987)
Claire Panter: Go For It !
(SP87/26, September 1987)
Chris Barker, Bloomsbury Health Authority, and Claire Panter, BRD: You in Mind – An Evaluation of the Back-up Booklet (SP88/06, February 1988)
Karen Day: Public Attitudes to Back-up Literature
(April 1988)
Karen Day: Evaluation of Save-a-Life Campaign
(SP88/25J, August 1988)

Moira Bovill: Spelling it Out
(SP89/08, February 1989)
Gavin McKivragan: Attitudes of Recipients to Back-up Literature
(SP89/48, September 1989)
Moira Bovill: Wordpower
(SP90/09, February 1990)
David Bunker: Radio 1 — 'The Line'
(SP90/38, July 1990)
Maureen O'Brien and Jan Lauder: Help your Child with Reading — Evaluation of Booklet
(SP91/25, May 1991)
Irene Shaw, BRD, Chris Barker, Nancy Pistrang,
Bloomsbury and Islington District Psychology Department:
OK2 Talk Feelings
(SP91/46, August 1991)
Gavin McKivragan: Television and the Learning Society
(March 1992)
Irene Shaw: Second Chance
(July 1992)

2. From Broadcasting Support Services:
   [Address: 252 Western Avenue, London W3 6XJ; UK]

Stephen Holland: Moneyfax '91 — Report on Helpline
(December 1991)

3. From Social and Community Planning Research:
   [Address: 35 Northampton Square, London EC1V 0AX; UK]

Clarissa White: Drug Alert 1991 — An exploratory Study
(P5189, December 1991)

Chapter 5:
Alternative Ways of Offering and Financing Cultural and Educational Programmes

Dietrich Schwarzkopf

The European Cultural Channel – Culture Without Borders?

In the last few weeks there has been much talk of the European cultural channel ARTE in the German and even more so in the French press. Nevertheless, it would seem to me useful to make a few introductory remarks on it in case you have not yet come across ARTE. Since 30th May 1992 ARTE has been transmitting from Strasbourg in German for German viewers and in French for the French ones every day from 7 pm to midnight or later, and in the near future with repeats before 7 pm.

In Germany ARTE can be received by cable, i.e. in about 10 million households. Unfortunately, there is at present still a gap in the supply in the Cologne/Bonn area. I very much hope that it can soon be filled. In France, ARTE can currently also be received by cable. There it can be seen in considerably fewer households, namely about 800,000. As from September 1992, ARTE is to be additionally transmitted via La Cinq, a terrestrial channel in France. Then the programme will be available to some 20 million French households, about 80 per cent of all viewers in France.

The abbreviation ARTE stands for 'Association Relative à la Télévision Européenne'. ARTE's legal form is a European Economic Community of Interests. The partners are, on the German side, the Baden-Baden-based ARTE Deutschland

TV GmbH and the French cultural channel La Sept based in Paris. The partners of ARTE Deutschland are the nine West German regional broadcasting stations of the ARD as well as the ZDF. The East German regional stations are invited to join, but will no doubt not do so before the licence fees in the new federal states have reached the level of the fees in the old ones.

The basis of ARTE is a treaty signed in Berlin on 2nd October 1990 between France and the West German federal states, which in the meantime has been ratified. The treaty is open not only to the other German states to join, but also to any member state of the Council of Europe and any party to the European Cultural Agreement, so it is explicitly not restricted to members of the European Community (EC).

ARTE is managed by a President, at present by the Frenchman Jérôme Clément, who at the same time is the President of the ARTE member La Sept. The other members of the Board of Management are the Vice President, with whom the President has to agree on all important decisions, the Programme Director and the Administrative Director. This composition will remain in force for the first three years. After that the Programme Director is also to be the Vice President.

The Supervisory Board is the Members' Meeting, currently made up of six German and six French representatives. A Programme Advisory Board of representatives of the cultural life of the member countries advises the Board of Management and the Members' Meeting on programme matters.

ARTE is at the moment funded in equal parts by the German and French sides. The 1992 budget amounts to DM 338 million. The source of funding on the German side is the sum of DM 0.75 from the monthly licence fee. The same share comes from the French national budget, into which the licence fees are paid, of course. For broadcasting by means of the terrestrial chain La Cinq, France has made additional funding available.

ARTE consists of the Strasbourg-based Head Office and at present two national poles, La Sept in Paris and ARTE Deutschland in Baden-Baden. The Strasbourg Head Office has a staff of 143, 60 of whom are German and 83 French; 27 people are employed at ARTE Deutschland.

ARTE's information programmes and a few programmes from other sections are produced in Strasbourg or commissioned from there. All the other contributions are supplied from outside, half by La Sept and half by ARTE Deutschland. Half of the German contributions are, in turn, from the ARD and half from ZDF. Within the ARD's share, compulsory proportions from the individual Laender broadcasting stations have been agreed upon; they range from 12.5 per cent from the Westdeutscher Rundfunk to 1.5 per cent from the Saarländischer Rundfunk and Radio Bremen (that is 6.25 and 0.75 per cent respectively of the total programme). The percentage division is also to apply to the individual programme sections. It

174

s obvious that the compulsory shares of the ARD stations result in coordination problems. The Director General of the NDR and next ARD Chairman, Mr. Plog, as therefore quite rightly urgently requested the ARD to bundle its contributions o ARTE.

Decisions on the programmes to be offered by the member suppliers are taken at he monthly ARTE Programme Conference in Strasbourg, which is attended by representatives of the Head Office and of the members. Decisions are passed by a two-thirds' majority, so that neither the German nor the French side can be outvoted. Once the Programme Conference has made its decision the members produce their contributions independently. It should be a matter of course that this is done in collegial cooperation with the producers at the Strasbourg Head Office, who are responsible for the overall picture of the programme and who additionally have to pay attention to the suitability of the contributions for the viewers in Germany and in France and later in other countries, too. It is not surprising that this occasionally results in tension.

ARTE pays for the suppliers' programme from the funds at its disposal according o agreed rates. Inasfar as new productions are concerned – of which as large a proportion as possible is aimed at – the first transmission takes place in ARTE. This is important for the German suppliers, for *La Sept* is no longer a broadcaster. The second transmission takes place in the ARD and ZDF. In this way programmes are produced for these organisations which would not have been made but for ARTE's existence and funds. Nevertheless, it would be wrong to see in ARTE merely an instrument for optimising German cultural broadcasts.

The supply system in its present form means, admittedly, that the production departments in Strasbourg – apart from the information section – have for the most part coordination tasks and not programme-production tasks of their own. The Strasbourg Head Office cannot place any programme commissions of its own which are not in the information area, either. This state of affairs seems to me o be in need of correction, to give the Head Office in Strasbourg greater independence in making programmes, with a sensible balance between Strasbourg's own or commissioned productions and the suppliers' productions.

The topic of this paper is the question as to whether the establishment of a European cultural channel already means culture without borders or whether this is an objective to be aimed at with the help of the cultural channel. I should like to present ten theses on this:

1. Large parts of culture are national in origin, especially when the language is its means of expression. It cannot be the task of a European television cultural channel to blur or artificially internationalise national origins.

2. The European cultural channel ARTE must originate from national sources. It is its task to spread nationally characterised culture internationally and to promote an understanding for it internationally. At ARTE this begins organisationally on a Franco-German basis, which is soon to be expanded by other European participants joining in; as far as content is concerned, ARTE opened itself to the culture of other European peoples from the outset.

3. The term culture and understanding culture are also largely of a national character. That is why, from the outset, ARTE has refrained from finding a common Franco-German definition of culture. ARTE's cross-border task, aiming at overcoming borders, consists in contrasting different ideas of culture, comparing them with one another, making them the subject of information, discussion and critical analysis, in order to thus promote an understanding in other nations.

4. Imparting knowledge and understanding helps to break down the prejudices and psychological borders they have drawn. ARTE has set itself this goal in Franco-German relations and throughout Europe.

5. Knowledge and understanding are imparted most effectively when authors from one country deal with circumstances in another and authors from third countries add their viewpoints. In this way a 'composite view' emerges which can create new cognitive connections and new dimensions. This aim is served in ARTE above all by the 'theme evenings' or 'title days', on which in each case a whole programme evening is devoted to one and the same subject from a whole variety of different angles and approaches.

6. ARTE sees itself as *European* especially in the sense that by Europe not only the member states of the European Community or Western Europe are meant. ARTE explicitly and emphatically includes Central and Eastern Europe. That is why the first theme evening was programmatically and quite deliberately devoted to the old Russian capital of St. Petersburg.

7. ARTE offers itself as a forum for the major issues which are preoccupying the whole of Europe: nationalism, sub-nationalism, the growth of violence in the political debates, migratory movements and xenophobia, the future of democracy.

8. The term 'European' means for ARTE not a dissociation from American culture or other European cultures. ARTE attaches importance to presenting in its programme the connection, the interplay and growing links between culture in and outside Europe.

9. ARTE also wants to dismantle and overcome borders not by running the risk — for example, by being elitist or making boastful claims — of excluding or

offending viewers. For ARTE, 'culture' has to be understood in the widest and broadest sense; thus humour and lifestyle, for instance, are naturally also part of it. ARTE does not want to offer leisure-time culture, but culture to help people become acquainted with one another, to astonish them, to let them enjoy themselves, even to be annoyed at times perhaps, at any rate to make them talk with one another about it.

10. Like most television organisations, ARTE is a child of politics, but not its instrument or its mouthpiece. ARTE pursues neither German nor French cultural foreign policy and is not the organ of European organisations, but endeavours, independently and on its own, to overcome borders, including those of the official understanding of culture.

Whoever, as I have done, talks about the national origin and the national understanding of culture, has to answer the question as to what remains of the integrative aspect at ARTE.

First, the familiarisation with the culture of other nations and the arousing of understanding for them are important requirements. Even in Franco-German relations these requirements have not yet been fully met. The knowledge of the average television viewer in both countries about the other country is quite limited. ARTE offers German viewers the chance to find out what is important for French viewers and for what reasons, and vice versa.

For many French viewers the way German television productions are made, their presentation as well as frequently hearing German on television are strange, even so strange that rejection can easily set in. The converse may be similar. French viewers quickly tend to find German programmes too heavy, too old-fashioned, too didactic. German criticism of French programmes is: too highly-strung, too hectic, too subjective. It is part of the process of mutual understanding that each becomes accustomed to the other, comes to know and tolerate the different taste, then, hopefully, even becomes curious to learn why the other one is so different, and finally is prepared to find something interesting and attractive about the other.

These considerations play a part in the transmission of ARTE that is planned on the terrestrial chain La Cinq in France. The Conservative opposition has described the Socialist Government's decision to transmit the ARTE cultural programme on a channel which was used to transmit a commercial programme up to 12th April as 'idiocy' and has announced that, when it comes to power, it will cancel the decision. Added to this is the fact that ARTE is to be broadcast via La Cinq only from 7 pm; no decision has yet been taken on the day programme.

On the La Cinq channel ARTE enters into competition with the French national television channels, the public service and the private ones. It is indisputable that even in this competitive environment ARTE will remain a European cultural programme. A French observer has quite rightly remarked that ARTE will have to develop its distinctive features even more strongly, for if ARTE tries to adapt itself to the others it would have to carry out this adaptation with financial mean which are inadequate for this purpose, and this would involve the risk of failure

The emphasis on the distinctiveness by no means rules out flexibility in the programme planning. On the contrary, flexibility means programme changes to take current events into account – a good opportunity to make it clear to one national audience what the other regards as a current event. Flexibility also mean the inclusion of lighter programme forms. ARTE will not offer any big entertainment shows, such as the ARD and ZDF audiences are accustomed to or Thursdays and Saturdays, no live broadcasts of sporting events, no American serie of the kind one encounters everywhere all the time. But programmes on lifestyle for example, on everyday culture, can contribute much to an understanding of othe nations.

Contributions from other European countries (as well as from non-European ones can be taken into the ARTE programme, if they are brought in as a share of one of the present partners, i.e. of the ARD, ZDF or *La Sept*. That will change when other European broadcasting organisations join ARTE. RTBF, television of the French-speaking part of Belgium, has formally applied for membership. Nego tiations are being conducted on the suitable form for RTBF's participation. One difficulty is that the ARTE contract provides for the members to make contribution both in money and in programmes and staff. RTBF is finding the financia contribution difficult at the moment. On the other hand, ARTE has a lively interes in obtaining RTBF's participation, since in this way Brussels, with Strasbourg one of the European 'capitals', would be brought in. If an appropriate solution is foun for RTBF's participation this example might well be interesting for other Europea broadcasting organisations, first and foremost the Swiss SRG.

Since any language other than German or French, which are planned for the start would incur not inconsiderable extra costs it is obvious that ARTE wants to enlis members in the first stage in whose service area these two languages are spoken This raises the question of what attitude the Austrian ORF will adopt to ARTE The impression up to now is that the ORF is currently concentrating on it involvement with 3Sat, because it is there that its considerable contribution is mos effective and noticeable. Cooperation with ARTE is by no means likely to b impossible for this reason, but should, rather, be more obvious.

Negotiations on the participation of European broadcasting organisations with languages other than German or French are planned as the next step. If a majo broadcasting organisation joins, the structure of ARTE, which is tailored to th initial stage of Franco-German parity, would have to be thought over again. Each new partner that joins reduces the share of the present ones, but also makes it clea hat the beginning of transmissions at 7 pm must not become a permanent arrangement. When further members join it must be possible to extend ARTE into he day, the total transmission time, of course, being sensibly divided up between ll the participants and not having new members slotted into the early evening, vhile the prime time in the evening remains a Franco-German domain.

robably Central and Eastern European countries would like to join ARTE, lthough they are unable to raise the necessary funding. ARTE will want to avoid situation in which the German and French partners alone bear the main financial urden of the undertaking, while other members are exempt on account of their inancial straits. So ARTE will also be interested in more financially strong partners.)f course, the cultural channel aims to expand into Europe beyond the Franco-ierman beginning, and nowhere does it say that if you are poor you cannot join n, or that there has to be a certain balance between members who are financially etter off and those that are worse off. But nor should the practical side be lost ight of, if only in the interest of the functioning and development of the channel. o different forms of participation will have to be sought which take account not nly of the interests of the present partners but also of those who join subsequently.

RTE's Programme Director André Harris has described the channel as "the last reat television adventure". The attempt to overcome borders is always an dventure. Technically television is without borders today, but this does not apply o reception. Here are the borders that have to be overcome, here is ARTE's rincipal task.

Pierre Trincal

Technology Support for the French Educational System: The Centre National de Documentation Pédagogique

The *Centre National de Documentation Pédagogique* (CNDP) is an officia
establishment placed under the supervision of the Ministry of National Education
The CNDP has three tasks:

- The first is to carry out *pedagogic documentation*, i.e. to make available t
  everyone, starting with teachers, official regulations that concern educatio
  (curriculums, timetables, examination syllabuses, competition regulations etc.)
  as well as material and information needed by teachers in their profession.
- The second task is that of *publishing*, in the print, audiovisual and compute
  media.
- The third field is concerned with *'educational engineering'*; this involves keepin
  itself up-to-date with technological developments in the techniques of infor
  mation science and communications, and being able to provide informatio
  about the new opportunities that they offer to the teaching profession.

The CNDP was subject to a major reform in January 1992. It was split up int
29 independent organisations, the Regional Centres for Pedagogic Documentation
(*Centres Régionaux de Documentation Pédagogique*, CRDP) – coordinated witl
each other by the CNDP, which at the same time was reduced to providing service
for Paris only.

To deal with the subject that concerns us here, i.e. the tasks of audiovisua
publishing, I asked the Minister to set up alongside myself a National Publishin
Committee (*Comité national de l'édition*, CNE) on which seats are held both b
the directors in the Ministry responsible for school and university syllabuses, an
by the publishing professionals who are concerned with the print, audiovisual an
computer publishing media.

I will now come to the survey I have been asked to give concerning the educationa
audiovisual sector.

On behalf of the French educational system, the CNDP has analysed the problem
involved and has developed a new publishing strategy. From the first meeting o
the *Comité national de l'édition* in December 1990, its members emphasised th
already acknowledged role of the visual image in teaching, and invited the CNDF

o play an active part in developing this image. It is from this point of view that he CNDP has since then refined its strategy and modified some parts of its work.

These ideas on the CNDP's role in the educational audiovisual sector occur at a ime when the French audiovisual landscape is striving to redefine itself, and when he school and the audiovisual sector are coming closer together as a result of echnological developments that are introducing greater flexibility in the use of audiovisual teaching aids in schools and that will in future provide teachers with greater control over these tools.

As a producer of programmes and as a provider of educational engineering services, he CNDP is not content to simply watch this development happen – it is trying o speed it up. During a period of some years, it has advanced from having its programmes broadcast by the TV channels alone to a very diversified form of broadcasting. It now employs cable, satellite, video cassettes, video discs, etc.

The production of broadcast television

During the same period what has been changing is not simply the method of broadcasting but the products themselves. Users will ultimately be able to receive programmes directly broadcast or call them up on their screens whenever they want them. It is the entire educational audiovisual sector that is undergoing a process of change in its technical and economic foundations, in the nature of its productions, and in the part played by those involved in it.

The CNDP therefore started out by transmitting only on-air over television channels. This was its point of departure. Until the middle of the 1980s, the essential part of the CNDP's audiovisual work consisted in producing programmes for broadcast transmission.

But since then the appearance of new broadcasting aids and the widespread use of video recorders have caused the CNDP to rethink its strategy as a producer of television programmes and as a provider of assistance to teachers in their use of general interest television.

The CNDP continues to produce television programmes. The production of broadcast TV programmes today still accounts for a large part of the funds that the CNDP allocates to audiovisual media (about 75%), since at the moment broadcast television remains, by a considerable margin, the only means of reaching on a large scale the huge number of educational establishments in France that are spread over the whole country. There are 64,000 primary schools, a certain number of which are situated in rural and mountain areas which can only be reached by on-air television.

181

School television in France consists of the programme *Parole d'école*, transmitted for 78 hours every year on the *France 3* channel (the former FR3). This television programme conforms to the aesthetic requirements of every televised programme. It differs from other types of programmes not by formal aspects but by the aim that it pursues and the subjects it deals with. If these subjects have to be presented in the form of a TV show, this does not mean in any way that concessions are made and productions become superficial or trendy. The principles of classroom teaching have to be strictly observed.

This kind of programme can be viewed by quite a large television audience — that of the morning hours, which is very diverse in nature. But this type of programme meets above all the expectations of teachers who need awareness-creating programmes in order to motivate their pupils and make them ask questions.

The majority of programmes produced for school television are not simply of ephemeral interest and are suitable for repeated showing. Out of 5O hours of new productions for television broadcasting in the period 1991-1992, 34 hours were devoted to fiction, documentaries and news reports, and only 16 hours to studio programmes.

This kind of production policy is the reason why the CNDP is now organising an 'image bank' of programmes to increase the value of its programme archives and to acquire resources.

Thus certain series, for example the *Badaboks* series for the very young (3 to 7 years old), have been acquired by the French channels and many foreign stations.

So which channel can the CNDP have its television programmes transmitted on? Here it is important to remember what kind of regulatory system French TV stations operate under.

Broadcast legislation in France

Television in France is governed by the law of 3Oth September 1986 on audiovisual communications together with its numerous implementing decrees or regulations. The public channels had previously been defined by the decrees of 1982, whilst the private stations were defined and authorised by the decrees of 1987. What must be emphasised is that all these texts together correspond to the spirit of the 1986 Act, which is one of the major documents organising public rights in France. Its exact title is the 'Law relating to the freedom of communication'.

In fact, this law is intended above all to preserve French citizens from the risks that could arise in the provision of audiovisual information by the pressures exercised by the political and financial powers, by political, ideological or religious groups, and also by advertising, amongst others.

This law is also intended to preserve equality of access to the media and equality of treatment on media of this kind for political, economic, religious or social information, so as to prevent the media power of television being used for propaganda purposes of any kind whatever. The creation of a politically independent authority now known as the *Conseil supérieur de l'audiovisuel* (CSA) to allocate broadcasting frequencies and to monitor the proper application of the law is also a guarantee of the rights of French citizens.

The public interest, it is true, caused legislators to make it mandatory for public or private TV stations to devote a minimum of time to cultural and educational activities or to consumer protection (laid down in Article 28, 4th paragraph, of the 1986 Act). Of course, the law also imposes general educational, cultural and social aims on the public channels in which the state holds the entire capital and controls the board of governors.

Then there is the exception formed by ARTE, which has been discussed here. This does not conform to a French law, because it is the result of an international agreement imposed on French legislators. All this means that French television should be a marvellous support in spreading the message of education.

And yet it is nothing of the kind. If one refers to the texts of the implementing regulations, notably the charter specifying aims and duties approved by decree for all public television channels, one will note that the educational audiovisual sector is very badly treated. It is in fact stated precisely (in general Article 23 of the charter) that the system of cooperation between the channel and the Ministry of National Education and its subordinate organisations, i.e. the CNDP, are the subject of an agreement, the resulting costs having to be borne by the Ministry of National Education or its subordinate organisations.

Thus the costs of production and also of transmission are to be borne by the Ministry of National Education. This arrangement, intended to be favourable to the educational audiovisual sector, has in fact revealed itself as being very unfavourable, since it makes the Ministry responsible for what is normally regarded as a channel's functions − in particular with regard to transmission, since the channel may have to decide to broadcast any time round the clock. The Ministry, however, has not been granted a preferential right of access to programme schedules, which remain in the absolute control of the channel. This means that the Minister has a right to make educational programmes on condition that he pays for everything, and in exchange he has no kind of advantage, either preferential access to television transmission or a reserved slot in schedules.

So obviously the CNDP had to adapt, and from 1990, shortly after my arrival, it chose to negotiate with France 3 not on a legislative and regulatory basis but on a contractual one. It refused to pay for television transmission and assumed the role of partner to the channel in putting forward its own ideas about its productions and in providing the channel with educational programmes. In exchange, it claimed the status of coproducer, since it provided finance.

The channel agreed to transmit CNDP's programmes, ensuring that they will be harmoniously integrated into its programme schedules, and has granted CNDP distribution rights on cassettes for the educational system of certain of its programmes, selected by common agreement. France 3 has also committed itself to including in the purchase and production contracts for programmes that it places with the production companies and authors' rights societies a clause providing for the use of these programmes in the educational system.

If at the moment CNDP's programmes are transmitted on *France 3*, this is because this public service channel is, together with *La Sept* or ARTE, the channel that shows most openly a desire to develop educational and cultural programmes.

The CNDP, however, does not exclude a partnership with other operating companies. Thus it has coproduced with VM Production a science programme entitled $E=M6$, which is being transmitted at the moment of the 6th French channel.

Financial arrangements

How can the CNDP finance its programmes? On the French audiovisual market, the CNDP is a producer of not insignificant size but it is somewhat untypical. Its status as a public establishment of administrative character in fact makes it subject to a particular financial logic, which is nothing if not inconvenient in the current crisis that is shaking the sector (financing depends entirely on the budgetary funds made available by the CNDP). It is true that an important part of its resources is provided by state subsidy but this is not even enough to meet its personnel costs.

The fact is that in the last few years budgetary stringency has been imposed on the CNDP as on all French official organisations and establishments. Moreover, the CNDP is at a disadvantage as it has no access to certain sources of finance, such as the assistance provided by the *Centre national de la cinématographie*, the national cinematography centre (CNC), and of course it has no recourse to bank loans. The result is that the CNDP has to use its own resources to assist its productions. Although being increased, these funds are still very limited, for until recently general attitudes in the public service in France rejected the idea of profitability.

Today, the modernisation of the public services allows new economic criteria to be introduced closer to those of the corporate sector in production choices and in the commercial exploitation of products.

Nevertheless, the CNDP continues to be confronted permanently by a real problem in financing its audiovisual activities, which hinders its development. This is why - like all audiovisual producers at the present moment - it is also trying to share costs with other partners.

At the national level, coproduction in mounting projects is becoming a necessity more and more frequently, whilst at international level some recent operations show that it is possible to bring together educational producers following the same aims. An example of this is a series entitled *Panoramic*, produced on the initiative of the CNDP and the Agency for International Technology (AIT) in the USA.

It is essential to harmonise conditions so that the supply of educational audiovisual programmes attains a significant volume. Below a critical threshold, the programmes supplied do not have the diversity required to meet the expectations of a potential heterogeneous public, which is varied in the teaching levels required, is interested in different subjects and requires different teaching approaches.

The enlargement of supply will thus to a large extent influence decisively the popularised use of television and the emergence of needs, for today one can only note the decline in the number of hours of school television: in 1970 there were 10 hours weekly broadcast, in 1992 two regular hours.

Engaging in an educational TV channel?

There is in France, it is true, a project for an educational channel, which is not yet properly developed. This is a project announced by the President of the Republic and the current Minister of Education, Jack Lang. It would consist of an allocation of the frequency formerly used by the 5th Channel, which has disappeared, to a new television channel for education and training, to be on the air in the hours before 7 pm. At present, only the evening hours of the old French 5th Channel, the time after 7 pm, are used by ARTE, but ARTE, having the natural ambition of wanting to increase the participation of the other European states, will itself also claim these day-time hours to broadcast television.

It is up to the CSA to allocate these hours to a limited company, set up under the provisions of the 1986 Act, for running an educational channel. Of course, the CNDP would be delighted if this project is realised with our participation, and we would then be competitors of ARTE. As far as I am concerned, while I have a lot of respect for cultural activities, I do not forget that educational activities are also a way of bringing nations closer together and I would not find it normal if I were to be condemned to sign agreements with the FWU in Germany and the BBC in Britain for the sole exploitation of cassettes, for example, when we could also, perhaps, set up an educational channel in France with the assistance of these foreign colleagues.

Be that as it may, this is a project dear to the Minister's heart but one faced by the obstacles I have just mentioned. The obstacle represented by competition with ARTE is not the worst. There are lots of other obstacles, financial and legal ones that I will not venture to refer to here.

If the CNDP could benefit from an educational channel of this kind, it would certainly not modify its strategy, but would, of course, have to develop it production activities considerably, and it would be considered by this channel, which itself has been given responsibility for educational programming, to be a – certainl privileged – producer, but also one producer among many others.

Making better use of television

I would now like to say some words, still on the subject of television, concernin another of the CNDP's fields of activity that is at least as important as its rol as a producer, and that is helping teachers to make better use of television.

Television in fact shows CNDP programmes, but there are also many othe programmes in the programme schedules, general-interest television programme of high quality, that could be used profitably for educational purposes.

Many ARTE programmes, for example, which were not originally conceived fo use in class, are nevertheless very suitable for such use. Among the examples t be quoted are large-scale historical portraits such as *Nuremberg à Nuremberg*, *Le années Algériennes*, *Histoires parallèles* or scientific documentaries such as *Th Life of the Plants*, or *The Miraculous Planet*, that very beautiful Japanese film

Teachers of history and geography or economics could use current affairs magazine such as *Envoyé spécial*, *Reportages*, *24 Heures*, to provide up-to-date audiovisu material on countries and on the major issues in society. *Continentale* on Franc 3, which is an interesting programme familiarising the French public with th languages of Europe, would be another example.

Evening news on *Canal +* every day provide language teachers with extracts fro foreign televised news programmes. The paucity of programmes for children tha can be re-used in the elementary school is often, in fact, simply the consequenc of the commonly acknowledged mediocrity of French programmes for youth.

On the other hand, the contents of the TV channels' programmes are often fu of information, but an understanding of the problems raised requires a minimu of cultural knowledge and experience that pupils do not always possess. The us of general-interest television programmes in class, to be fruitful, therefor presupposes real work by teachers, viewing programmes in advance to find ou which of them are suitable, and then to analyse and determine how these programmes can be integrated into the teaching plan of their lessons.

This is why the CNDP has established a weekly press organ entitled *Téléscope*, which provides teachers with methods of using television rationally. It points out to them which programmes are usable in class and shows them ways to use them.

Téléscope is also intended to popularise the idea that using television is not simply a way of making life easy for teachers. It is a demanding exercise, which could be useful for courses involving intensive learning. This magazine has been very well received and the number of subscribers is growing regularly.

Legal considerations

Finally, the use of television programmes for audiovisual teaching matter at school presupposes that the teachers or librarians have the right to receive these programmes in class but also that they will be able to tape them on video cassettes without infringing the rights of authors, publishers, producers, performers etc. In this field we come up against the French national regulations covering authors' rights, which is based on the Lausanne Convention.

The use in class of television programmes is not comparable to private use, for example in the family home, when rights are not assigned to authors. The use in class of protected works is subject to a settlement of authors' rights. For a very long time there has been an impasse on this problem in France, and now the decision has been taken to negotiate with the authors' rights societies, because nobody wanted to modify the French law, which seemed to be too difficult a venture. This law has been discussed so much that the Government has little inclination to re-open a legislative debate on a delicate case.

On the other hand, as the Director General of the CNDP I have been given by the Minister the responsibility of negotiating with authors, on a contractual basis, the method of paying lump sums or flat rates. This is a way of purchasing on behalf of teachers the right not only to receive but also to record on cassettes the programmes that teachers want to use in class. The system will be a kind of insurance against any right of recourse to litigation on the part of the authors' rights societies.

A general agreement with the latter, signed by the CNDP, will then be put forward to the educational establishments, which would become parties to it by paying a flat rate subscription.

Non-broadcast distribution of audiovisual material

I would now like to deal with the one outstanding innovation introduced by the CNDP – distribution using media other than broadcast television.

Modern computer and communications technologies are in the process of modifying the audiovisual landscape throughout the country. It is not sufficient, however, to equip educational establishments with receivers if we want to see practical teaching methods develop. It is also necessary for teachers to be in possession of products to make this equipment operational.

Today, the CNDP's publishing policy is to exploit to an optimum degree the potential of the different audiovisual broadcasting teaching aids and to supply programmes well suited to each kind of aid. Broadcast television, in our opinion, is capable of reaching a wide public and it therefore remains the preferred media for the transmission of awareness-creating and motivational programmes.

On the other hand, cable as well as video cassettes and soon, perhaps, Compact Disc Interactive (CD-I) are better adapted to reaching specific audiences, since more didactic contents aim at the acquisition of precise knowledge of a specialised nature, or at the promotion of self-training and self-evaluation activities.

The CNDP therefore wishes to supply an enlarged range of products to the French educational system: a diversified range of awareness-creating and motivational programmes that it can, to some extent, find in the programmes of the television channels, but with an unequal allocation of resources depending on the subject.

I do not know what the situation is like in Germany or Britain, but I believe even so that in general it is easy to take transmissions concerning history and geography from the general-interest programmes.

This is not so much the case with science programmes. Pupils in class need such programmes of a didactic nature intended to provide knowledge or methods. These programmes therefore have to be produced for the specific use of the class. They will be available on cassettes, preferably, as this is the most flexible media.

The demonstration of the theorem of Pythagoras, for example, or an explanation the rule of three as learnt at the primary school, which is a stumbling block for numerous pupils, should thus be made available on cassettes, not as broadcast programmes.

The CNDP already possesses a generation of didactic programmes for exclusive use in class or groups together with a teacher-intermediary, who integrates the programmes into the plan of his or her lessons, makes use of it and brings out its real meaning. This was the case above all with short films concerned with the natural sciences distributed on Super 8.

A second generation of didactic programmes is now being produced, this time being targeted at the pupils themselves, for independent use. These programmes can thus be part of a process involving the individualisation of training courses; they can also serve as self-instructional material or to complement a course by providing support or more detailed knowledge. The targeted audience could be pupils making use of the documentatation and information centres *(Centres de documentation et d'information, CDI)* that are attached to practically all of the ten thousand or so educational establishment in France. But they could also be targeted at adults who would find these programmes at the resource centres.

Finally, the CNDP hopes to reach private homes themselves. The cassette is naturally the most convenient format to distribute programmes of this kind. But cable could also become an excellent means of directing them towards training centres or even private homes.

The CNDP is thus aware that in this way it can increase the range of different services it is offering, while trying to make them more profitable. In contrast to broadcast television, the new means of distribution could also generate resources for the CNDP. The market for training video cassettes is being developed. Educational establishments and training organisations have been buying more since they began to be financed by the local authorities. There is a market for continuous training.

Families are potential customers and naturally they can be numbered in millions. In the modern language, documentary and domestic service sectors, there are already distributors of video cassettes who are beginning to create a market. The television channels themselves are creating specialised subsidiaries, and some of them have approached the CNDP to build up their catalogues of educational cassettes.

Each of these formats that the CNDP is thinking of using to make programmes available must in fact find its own financial equilibrium, and when the same product can be distributed in various formats steps must be taken, of course, to ensure that multi-distribution does not cause competition between the different systems. It may thus be worth discussing what effect making video cassettes simultaneously available for hire in video libraries and also via cable will have on their sales.

This range of products being offered comes, of course, from different sources. The CNDP could no longer be satisfied with making available its own stock of programmes stemming from its production activities. It must therefore enlarge its acquisitions, which is the reason for our presence here at MediaNet, as we can never obtain enough if we intend to supply a country's entire educational system.

The CNDP is thus moving on from being a producer to becoming progressively both general supplier of services and programme planner, and, in line with its publishing priorities as defined by the *Comité national de l'édition*, it is adopting an active attitude in seeking titles available on the international market. Naturally it is also negotiating with the authors' rights societies, the association of audiovisua producers and the television-operating companies to obtain advantageous condition to benefit the educational system.

Cable transmissions

Finally, I would like to say a few words about cable and video libraries. The CNDI has been interested in cable since very early on, since 1987. But as you know cabl in France is meeting great difficulties, largely due to excessive initial technica ambitions and then to the fact that, after having made large investments, cable operators are not perhaps making enough effort to advertise or to provide ar interesting range of programmes.

CNDP's specialised cable channel, *Educâble*, is undergoing a growth crisis at the moment. The slow installation of cable in France has not created the dynamic development required to encourage specific production. The programme bank o 6OO films was initially set up starting with programmes produced for televisio and so certain titles are dated.

Thus the CNDP is faced today with a certain number of questions and in some months answers will have to be found to them:

- Is it necessary to distinguish in the programme bank between the different level:
  - schools, grammar schools, or colleges - or to keep all levels withou differentiation?
- Does this specialised cable channel, which at the present moment is financec by agreement and by subscriptions, have to be opened up to being rented ir some way to the local authorities?
- Should it be entrusted to the cable-operators and the aim be to distribute it tc homes?

The latter issue is based on a hypothesis that is dear to me. I believe that cable': future does not lie in distribution exclusively to educational establishments. Quite obviously, cable programmes have to be supplied to homes. But this means tha the CNDP will have to buy supplementary rights, as its current bank of programme: is not free of all rights: the rights for distribution to the general public have no yet been purchased, but only for distribution to educational establishments and only for a small number of titles.

So it will be necessary either to acquire the rights or to change the titles; and finall we will doubtless have to develop the contents of our programme bank *Educâbl* so that it does not duplicate the programmes of the broadcast educational TV channel, if this channel is to be created in France.

Here too, the CNDP has a very clear strategy. In our broadcast TV transmissions, it is up to us to transmit awareness-creating programmes providing general information that can be viewed by the general public. For cable we would no doubt have to reserve much more specialised didactic programmes providing self-instruction or self-evaluation, approximately the same as those currently being distributed by video cassettes.

In recent years regional video libraries have experienced a very noticeable development in their lending figures. There is considerable variation in the demand for different titles, however. Marketing has not yet been developed enough in France for it to be possible to modify the contents of these video libraries as information is fed back. This information on the quality of the titles borrowed is insufficient either in quantity or in quality to allow us to restructure the contents of the video libraries.

It does, however, seem that there is a very strong potential demand in this field, and the CNDP is looking into the matter of how it can rapidly build up its video libraries. Let me remind you that it possesses a network of video libraries at 115 points distributed nationally in the country, which rent programmes to educational establishments and schools.

This is what I wanted to say concerning the strategy that has been developed by the CNDP to make available to educational establishments, and in a more general manner, to learners, different audiovisual programmes meeting the expectations of these different audiences. Of course, the very slow development in the use of audiovisual media in schools can no longer be attributed to possible conflicts between an image-based culture, i.e. television, and a culture based on the written word, i.e. the school. This conflict is over and no longer amounts to very much. It simply provides material for some academic speeches. The fears have also disappeared that television will one day replace teachers. In France nobody believes any longer that this will ever be the case.

In fact, there are more profound reasons for the slow penetration of audiovisual media into the practice of education. The visual image is relatively expensive. Access to it is not easy. There is no catalogue for it comparable to those found in libraries. And even if catalogues are beginning to be developed, subsequent access to the visual image, in the proper sense of the word, involves renting or buying a video cassette recorder, for example, and is thus not automatic.

In conclusion it may be predicted that educational audiovisual media will undergo real development in schools when teachers are better acquainted with the methods of using the new technological media (video discs, video cassettes, video recorders etc.), when the educational audiovisual sector is able to make use of all channels of distribution (television, cable, video) and when the word 'television' no longer designates a transmission but simply a receiver which can show both television and cable programmes, as well as any product on video disc or cassette that teachers will have been able to procure.

Nick Comer-Calder

The Learning Channel and Discovery Europe: Educational Programmes via Cable

I thank for being invited to speak and for the opportunity to discuss *The Learning Channel UK* and its sister channel *Discovery Europe*. Let me start with the ownership of the two channels. Both channels are owned by the American company *The Discovery Communication Inc.* (DCI), which is the parent company of both *The Discovery Channel* and *The Learning Channel* in the USA.

There, *The Discovery Channel* was launched in 1985 with approximately 156,000 subscribers, with a mission to provide the very best of documentary television from around the world. It is now received in 58 million households across the USA. *The Learning Channel* was launched in 1990 and acquired by DCI in 1991 and now provides highly accessible educational programming for adults as well as an early morning educational service for pre-school children.

Discovery Channel Europe

The Discovery Channel Europe was launched in 1989 and is editorially entirely independent of the American parent organisation. It is an all documentary cable channel that transmits 8 hours a day – from 4 in the afternoon until 11 at night. It is satellite-delivered to cable operators from Intelsat VI and is received – via cable – in over 2 million homes in Norway, Sweden, Iceland, Denmark, Holland, Belgium, Ireland and the United Kingdom. Of Discovery's programmes, 60% are subtitled in Swedish, 50% in Danish, and 40% in Dutch.

Discovery Europe acquires programmes from British, European, American and Australian broadcasters and independent producers. In the future Discovery Europe will work closely with the Discovery Channel in the USA on international co productions.

The Discovery schedule is made up of the following five genres: People and Places, Human Adventure, History, Nature, and Science and Technology.

Examples of the programmes that go in these genres are as follows:

World Leaders, a series of biographies of world-leaders like Stalin, Churchill Gorbachev, Bush and Saddam Hussein – for People and Places;

The Route, a historic reconstruction of an expedition on foot to the North Pole – for Human Adventure;
The Great Moghuls, the story of India's ancient rulers – for History;
Swift and Silent, the story of the natural world's most dangerous predators and their struggle to survive as their environment is destroyed – for Nature;
Equinox, an award-winning series covering a wide range of scientific topics from black holes to Japanese car design – for Science and Technology.

As to the style of our programmes, it can be said that the presentation of Discovery emphasises the drama and excitement of the programmes rather than the educational content. However, much of the programming is educational and the channel is used extensively in schools and colleges in the UK.

The Learning Channel

The Learning Channel (TLC) was launched on March 2nd, 1992 – thereby making television history: for the first time the UK has a television service devoted entirely to adult learning.

The channel transmits from 12.00 noon to 3.00 pm every day and is delivered by the same satellite as Discovery Europe. Because so much educational material is culturally specific, TLC is a service for the United Kingdom only.

By the end of 1992, The Learning Channel was carried by all cable systems in the UK, giving us access to 300,000 households spread across the country. In areas not cabled TLC can be received direct from satellite using a 1.8m dish.

TLC is part of the Basic cable package, as is Discovery. This means that cable subscribers do not have to pay over and above the basic cable subscription to receive the two channels.

At the present time, TLC acquires all its programmes from C4, ITV companies, UK independents and to a very small extent the BBC. In the future we hope to commission and co-produce our own series. Like Discovery, we have an arrangement with Broadcasting Support Services (BSS) to provide printed back-up where available. We also produce our own back-up.

The back-up typically takes the form of paper-back booklets which contain information complementary to the television series. In some cases back-up is produced by BSS in conjunction with the broadcaster (e.g. BBC or Channel 4), BSS are the distributors.

TV companies produce and distribute their own materials. The booklets may offer background information which will give the series a wider context, or it may offer more detailed practical information – e.g. recipes in the case of a cookery series. Prices of booklets are usually in the area of £3 to £4. For some programmes back-up in the form of a video tape is available. To date take up from The Learning Channel has been small, but we hope that as the channel becomes better known this will increase.

TLC's schedule is divided into three hour-long strands. The first hour covers *Family, Health and Social Issues*; the second carries 'How-to'-programmes on *Leisure, Do-It-Yourself and Hobbies*, and the third hour, the 'study hour', covers *Science, Arts, and Politics, Geography, History* and other more formal learning subjects. So with three hours a day we cover the whole range of adult education topics from heavy to light, serving both formal and informal learners.

Our on-air promotion of The Learning Channel has the following main features:

1. In the generic promos we are completely up front about what the channel is about. We are saying this is an educational channel. We are not being 'stealthy' about it – we're saying it loud and clear, and this because we believe there is an audience out there that wants this sort of clearly defined programming.

2. We are trying very frankly to establish a relationship between the viewer and the channel: "We are here for you and your family." The tag lines "really useful television" and "from viewing to doing" are not just glib lines of copy – they encapsulate our commitment to engaging with the viewer.

3. Because we are a dedicated educational service, we can encapsulate the whole range of adult education in one 30-second promo. – By so doing we're trying to capture the whole range of viewers from informal learner through to formal.

4. The style of the promos is intended to signal just that diversity; we are saying: "Look, this is interesting, inspirational, good-humoured".

It would seem that we are doing the right thing. Given the relatively small size of our subscriber base, the feedback has been little short of astounding. Almost every day we receive letters and phone calls from people saying how delighted they are to have something worthwhile on daytime television.

And they want more: more on history, more on personal development, more 'How-to' series. In a small survey for internal use, taken only weeks after we started transmission, 11% of subscribers said TLC was one of the main channels they watched (out of a choice of more than 30) and 25% said they would be very disappointed if TLC were not longer available.

No doubt, part of the reason we get so much feedback is because we ask for it.- Every hour we put out a viewer relations announcement asking for comments from viewers and suggestions about what they would like to see.

It is very early days yet, but I have a notion that these announcements, combined with the level of viewer participation involved in choosing TLC from the many channels available is fostering – at least in some people – a sense that TLC is their channel. We will not be able to judge if this is the case until we start the audience research later this year, but I hope I am right because such a development would be a great step towards achieving the goal of educational television as 'a conversation between equals'.

As a newcomer to cable it is not only the viewers we have to satisfy. In this crucial early period we have to convince the cable operators that by carrying TLC they will attract more subscribers and hence earn more revenue. On the whole, cable operators are a hard-nosed bunch. Not unlike some UK channel controllers, they are inclined to think of adult education television as one big bore.

Fortunately, cable operators at least have a craving for respectability – in so far as it will improve their image with politicians. This, combined with our determination to avoid a dull and pedagogic image, has brought most of them round to our side. However, cable – like the rest of television – is fiercely competitive and we will have to be particularly mindful of the needs and perceptions of the operators until our viewer base is firmly established.

It is for this reason that there are some areas of adult educational television that we will avoid. I cannot see that we will schedule series aimed specifically at special needs groups – people who are unemployed, on low income, disabled, or otherwise disadvantaged.

We are not ignoring these people – already we have scheduled a number of series on mental health, coping with long-term illness and AIDS. But it is much more important that we secure our position than we strike an ideologically sound posture now which might permanently stunt our growth by alienating cable operators.

So that is how matters lie with our viewers and cable operators, but there are other players in the game, namely the broadcasters from which we buy our programmes. Let me first of all make public my thanks to all the people present from the big broadcasting companies for their interest, enthusiasm and support. In terms of doing business the response has been – on the whole – very encouraging. Companies are not only selling to us, they are talking about long-term output deals.

Adult educational television is being increasingly squeezed to the margins of terrestrial broadcasters' schedules. The Learning Channel offers broadcasters a showcase for their adult educational output (of course there is money as well but we do not have a great deal of that at the moment). It seems to me that educational television is not an area for competition but for looking for services which can complement each other. TLC will not cut into the viewing figures of terrestrial broadcasters – rather it will offer educational producers a secondary vehicle to carry their output.

As I say to date, we have a good deal of encouragement from within the industry, but I am anxious about the noises coming from some managers of independent broadcasting companies who want to prevent sales of programmes to UK-based cable and satellite companies. We would propose that educational programming must be made available to the widest possible audience, that education is an area for cooperation between cable and satellite and terrestrial broadcasters. It would surely be a terrible waste to have hundreds of hours of educational programmes lying on library shelves when now there is a channel specifically designed for just such material.

To finish, a few brief words about our future plans. We intend to broadcast more hours of course; from January 1994 we plan to broadcast six hours a day. We also intend to have more areas covered – in particular I think we should cover vocational training. We are working hard at developing links with adult education institutions. We are talking with the National Association for Adult Continuing Education (NIACE) and the National Council for Educational Technology; we have joined the Educational Television Association. I would like to develop some kind of adult education access slot, perhaps a monthly series made by adult education student showing what they are doing.

We will be working closely with local cable operators, taking up Rosemary Bristow's point about viewers wanting more information about local resources. This is exactly the sort of thing cable can do very well. And then there is interactive television. Already we have been approached by a cable operator in South London who has an interactive service up and running: they want to know if they can acquire or develop programmes that would make use of this facility.

So there you have it: *The Learning Channel* – really useful television now – and even more useful in the future.

PART II

Background Information

Belgium

Belgische Radio en Televisie, Nederlandse Uitzendingen (BRTN)

In the brochure *Visitors' Guide to the BRTN*, the Administrator General Cas Goossens presents his organisation as follows:

"The BRTN, the broadcaster of the Flemish Community in Belgium, plays an important role in Flanders; it is responsible for producing informative, entertaining and educational programmes for 5.7 million Flemings. In the face of increasing competition, its identity as a Flemish broadcaster in a country with 90% cable penetration is especially significant, because the network is the foremost reflector of Flemish life in all its dynamism.

The Flemings who live in Northern Belgium and speak Dutch have the great privilege of living and working at a crossroads of cultures: the Netherlands, Germany, France and England are quite close. In fact, Belgium lies at the point where the Germanic-Anglo-Saxon culture of Northern Europe meets the Latin-Roman culture of Southern Europe.

Flemings speak a Germanic language and are part of the Germanic culture, but they are also in permanent and enriching contact with the Latin culture. They are proud of their contribution to Europe's common patrimony.

The biggest evidence of their receptivity is the open policy with regard to media. At a time when television around the world was bound by national frontiers, Flemings could already watch Dutch, English, German, French and Luxembourg channels, helped by the smallness of the territory. And since cable made its appearance, Flanders has become the country with the largest cable-penetration in the world; 90% of the population can pick up 20 channels of various languages and origin. They have become used to living, in miniature, as the realisation of the European ideal: diversification in unity and unity in diversity."

BRTN and its Belgian background

The three Belgian communities have been made largely autonomous by different laws, the result of a gradual process of devolution that took its final shape on January 1st, 1989. The autonomy is especially felt in the field of culture, in which the Dutch-speaking community, the French-speaking community and the German-speaking community are independent not only of one another, but also of the national authorities.

Each community has a large degree of proper legislative competence, including legislation about the respective broadcasting organisations. Thus, while the Belgian broadcasting situation is profoundly affected by international and technological changes, it is in many ways the result of Belgium's unique linguistic compilation.

Each community runs its own public-service broadcasting company, which answers to the respective regional parliament or council. Each has developed its own legislation and financing, which explains the increasing difference between the Belgian stations:

The *Belgische Radio en Televisie, Omroep van de Vlaamse Gemeenschap*, the BRTN, is Belgium's Dutch-language radio and television network which supplies an audience of 5.7 million Flemish people with six radio stations and two television channels.

The *Radio Télévision Belge de la Communauté Française*, the RTBF, is the BRTN's French-language counterpart with two television channels and roughly the same number of radio stations.

For the 66,000 people of the German-language community in Belgium, there is the BRF, the *Belgisches Rundfunk- und Fernsehzentrum der Deutschsprachigen Gemeinschaft*, which broadcasts radio programmes from a small town called Eupen.

To be complete, one should mention the existence of the two Belgian commercial television stations: VTM in Flanders and RTL-TVi in the Walloon provinces. VTM is a privately owned commercial TV-station that was made possible when the Flemish Council abolished BRTN's monopoly in 1987. The station became operational on February 1st, 1989.

Legal statutes

The BRTN is an independent public institution with a legal personality. It is directed by a Board of Governors appointed by the Flemish Council or Flemish Parliament. The organisation has the task of providing three categories of programmes for the Flemish Community: educational, informative and entertaining programmes.

The BRTN has its own radio and television channels, its own technical facilities, administrative departments and orchestras. The BRTN also has its own general budget and its programming is independent.

Educational Broadcasting

BRTN's department Educational Broadcasting *(Instructive Omroep)* comprises three production areas : Adult Education, School Broadcasts and Vocational Training. A multi-media approach is used, meaning that the same subject is dealt with simultaneously in various ways. Thus, slide series, handbooks, records, video and audio cassettes, computer software and programme sheets complement the radio and television programmes. All the accompanying material is produced by a common section.

The School Broadcasts are aimed at pupils from the first year of primary school (6-year-olds) up to the last stage of secondary education (18-year-olds). A wide range of programmes, mostly television programmes, support educators. However, it is felt that radio remains important for language teaching, music and current affairs.

The Adult Education department produces programmes for specific target groups: consumers, employees, farmers, gardeners, parents and others. They are particularly aimed at disadvantaged groups with a low training background and deal with factual knowledge as well as relationship training.

Adult Education programmes generally come in serials and use all the guidance media mentioned above, as well as exhibitions and the organisation of group meetings. The multi-media approach is not compulsory, however, and each of the media can be put into action separately. With a few exceptions, adult education programmes belong currently to the category of 'non-formal education', which means that they do not aim at leading to certificates.

In 1992 FOVOP (Fund for Education and Training) was created, a self-supporting department of Educational Broadcasting. It is specialised in vocational training, conceiving and producing multi-media projects, as a whole or in part, that fulfill specific purposes and help to satisfy the growing demands of audio-visual material for training and continuing education in both public services and private companies.

The projects are basically audio-visual productions. However, due to their multi-media character, some of the course elements — such as books and other publications, computer software or interactive course material — are particularly adapted to the specific needs of the target groups and can be used independently of the broadcast programme, which adds to the value of the basic conception of a course.

The range of topics covered by FOVOP is becoming increasingly wider. It does not only include clips intended as incentives, but also programmes to back up training in new technologies, computer courses for teachers and programmes on integrated quality control and energy saving. Furthermore, FOVOP has also been involved in training programmes for civil servants, videos on how to apply for a job, programmes on relational aptitudes, etc..

Contact:

Mrs. Léa Martel
Managing Director
BRTN – Educational Broadcasting
52, A. Reyerslaan
B – 1043 Brussels
Belgium

Tel.: +32-2-741.52.92
Fax: +32-2-741.93.51

France

Centre National de Documentation Pédagogique (CNDP)

Dedicated to public education and committed to educational advances, the CNDP, a research and publishing group associated to the French Ministry of Education, contributes to the field of education by

- providing information,
- publishing magazines and producing audio-visual materials,
- promoting the use of new forms of technology.

A nation-wide network

The national centre (CNDP) is assisted by 116 regional (CRDP), departmental (CDDP), and local (CLDP) centres.

2,250 teachers, librarians, civil servants, audio-visual and computer software producers and designers bring invaluable assistance and information to the education community. They also produce teaching aids and promote the use of the latest technology in the educational environment.

CNDP relies on the expertise of other departments:

- SFRS (*Service du film de recherche scientifique*) produces and distributes scientific films for higher education;
- CLEMI (*Centre de liaison de l'enseignement et des moyens de l'information*) is specialised in the analysis of the media at school, out of a desire to create in pupils a spirit of citizenship.

Documentation

CNDP dispatches educational and administrative information. It also selects and analyses pedagogical tools, such as videos. An easy access to these materials is offered through a network of 116 bookshops and libraries.

Publishing

CNDP produces educational radio and TV programmes for primary and secondary schools. 1992 will see CNDP's 'image bank' meeting the specific needs of every audio-visual material users . This comprehensive image bank already features more than 7,000 titles, thousands of hours of programmes: the result of 40 years of striving to attain the highest standards in the field of education.

CNDP publishes and distributes periodicals, brochures, slides, computer software and video discs. The CNDP national catalogue features 1,800 titles covering a wide variety of subjects at all levels of education.

Technological applications in education

In order to facilitate the use of new technologies for educators and administrators alike, CNDP advises on the choice of equipment. By keeping in touch with the education community, CNDP enhances the development of new educational technologies.

CNDP tests new educational hardware and publishes technical specifications in order to help users. It also offers training courses in up-to date technologies.

Finally, CNDP suggests applications for the latest forms of modern communication systems, such as cable and satellite broadcasting. CNDP's expertise and contributions to the field of education is recognised worldwide.

Being a member of the European Broadcasting Union's Working Party for Educational Programmes and of the International Council for Educational Media (ICEM) leads CNDP to contribute to educational television, theoretical analysis, and innovation.

CNDP may be consulted for expertise, or co-production ventures. It is also open to the acquisition, selling and exchange of educational programmes.

Contact:

Mme. Michèle Cohen
Relations Internationales
Centre National de Documentation Pédagogique (CNDP)
29, rue d'Ulm
F − 75230 Paris Cedex 05
Tél.: +33 1 46 34 92 97
Fax: +33 1 46 34 55 44

ARTE: the European Cultural Channel

Background

On 21st October, 1990, an international treaty between Germany and France was signed, and this constitutes the basis of the European Cultural Channel. The foundation of the broadcasting station goes back to an idea of the former Minister President of Baden-Württemberg, Lothar Späth, and of the French Minister of Culture, Jack Lang. The programme requirements are "to consolidate understanding and rapprochement between the nations in Europe" and "to contribute to presenting Europe's cultural heritage and artistic life".

Organisation

The station is responsible to the company ARTE G.E.I.E., which is organised in the legal form of a Strasbourg-based European economic community of interests. The Head Office is in charge of programme policy, production of the news and information broadcasts, press and public relations work and relations with foreign countries. The staff comprises about 130 people.

The Head Office coordinates the cooperation with the stations's National Offices, which are currently ARTE Deutschland TV GmbH in Baden-Baden, where the ARD und ZDF contributions are coordinated, and *La Sept* in Paris. It is the aim of the national offices to allow ARTE to have as large a share of first transmissions as possible. The German and the French shares of the programme at present amount to 50 per cent each.

The participation of other European broadcasting stations is also envisaged. RTBF, television in French-speaking Belgium, has already applied for membership.

Broadcasting area

In Germany the ARTE programme is transmitted using the PAL system via the satellite Copernicus and the wide-band Telecom network. As the cable input of the programme is not uniform, users can obtain information as to the cable assignment from their local Telecom office. Individuals can receive the programme via Copernicus, orbital position 23.5 East Channel B1, frequency 11.548 GHz.

The programme

Theme evenings

One of the major innovations on ARTE are the theme evenings. On Tuesdays Thursdays and Sundays one subject is dealt with from a very wide variety of angle during the whole television evening. Feature films, reports, interviews offer different, varied way of looking at the subject.

Feature films

Monday evening is reserved for the quality feature film. The spectrum of Europea as well as non-European films is intended to cover not only 'classics' but also thos films which otherwise would be submerged in the mass of American features.

Contact:

Mr. Dietrich Schwarzkopf
Vice President
ARTE G.E.I.E.
2a, rue de la Fonderie
F – 67080 Strasbourg Cedex
France
Tel.: +33-8852 2222
Fax: +33-8852-2200

Germany

The Adolf Grimme Institute (AGI)

The Adolf Grimme Institute, founded in 1973 as a Media Institute of the *Deutscher Volkshochschul-Verband* (German Adult Education Association) is dedicated to the study of the relationship between educational and media systems, and to the creation of practical media models for continuing education. The fact that the 'curricula' of mass media, technical communication as well as educational institutions all work together (and influence the perception of the recipient in such areas as cognition) is well known; how these processes are concretely achieved however, and how they should be dealt with while democratic guidelines are maintained, must be constantly re-examined.

The results of the Institute's work serve the adult education institutions across Germany, as well as numerous other institutions for continuing education and culture: as announcements of special programmes, but moreover, as a model for the innovative approach to and use of the media, and for the qualification of their personnel in questions related to the media.

Last but not least, the AGI also advises networks in the question of how superior programming may be produced, within the context of educational public broadcasting, and how such programming may be applied in specific learning situations.

With its television competition *Adolf-Grimme-Preis* the Institute has organised a respected model for the cooperation between institutions of continuing education, the communication sciences and the field of journalism. This work is complemented and extended to an international context by the *Marler Tage der Medienkultur* (The Marl Days for Media Culture).

With conferences, seminars, training workshops and publications, the Institute keeps the debate on broadcasting and on the role of the media in our society very much alive and controversial.

The Adolf Grimme Institute is financed by the *Land* North-Rhine Westphalia, by the City of Marl — and, within the framework of temporary model projects — by the German Ministry for Education and Science and by the *Westdeutscher Rundfunk* (WDR), the North-Rhine Westphalian public service broadcasting company.

The Adolf Grimme Award

The *Adolf-Grimme-Preis* (Adolf Grimme Award), originally instituted by Dr. Bei Donnepp, former director of the Marl educational centre *'Die Insel'* (the island has been awarded annually for excellent television productions since 1964. It is see as *the* German television award. Three independent juries, comprised of journalist media scientists, cultural experts and representatives of continuing education decid on the presentation of the Award for three independent categories, i.e. 'genera programming', 'series and multi-part presentations' and 'special'.

Selections come from two areas: from among programmes submitted by th networks as their best television productions, and from viewer suggestions: anyon may suggest a television programme for an Adolf Grimme Award.

Following the Award, producers of award-winning programmes visit institution of adult and continuing education, putting their productions for discussion (*Adol, Grimme-Preis unterwegs* – the Adolf Grimme Award on the road).

Publications

The Adolf Grimme Institute publishes the journal *Agenda – Zeitschrift für Medier Bildung, Kultur* (journal for media, education and culture).[1] This magazine i published six times a year, with emphasis on a single topic related to the medi and currently under discussion, with news, facts and background information fror media/culture/education. Supplementary, programme-related information i offered in a monthly information bulletin *'Agenda Service'*, with, among othe things, a long-term preview of select television programmes.

For special topics as well as for the documentation of conferences, furthe publications appear irregularly in the series *'W&M Materialien'* (Materials).

Conception and development

In order to guarantee the confluence and further development of the Institute' varied tasks and working areas, constant reflection, the dialogue on curren development, and the conception of new forms of programmes are all necessary This occurs, beyond internal communication, through the specific dialogue wit external professionals, the cooperation with both research and university institutions and the presentation of colloquia on central questions of the Institute's work.

---

[1] formerly *'W&M – Weiterbildung und Medien'* (Continuing Education and Media)

As "the development of models for the cooperation between institutions of continuing education and the media" is set out in the Institute's statutes as its central task, this necessitates – in addition to concrete measures for consultation and service – specific intellectual efforts. These include:

- the observation and evaluation of programming developments and structural changes of the media system in both a national and an ever-increasing international context;
- the discussion on changing forms of reception for the media, especially with regard to their importance for the educational and learning processes; and finally,
- the analysis of organised and institutional correlations between education and media – be they new attempts at integrated media systems, concepts for media education or the realisation of contemporary educational programmes within the broadcasting networks themselves.

Such conceptual and rather theoretical efforts are expressed in the Institute's varied events. They are the result of as well as the prerequisite for the development of new models. They are also, which is of notable significance, presented for public debate in the numerous publications of the Institute. Such analytic resources also go into the creation of evaluations, expertise and consultations with other cultural and educational institutions concerning media events and media-specific activities.

Even though the Adolf Grimme Institute does not represent a research institute in the university sense, its mediator position between science, journalism, education and culture directly results in its specific importance as a centre for research, dialogue and reflection.

'Medienverbund' – integrated media compounds based on cooperation

In close cooperation with public service television companies, integrated media compounds comprising television series, accompanying print material and courses for continuing education *(Medienverbundsysteme)* are developed. The following are a few examples:

- *'Un-Ruhestand'* (Restless retirement), a series for senior citizens who are still active and busy even beyond retirement (with ZDF);
- *'Ausländer – Inländer'* (Foreigners – nationals), a series on questions and problems of a multicultural society (with NDR, HR, and WDR);
- *'Kindsein ist kein Kinderspiel'* (Being a child is no child's play), examples of the changing situations and perspectives of today's youth (with NDR, HR, and BR);
- *'Alphabetisierung'* (Literacy campaign), a campaign aimed at motivating the

estimated 750,000 to 2 million illiterates in Germany to attend evening classes and increasing, at the same time, public awareness on this issue.

As a service for continuing education centres, the Institute has compiled so-called 'Medienpakete', i.e. media packages for selected topics such as 'Erwachsenwerden' (Growing up); '40 Jahre Mediengeschichte der Bundesrepublik' (40 years of media history of the Federal Republic of Germany).

In view of the political changes in the fields of media and education, the relationship between the two has also been redefined. Integrated media projects today have a different form, and, in some cases, a different target audience. Current developments in the media landscape (from the local to the international context), new demands for qualifications and the changing reception for media are all coming to the fore creating in turn the Institute's new projects:

– 'Partizipation und Hörerbeteiligung' (Participation and the active listener) Based upon the radio as a medium, the question of whether participation from the listening audience opens new possibilities for continuing education was examined.

– 'Volkshochschule und publizistische Praxis' (Adult education centres and journalist practice) In a nation-wide model for cooperation, topics from among local VHS participants were researched, worked up, and, with support from local editors, published in newsprint.

– 'Weiterbildung und Lokalfunk' (Continuing education and local radio) In order to enable citizens to access open channels in local broadcasting, the Institute initiated a project which provides expertise in the politics of communication and in journalism.

– 'Unsere Medien – Unsere Republik' (Our media – our republic) Based in the 40th anniversary of the Republic, this project focuses on media history as a historical perspective for Germany. A study of the media history of the former GDR is in progress.

– 'Bildung und Medien im Kommunikativen Netzwerk' (Education and the media in a communication network): In view of the deep-reaching changes in both the media landscape and the form of reception, this project serves to probe new possibilities for the cooperation between education and the media.

– 'Eine Welt für alle' (One world for all): This project accompanying the television production 'Eine Welt für alle', in which major international public broadcasting organisations participate, will initiate new concepts for development-related educational work, as well as provide accompanying material for direct application in continuing education.

And who was Adolf Grimme?

Adolf Grimme's life-work stands for the cooperation between continuing education and television. He was the last Prussian Minister of Science, Art and Public Education before the 'seizure of power' by the National Socialists. He was arrested by the Gestapo in 1942 and imprisoned for 'non-disclosure of intended sedition'. Following the war, Adolf Grimme was appointed as the first Minister of Culture for Lower Saxony. In 1948 he was elected Chairman of the Board of Directors of the Nordwestdeutscher Rundfunk (NWDR) in Hamburg, and served as its Director General until 1955. Adolf Grimme died on August 27, 1963 in Degerndorf am Inn. In 1964, the television award of the Deutscher Volkshochschulverband, bearing his name, was presented for the first time.

Contact:

Dr. Hans Paukens
Adolf-Grimme-Institut
Eduard-Weitsch-Weg 25
D – 4370 Marl
Germany

Tel: + 49-2365-918944
Fax: + 49-2365-918989

Nederlandse Onderwijs Televisie (NOT)

Statutory basis

The foundation *Nederlandse Onderwijs Televisie* (NOT) is responsible for the provision of school television programmes and accompanying material for the Dutch educational system. It is the cooperative body of three national organisations of public and private education which also form the executive Board of NOT, i.e.

- ABOO (foundation Audiovisual Communication for Private and Public Schools);
- ACKO (foundation Audiovisual Communication for Roman-Catholic Schools)
- APCO (foundation Audiovisual Communication for Protestant Schools).

The 1987 Media Act, which provides for the organisation of radio and television programmes in The Netherlands, enables educational broadcasting companies to obtain broadcasting time for radio and television transmissions.

According to this act, an educational broadcasting company must comply with the following requirements:

- the organisation is a body with full legal capacity;
- the organisation has as its objective the issue of broadcast programmes in the field of education, teaching and training.
- the organisation has a board which defines programme policy; this board should be composed in such a way that experts from representative national organisations in the field of education, teaching and training are members of the board.

In fact, it is the governmental *Commissariaat voor de Media* (Media committee) that allocates the air time to the foundation *Educatieve Omroepcombinatie* (Educational Broadcasting Corporation), the cooperative body of the three Dutch educational broadcasting organisations NOT, RVU and Teleac.

The *Educatieve Omroepcombinatie* distributes air time for television broadcast to its three affiliates in the following way:

- 190 hours and 40 minutes (= 37%) per year for NOT, Hilversum;
- 52 hours (= 10.3%) per year for RVU, Hilversum;
- 207 hours and 8 minutes (= 40.9%) per year for Teleac, Utrecht.

The main activities of NOT

With its approximately 60 permanently appointed employees located in Hilversum, NOT is charged with the following:

- developing school television programmes and composing accompanying material: NOT has 14 qualified educational specialists with a permanent appointment at its disposal;
- producing, directing and broadcasting all school television programmes: For this purpose NOT has 8 qualified, permanently appointed TV directors at its disposal and a varying number of freelance directors;
- producing and distributing accompanying material at cost price: NOT has its own publishing company with an annual turnover of approximately one million pupils' books and manuals; the financial annual turnover amounting to approximately four and a half million guilders;
- giving information on school television: Twice a year NOT distributes its own school television guide to all schools; moreover, the Information Department distributes press information, organises press presentations, inserts advertisements, produces articles and folders and is present at educational events;
- conducting research regarding participation, evaluation and effect of school television: Since 1989 the Research Department together with Intomart has installed an Electronic School Panel (ESP). One hundred primary schools inform NOT each week by means of their own computer of the school television programmes they have been watching that week. In this way the NOT receives up-to-the-minute information which may be important for the makers of the programmes when composing new broadcasts.

General and specific programmes

70% of all school television programmes made by the NOT are destined for all kinds of schools. These programmes are called 'general programmes'. The remaining 30% are made by the programme committees of the three foundations ABCO, ACKO and APCO and employees of NOT. These programmes are called 'specific programmes'. They are particularly destined for Private and Public Schools, Roman-Catholic Schools and Protestant Schools.

What does NOT look like?

The foundation occupies a modern office building in the centre of Hilversum. Here approximately 60 employees (and a varying number of freelancers) realise school television. The company has four business units:

- the Magazines Department
- the Project Department
- the Internal Management
- the General Manager and Staff Department.

How are NOT programmes made?

Subjects for school television series are to an important degree extracted from the investigation among primary and secondary schools concerning their needs Supported by an advisory council (the *'Programma-Advies-Raad'*), NOT also chooses subjects on the basis of their social relevance.

About 70% of the annual programme output is new; 30% are re-runs from earlier school years, chosen on the basis of research on the use of these programmes.

For each project various professionals work closely together. A project is first of all developed on paper by an education expert. After approval from the Board and the management, a project group is composed in which persons from various departments start working under the supervision of a project leader. The programmes are produced in cooperation of the *Nederlandse Omroep produktie Bedrijf* (NOB), the Dutch Broadcasting Production Company in Hilversum, and other production companies.

Nine out of ten times the project leader is also the author of the accompanying educational material. The producer from the publishing department sees to the production of the educational material, together with freelance illustrators, designer and printing companies.

The Information and Public Relations Department invents and realises information activities aiming at promoting the 'product' school television.

How many programmes does NOT broadcast?

Each year the NOT broadcasts about 350 programmes, which means that there is school television almost every school day on the channel *'Nederland 3'*. Each programme has an average length of 20 minutes; altogether the broadcast time amounts to 191 hours per year for both primary and secondary schools.

The broadcasts start at 10.00 a.m. on Mondays and Tuesdays and at 9.00 on Wednesdays, Thursdays and Fridays. On Mondays and Tuesdays there are also broadcasts at 2 p.m. The programmes start on the hour and on the half hour. In the broadcasting week almost all programmes are broadcast a second time.

Linking up with the regular school curriculum

NOT's programme output links up with the regular school subjects in primary and secondary schools. There are programmes for the following subjects: Geography, Professional Orientation, Biology, English, History, Religion, Computer Science, Social Science, Music, Physics, Social and Emotional Training, Chemistry, Drawing, and World Studies.

Each school year the NOT produces special series for the subjects Geography and History for classes preparing for the Central Written Final Examination.

What are NOT projects like?

School television is more than a number of televised programmes aiming at providing information and stimulating activities in the classroom. Almost every series is accompanied by written material, usually a manual for the teacher and – in most cases – learning material for pupils.

Depending on the set-up of the project, the following may also be included: a poster, a sound cassette, a series of slides, a grammophone record, playing and exercise material, papers to cut out, etc.

How many schools can receive us?

Mid 1988 the following numbers of schools (in %) had one or more colour television sets and video recorders at their disposal:

	TV sets	Video recorders
Primary schools	97%	92%
Secondary schools	97%	97%

In the school year 1987/1988 the following numbers of schools participated in one or more school television projects:

	Participation in %
Primary schools	90%
Secondary schools	83%

215

How is school television evaluated?

On the basis of a random sample from secondary schools, a survey is carried out twice a year to assess the number of schools participating in the individual school television projects.

The table below shows figures indicating the usefulness of the series broadcast in the school year 1987/1988. They were classified according to three marks: 'good' (over 7.5), 'sufficient' (between 5.5 and 7.5) and 'insufficient' (under 5.5).

	Number of series
good	41
sufficient	16
insufficient	0

Since 1st January 1989 the Research Department of NOT has used what is known as an Electronic School Panel (ESP). It consists of 100 primary schools that supply NOT every week with data on the utilisation of our series and their appreciation by the teachers.

Information on the NOT programmes

Four times a year all schools in the Netherlands receive a school television guide. In this guide all TV projects for the period to come are extensively announced.

The first guide of the school year contains a complete broadcasting schedule in the size of a poster to be hung in the classroom. Each guide also contains an order form for the accompanying material, which can be returned to the NOT Sales Department post-paid. Orders can also be made by telephone.

Contact:

Mr. Leo Both
Public Relations Officer
Nederlandse Onderwijs Televisie (NOT)
Noordse Bosje 18
NL – 1211 BG Hilversum
The Netherlands

Tel.: +3135 723611
Fax: +3135 210143

The Teleac Foundation

The Teleac Foundation, or Teleac for short, is the Dutch broadcasting corporation for adult education and training offering a wide range of multi-media courses. The Foundation's bye-laws state Teleac's main aim as providing education and training according to the principles of permanent education.

Teleac broadcasts its courses on open-net television and radio. Annually, Teleac controls 233 hours of television air time and 260 hours of radio air time, assigned to the Foundation through the Educational Broadcasting Combination, EDUCOM. Students study at home with their Teleac course material which may consist of text books, audio cassettes, software, and so on. They are also encouraged to participate in classes, excursions or summer courses which accompany some courses. Teleac is a non-governmental, independent foundation financed by the national broadcasting budget and the revenues of course material sales. Teleac's aims are often achieved in co-operation with schools, universities, other institutions of education and training and various organisations from society.

In this brochure some light will be shed on the history and development of Teleac, its organisational and financial structure, its students and its multi-media courses.

History of the Teleac Foundation

On 20 October 1960 an exploratory meeting was held at the offices of the Trade and Industry Association of the Netherlands in Haarlem, which was attended by representatives from national government, trade and industry and other sectors of society. This exploratory meeting resulted in the founding of the Teleac Television Academy Foundation on 10 December 1963. The first Board of Governors of the new Foundation was convened a week later.

Teleac was formally launched one and a half years later by the then Minister of Education, Culture and Science, when the first course, *Accidents in and Around the Home*, was broadcast in 1965. This first Teleac course attracted 1,440,000 viewers and 3,516 students.

Initially Teleac emphasised television as its teaching medium and acquired the image of a 'blackboard-and-chalk television academy'. Yet even then Teleac laid the foundations for its future development as a multi-media educational institute by offering students written material in the form of a course syllabus. This policy was continued until 1967, when the first truly multi-media course package was offered.

Students of the Russian language course, 14,390 in total, were supplied with coursebook and a record. This project turned out to be the launch of Teleac a a publishing house, publishing its own books, records and audio cassettes.

Over the years more broadcasting time was assigned to Teleac and televisio programmes also had to be produced in colour. This resulted in the closure o Teleac's own small television studio, located in the former boiler house of th Technical University in Delft. From 1974/1975 all programmes were produce through NOS/NOB facilities in Hilversum.

In its first academic year (1965/1966) Teleac provided 99 hours of televisio broadcasting time. The television air time has now expanded to 233 hours a year In 1981 Teleac was allocated 260 hours of radio broadcasting time as a furthe expansion of its multi-media package. The radio programmes are broadcast o Radio 5, medium wave 298 m/1008 kHz.

The growth in broadcasting hours was accompanied by an increase in the stud materials made available to students. Records, audio cassettes and softwar complemented some course books. Seminars and excursions were organised all ove the country and summer courses were set up abroad. Moreover, with some course Teleac organised homework correction and tests.

Teleac has also grown in the number of people it employs: from twenty in 196: to about 120 permanent members of staff at present. Besides, Teleac appoints dozen of free-lancers and external experts every academic year. In 1965 Teleac was to small an organisation to contain different departments. Now it has a clea departmental structure which is described in a separate chapter of this brochure

During the first twenty-five years of its expansion Teleac outgrew its old imag of 'blackboard-and-chalk on television' which it had created with the slogan 'mak your armchair a chair for learning'. So, over a decade ago Teleac changed its nam from 'television academy' into 'Teleac, Foundation for Multi-media Adul Education and Training'.

Organisational structure

The Teleac Board of Governors consists of fifteen members representing variou sectors of society. The Board includes two government observers, one from th Ministry of Welfare, Health and Cultural Affairs and one from The Ministry o Education and Science.

The programming policy is controlled by a permanent Programming Policy Boar which in its turn is supported by the Programming Board for Multi-media Educatio and Training Projects. This Programming Board includes specialists from al branches and levels of adult education and training, academic and professional education and industrial (re)training, as well as media experts and representatives from the radio and television programming boards of NOS, the Dutch Broadcasting Corporation.

Daily management and execution of course projects are carried out by the Executive Management, assisted by two boards of staff members. Like other companies Teleac has a so-called Works Council which operates in compliance with Dutch legislation on company organisation as a body for negotiation and consultation with the Executive Management.

As Teleac is not only an educational institution but also a broadcasting corporation, it is involved in production and consultation as a broadcasting corporation. Teleac is therefore represented in all necessary boards and bodies within the broadcasting world. Teleac also has co-operation agreements with sister organisations such as NOT, the Dutch school television organisation, and the Radio University (RVU). There are working agreements with the Film and Science Foundation and the Dutch Institute for Audiovisual Media.

In 1978 the Minister of Education and Science officially recognised Teleac as an institute for correspondence education; Teleac is now a member of the Association of Institutes for Correspondence Education.

The organisations with which Teleac co-operates on a permanent or incidental basis are too numerous to name, as are the people involved in the various projects. Each year about fifteen new course projects are started up, requiring a great number of outside experts. At the feasibility stage of a project representatives from the relevant target groups are also involved.

Finance

For the so called open-net productions funds are made available to Teleac from the national broadcasting budget. Thus, Teleac has its own broadcasting budget for the development and production of television and radio programmes.

These funds are partly used to pay production companies like the NOB for the facilities they provide for the production of television and radio programmes. These facilities consist of studios, technical equipment, recording and editing facilities, set construction and personnel.

The production of course materials and the provision of student services are not paid from the broadcasting budget, but from the revenues of course material sales. For this purpose a special non-profit organisation with its own budget has been set up within Teleac to produce the materials and organise the activities. Occasionally these productions and activities are sponsored by interested parties in the form of warranties.

Teleac departments

Like any larger company, Teleac uses the system of line organisation which involves a complex set of relations between the Executive Management, the Staff, the departments and personnel. The departments form the administrative and technical apparatus required for course projects and general management activities.

This line organisation supports the development, production and distribution of multi-media educational packages. Actual development, production and distribution are carried out by teams of members from different departments. These teams are set up specially for each project and function relatively autonomously within the given conditions and assignments. Thus, Teleac is both a line organisation and a project organisation, the combination of which can be regarded as a matrix organisation. The organisation as a whole is managed by the Executive Management. Apart from the Executive Management Teleac consists of the seven departments described briefly below.

1. Research, Documentation and Archive

The main activities of this department are:

- policy research and long-term planning, market research, needs research and evaluation of courses;
- research for specific course projects, such as target group research, sampling, pre-screening of trial lessons, evaluation research; as these activities are product-oriented, members of this department participate in project teams;
- filing and managing books, magazines and reference works; collecting documentation for programming policy and specific course projects;
- management of all general Teleac files.

2. Television Production and Direction

This department is responsible for the production conditions and actual production of the television component of the multi-media educational package. It is divided into the production subdepartment, where production conditions are laid out, facilities arranged, and so on, and the direction subdepartment. The latter consists of directors and assistants who work in project teams with the responsibility of producing the television components of specific courses.

3. Radio Production and Direction

This department is responsible for the production of the radio component of the multi-media educational package. Radio producers who are product-oriented join project teams for the realisation of the radio component of a specific course.

4. Programme Support Department

This department is also product-oriented. Its activities cover all non-television and non-radio components of the multi-media course package, such as course books, audio material, other course materials, teletext, automation, classes, excursions and homework correction. This department also explores the potential of new media like the CDI.

Incorporated in this department are: the publishing office; the audio-visual office; marketing/sales; student services and the telematic group.

5. Didactics and Project Coordination

This department shows most clearly that Teleac can be seen as a project organisation, as well as a line organisation. The project co-ordinators are specifically in charge of, and responsible for, the management of all individual course projects, the co-ordination of the various activities and the attuning of the media. They monitor the qualities of the multi-media end product as regards didactics and content.

The five departments mentioned above are at the heart of the project organisation. The next two departments are either incidentally or partially involved with the realisation of the end product. Their main task is to provide support and service.

6. Internal and External Relations

This department has three main activities:

- *Personnel*, including staff recruitment and selection, training, and promoting employees' interests;
- *General services*, such as the canteen, telephone switchboard, mail and copying room, and the audio-visual bureau;
- *Information*, i.e. public information and student recruitment.

Information and recruitment are directly related to the various course projects; for these activities the department is represented on the project teams.

7. Finance

This department is most obviously supportive, servicing and administrative with respect to the production of the multi-media educational package. Its activities include accounting, wage administration, students' administration, budget management and financial reporting

Organisationally, all departments come together at management level in the Staff board for aspects of the line organisation and in the Project board (Planning, Programming, Co-ordinating and Evaluating Committee) for consultation concerning the project organisation. At the level of implementation, production and distribution of the multi-media educational packages, departments meet through their representatives on the project teams.

The Teleac multi-media package

When the Teleac Television Academy Foundation began broadcasting in 1965 television was the most important of the media used. Quite soon, however, the need for printed materials arose: scripts of broadcasts and even complete textbooks. Later, students began to ask for seminars and summer courses. More recently the range of media has further expanded.

Now, whenever a new multi-media course project is developed, a team of specialists decides which media are to be used and which role the media should play in the new project. As a rule, television is always included.

In principle the following uses are considered:

1. Television

Television is very suitable for presenting subjects visually and for showing students unusual examples. The weekly broadcasts also set the pace of the course.

2. Radio

Radio programmes are used for lectures, feedback, news, discussions and documentaries.

3. Written material

The written material generally contains the complete contents of the course. Apart from a textbook often extra documentation is supplied: magazines, background literature, reading lists and brochures.

4. Other course materials

Language courses always include audio material: records, cassettes or compact discs. Slides or do-it-yourself kits may be included in other courses.

ver the years Teleac has offered make-up kits with a stagecraft course, home
omputers with a microprocessor course, anemometers with a meteorology course,
microscopes with a biology course and a box of exotic seeds with a course on
evelopment problems.

. Seminar

or language courses seminars may serve to practise the language or they may take
he form of a summer course in the target country. With other courses extra lectures
ay be organised, or excursions, end-of-course seminars or special events.

. Homework correction

'he Written Instruction department of Teleac has officially been recognised by
he Ministry of Education and Science. It qualifies for this recognition by offering
course each year with the option of homework correction by computer.

Contact:

1r. Henny van der Eng
Iead, Publishing and Video Dept.
'eleac Foundation
aarbeursplein 15
JL – 3500 GK Utrecht
'he Netherlands

'el.: +3130-956911
'ax: +3130-941411

Sweden

Utbildningsradion (UR)
The Swedish Educational Broadcasting Company

Statutory basis

In the spring of 1992, the Swedish Parliament decided to break up *Sveriges Radio* the former Swedish Broadcasting Company, into three companies – one for television, one for radio and the third one for education. Parliament's decision went into effect on January 1, 1993. Since that date, *Utbildningsradion* (UR), The Swedish Educational Broadcasting Company, is one of the three companies within Sweden's public broadcasting system, a company of its own legal capacity.

Public broadcasting in Sweden is financed through licence fees, the size of which is determined every year by the Parliament. Currently, every household pays the equivalent of about 200 US dollars annually. The only commercially operated terrestrial TV station is TV4; in recent years a number of privately owned satellite channels have entered the media arena.

History

Educational broadcasting dates back nearly 70 years in Sweden. Its roots go back to the early 1920s: adult education on radio started in 1925, the first school radio programmes were broadcast in 1928. On television, educational programmes for adults started in 1956, and the first school television programmes were broadcast in 1961.

Utbildningsradion was launched in 1978. UR was created through the merger of the Educational Programmes Department of *Sveriges Radio* and the Governmental committee for TV and radio in education, then known as *TRU*.

Programme activities

The programme activities are regulated by the Radio Law and the guidelines in the Agreement between the State and UR. It states that the programme activities " . . . shall mainly concentrate on reinforcing, broadening and supplementing the educational inputs made by the public education system, and within voluntary popular education".

UR has no channel of its own, but it has the right to broadcast via Sweden's public service television and radio networks, i.e. two TV channels, 3 national radio channels and the 25 local radio stations.

To fulfill its tasks, UR receives about 4.7 per cent of the total sum that goes to public broadcasting in Sweden. It must not accept sponsoring or commercials.

Today UR produces and broadcasts TV and radio programmes for the entire educational community which includes pre-schools, schools, adult education, university education and distance education. Programmes are often combined with printed materials that are produced by UR or other publishers and correspondence institutes.

In 1992, UR produced more than 250 hours of television programmes, about 200 hours of national radio programmes and some 600 hours of regional/local radio programmes. Taking the total programme output, altogether 462 hours of TV, 590 hours of national radio and 706 hours of regional/local radio were broadcast during the same period.

As Swedish is a language used by a small number of people in the world, learning foreign languages is vital. Moreover, radio is still an important tool in foreign language instruction.

In recent years the importance of distance education has grown. Within the area of distance education students can remain in their homes, watch TV programmes, listen to radio programmes or tapes and read the necessary printed matter.

Programme support

About 50 titles of printed materials and other media for use with individual programmes series are produced by UR's Publishing Division, often in conjunction with other publishers.

UR, having its own teletext facilities, uses teletext to inform about its various programmes and to provide exercises and word-lists. Moreover, one transmission of all UR's programmes for adults is subtitled because studies showed that a sizable part of the audience has hearing impairments.

The role of television programmes is largely to stimulate an interest, to play a part in recruiting students and to illustrate certain aspects of the courses. Radio programmes are often integrated into the courses; along with the printed materials, they form the factual basis.

Sweden also has a network of more than one-hundred audio-visual media centres organised by the local municipal authorities and the Swedish Federation of Municipal Authorities.

Almost for any production, UR tries to acquire the non-theatrical educational rights to make it possible for these audio-visual media centres to record and copy UR's TV and radio programmes and to make them available without charge to the educational community, i.e. to preschools, schools, study organisations and public libraries.

Contact:

Mr. Frederic Fleisher
International Relations
Utbildningsradion
Swedish Educational Broadcasting Company
S – 115 80 Stockholm
Sweden

Tel: +46-8-784 4141
Fax: +46-8-660 3263

British Broadcasting Corporation
BBC Education

Educational Broadcasting – at its best[1]

Introduction

The magical story of a church bell that rang from under the sea; advice on how to develop your communication skills in the workplace; ways of designing and producing hygienic packaging for bread; and how to help your child to read during a trip to the supermarket . . .

Just four sides of the diverse world of BBC Education. This key part of the BBC provides a unique range of high quality educational resources for everyone from the toddler to the adult learner. These resources include major television and radio broadcasts acclaimed as foremost in their field, together with stimulating support materials which inspire both viewers and listeners to practical activity.

In the 1990s BBC Education is helping schools meet the challenge of the new curriculum. At the other end of the spectrum, it is motivating adults to new commitments to learning and training both inside and outside the workplace.

Throughout this process BBC Education maintains a constant dialogue with teachers, trainers, viewers and listeners across the United Kingdom, in order to ensure that all the resources produced are as appropriate and effective as they can be. In the development of certain series, BBC Education collaborates with many different external agencies, from the National Curriculum Council to the Employment Department. It also links into an international network of co-ventures. All these contacts broaden the range of its activity and audience.

Here is a brief introduction to the main areas of BBC Education, explaining what each department does and how they all fit together.

---

[1] What follows is the text part from a richly illustrated leaflet that describes BBC Education's departments and their activities as of 1992. In the meantime, BBC Education has been reorganised; the new structure is shown in the diagram following this text.

Supporting the Curriculum

School Television

School Television has been stimulating and inspiring British schools for thirty-five years, and has established itself as a key presence in every classroom in the country.

More than anything else, School Television brings a variety of experiences vividly and directly into the classroom. How else could you really explore the forests of Brazil or imagine the inside view of an atom? As a resource, it develops children's understanding, putting the school curriculum into a wider context and showing its relevance to the real world.

At present, both School Television and Radio are helping schools meet the challenge of the new curriculum, by providing up-to-the-moment coverage of curriculum areas. For the core subjects of English, Maths and Science, material is available for all age groups, including popular series like *Look and Read*, *Search Out Science* and *Mathscope*.

From a more general perspective, School Television has a vital role in developing the whole child, with stimulating and empathetic series such as *Scene* and *Sex Education* covering personal and social issues, and series like *Christianity in Today's World* offering new approaches to religious education.

In all its broadcasts, School Television promotes active viewing, with programmes leading to creative follow-up activity e.g. research, problem-solving, discussion, reading and writing. Just ten minutes of broadcasting can provide up to fifty minutes of follow-up work. It also offers comprehensive support in the form of teacher's notes, pupil's books, cassettes and videos (see *Educational Publishing*, below).

Finally, School Television helps teachers themselves keep up-to-date with educational change and new classroom practice through the developing range of Teaching Today programmes.

School Radio

Established in 1924, School Radio has performed, and continues to perform, a vital role in the process of helping young people to learn how to listen. Now in its new home on Radio 5 MW, School Radio goes from strength to strength, building on its powerful and unique qualities as an educational resource.

In the field of the expressive arts, School Radio holds an established place, with formative and innovative series in the areas of music, movement and drama. Popular titles include *Let's Move!* (used by over 980,000 infants), *Dance Workshop*, *The*

Song Tree and *First Steps in Drama*. Radio is also a natural stimulus for language development, and every day classrooms of children are captivated by imaginative and stimulating presentations of stories, poetry and plays, whether it be an evocation of the sights and sounds of a bygone age or the squelches of *Fungus The Bogeyman*.

Other strengths include materials for modern languages – sample a taste of a French breakfast radio programme in *Branchez-vous!* with its authentic vox pops, dialogues, news bulletins and music; and new insights into English literature, current affairs and religious education.

Like School Television, School Radio also provides a practical range of teacher's notes, pupil's pamphlets, readers and cassettes, to support their broadcasts (see *Educational Publishing*, below).

Motivating Adults' Learning and Training

Continuing Education and Training, Television

The newly renamed Continuing Education and Training department provides a broad spectrum of stimulating programmes for adult learners.

In the 1990s and beyond, the department's major new commitment is to the UK's training needs. Important broadcast initiatives such as *The Training Hour* and *Second Chance* begin in 1991 and 1992 respectively, produced in collaboration with the Employment Department and the Department of Education and Science. These initiatives will inform, guide and inspire viewers, through practical case-studies and examples, into new training opportunities.

Other areas of sustained commitment are adult core skills (past successes include the popular *On the Move, Stepping Up* and *A Way with Numbers*); modern languages (major series in the European languages, as well as innovative departures e.g. *Japanese Language and People*); and multi-cultural issues (the unique five-year MOSAIC project).

Each year the department does major prime-time series on business, cookery, education for Europe, women's issues and disabilities, as well as day-time magazines such as *Bazaar* and *Advice Shop*. It is also responsible for the acclaimed *See Hear* series for deaf viewers.

Because the after-care of the viewer is paramount, Continuing Education and Training seeks to extend the learning experience long after the programme is over. This is achieved through a range of follow-up opportunities including coursebooks, training packs, cassettes, flexi-study courses, and above all, the pursuit and discovery of new interests.

Continuing Education, Radio

Acupuncture and addiction, the geology beneath our feet, a survey of creative writing courses . . . just three items you might hear during a week's transmissions from the Continuing Education Radio unit. Situated in its new home on Radio 5 MW, it offers a powerful and popular listening experience to appeal to adults across the whole learning and leisure spectrum.

Regular series include *Education Matters*, which reports on topical issues from the whole of the education world; and the popular magazine strand broadcast live every weekday morning. This strand covers all aspects of childcare and family life, as well as more general issues of the day, and offers advice on health and medicine and consumer affairs. Listeners are encouraged to participate actively by sharing their opinions and experiences both on and off air.

Other output covers targeted areas like languages (a particlar strength for the immediate and convenient medium of radio), popular history, multi-cultural Britain, science and training.

Finally, Continuing Education Radio — like its television counterpart — aims to extend the life of its broadcasts into practical activity. Listening combines with books and cassettes to provide structured multi-media courses, such as the highly popular *Get By In* and *When In* language packs (see *BBC Books*, below).

Open University Production Centre

The BBC Open University Production Centre, under a formal partnership between the BBC and the Open University, provides the video and audio components to support the Open University's internationally acclaimed distance learning project.

The programmes are broadcast on the BBC's national radio and television networks (primarily BBC 2 and Radio 5). Between February and October, when the majority of the series are broadcast, the television programmes have a reach of nine million viewers each week, some of whom take undergraduate or non-degree courses, or become Associate Students.

New series in 1992 cover a wide range of subjects and were filmed all over the world by the OUPC. For instance, *Third World Development*, a coproduction with the European Community through Oxfam, went on location to Brazil, India, Africa and South East Asia; and for *Evolution*, a film crew visited Svalbard, the nearest inhabited land to the North Pole, Ranthambhor Tiger Reserve in Rajasthan and the vaults of the American Museum of Natural History in New York.

Outside of the University's undergraduate areas, the educational provision continues to grow. New series include the *Rise of Scientific Europe 1500 – 1800*, produced n collaboration with several European co-producers; up-to-the-moment coverage of *Issues in Women's Studies*; *Understanding Modern Societies*, including programmes on USA and Poland; *Brain and Behaviour*, which looks at everything from mental illness in humans to the problems of bush crickets; and *Learning for All* aimed at anyone interested in the education of children and young people with learning difficulties.

So there's something to interest everyone in the Open University's programmes.

Covering all of the United Kingdom

BBC Education is committed to serving the needs of communities throughout the UK, with a particular focus on educational broadcasting for Scotland, Wales and Northern Ireland.

Scotland

Educational broadcasts, produced in Scotland, are designed to meet the particular needs of the Scottish education system. For example, at primary level, programmes resource teaching and learning in Environmental Studies, with popular, inspirational series such as *Let's See* and *Around Scotland* (used in over 50% of Scottish schools). In the secondary sector, there is a block of dedicated programming, led by the curricular Guidelines and geared to preparing pupils for the Scottish Certificate of Education .

The other key area of broadcasting activity, on both television and radio, is output for Gaelic education. This ranges from series like *Feuch E* for pre-school and infant children in a Gaelic-medium learning environment through programmes for learners of Gaelic as a second language, right up to innovative cross-curricular broadcasts exploring different social topics in Gaelic.

Continuing Education programmes, on subjects as diverse as anti-racism and management training, are also produced from Scotland, supplementing output from the rest of the UK.

Wales

BBC Education in Wales faces an exciting challenge peculiar to a society which has two linguistic cultures. Traditionally, its main focus has been on the Welsh language but the functions of the Welsh output are three-fold: to deliver education programmes across the curriculum for pupils whose mother tongue is Welsh; to offer resources for teaching Welsh as a second language; and to provide materials

231

for non-Welsh speaking pupils in Wales so that they become aware of their cultural heritage.

Currently, the Department transmits twenty-five radio series and ten television series a year. These include the popular *Pot Jam* and *Sang-di-fang* at Key Stage One; *Sioe Gerdd*, *Exploring our Past* and *Hawk's Eye* at Key Stage Two. The programmes for secondary schools provide resources and materials for teachers of History, Geography and Welsh at all levels.

For the general audience, *Gorau Arf*, the Welsh 'Education Matters' programme, presents items of educational interest and provides a forum for discussion of policies and developments in schools.

Northern Ireland

BBC Northern Ireland's Education Department reflects the distinctive Ulster culture and environment. In a divided society it is essential to establish common ground, and broadcasting is well-placed to fulfil this vital role.

For many years the miscellany series *One Potato – Two Potato, Today and Yesterday* and *Ulster in Focus* have provided a wide range of topics for local studies in primary schools. These series support the cross-curricular themes of Cultural Heritage and Education for Mutual Understanding, now integrated into the Northern Irish Curriculum.

In specialist subjects BBC Northern Ireland offers much needed resources in History, Geography, Literature, Language and Irish. The new *Study Ireland: History*, for example, provides a comprehensive archive of television programmes dealing with the major themes of Irish history in an unbiased way. The department also focuses on young people's issues with broadcasts such as *Tribes* (made jointly with School Television) which dramatises the dilemmas facing teenagers living in Northern Ireland.

BBC Northern Ireland is now developing a Continuing Education output on radio and television which helps explain the divisions of the past and soften the conflicts of the present.

Finally, the output for Irish language now spans the entire educational spectrum with series for primary, secondary and adult audiences.

Communicating with Users

The Educational Broadcasting Councils

The Educational Broadcasting Council for the UK, and its related councils in Scotland, Wales and Northern Ireland, are responsible for the policy which governs programmes for use in schools and colleges. They also advise the BBC on educational programming for adults.

Supporting the Councils are the Programme Committees, teams of dedicated educationalists and representatives from the worlds of industry, commerce and voluntary organisations. Each Committee specialises in a particular educational sector – primary, secondary or adult education, providing detailed input on all the programming planned, and ensuring that there is a constant link between the policies of the broadcaster and the needs of the users.

Educational Broadcasting Services

At a more detailed level, that all-important link between programme-maker and user is maintained by the work of the Education Officers from Educational Broadcasting Services.

Education Officers combine educational expertise and experience with knowledge of the BBC's output. Through their visits to schools, colleges, other educational institutions and user groups within the community, they provide valuable information about national needs which they then feed back to the BBC production departments. In this way, the priorities of users remain firmly at the heart of broadcasting development. At the same time, Education Officers also monitor the use of broadcasts in action and assess their effectiveness with users.

As a further extension of this communication with users, Educational Broadcasting Services also liaise with the BBC's Broadcasting Research Department, providing further feedback on audience's reactions to BBC Education's output.

Educational Developments and Information

Educational Developments and Information is a new and fast-growing department of BBC Education.It has two principle roles: the development of a range of non-broadcast materials targeted at specific educational markets; and the marketing and promotion of all of BBC Education.

In its first role, it has produced videopacks, audio-cassettes and publications developed from educational broadcasts in the following areas: governor training, nurse education, adult basic skills, health and in-service teacher training.

Alongside this activity runs a parallel publishing enterprise that develops suppor print for general output series such as *Tomorrow's World* and *Trials of Life*, serie which teachers are now legally able to use in their classroom teaching because o shifts in copyright regulations.

Finally, the marketing and promotion of BBC Education is focussed in thi department, covering production of all publicity items, support print, press advertising, exhibition coordination and a customer services unit. All these activitie ensure that customers are given vital information sufficiently in advance to enable them to plan the use of BBC Education resources in their learning and teaching programmes.

Providing Practical Support

Educational Publishing

Educational Publishing produces an increasing range of resources for teachers and pupils using School Television and Radio broadcasts. These include teacher's notes, pupil's pamphlets and a growing list of core textbooks developed in collaboration with the publisher Longman, all supporting the new curriculum.

In addition, there are inspirational readers, information books and activity packs linked to such well-known series as *Look and Read, Watch, Zig Zag* and the ever popular *Come and Praise.*

A new development is the production of video materials for teachers, providing exciting permanent resources for a variety of subjects including modern languages, geography, history, personal and social development, religious education and reading.

BBC Books

BBC Books has an extensive publishing programme to support series from Continuing Education. This includes cookery (popular titles like *Italian Regional Cookery* and Madhur Jaffrey's innovative range of cookbooks), a wide spectrum of self-help publications and the enormously successful language courses such as *A vous la France, Buon giorno Italia* and *España Viva.* Over three quarters of a million copies of the BBC's language books are bought every year, used extensively in colleges, adult education institutes and by adults learning at home.

Particular attention is paid in all these publications to producing resources that are of the highest quality educationally, but are also clear, accessible and inspirational for the user.

Training Videos

BBC Training Videos has grown rapidly over the last five years to become one of the UK's top four training video providers. Its current catalogue contains over fifty titles, featuring international business experts such as Tom Peters, Sir John Harvey Jones and Rosabeth Moss Kanter. Essential management skills are covered, such as interviewing, negotiating and presenting.

Much of the product range is sourced originally from broadcast programmes, but is extensively adapted and enhanced to meet the needs of the training market. In January 1991 *Speak for Yourself*, the first in a range of independently commissioned titles, was launched on presentation skills, and has already established itself as one of the UK's best-selling titles on the subject.

BBC Training Videos also has the exclusive distribution rights for the Video Management range from Belgium, featuring key academics from INSEAD and other leading business schools.

Award-winning BBC Education

1990
Sony Radio Award
Best Children's
Programme/Programming/Series
In the News

1990
Sony Radio Award
Best Education
Programme/Programming/Series
The Health Show

1990
Broadcast Designer's Association
International Design Competition
Silver Award
Europeans

1990
City of Basle Prize
Commendation
Europeans

1990
**25th Chicago
International Film Festival**
Gold Award
Imagina

1990
UK Technology Press Award
Best Television Programme
Electric Avenue

1990
Shell Cawston Prize
Where on Earth are we going?

1990
**XVIII International Festival of
Films and Television Programmes
on the Environment**
Diploma
Where on Earth are we going?

1990
Sony Radio Award
Best Children's Programme
Scottish Resources 7 – 9

1990
Royal Television Society
Best Education Programme
(Adults)
*Making Their Mark: Six Artists on
Drawing*

1990
British Medical Association
Gold Award
Quit and Win videopack

1990
Royal Television Society
Best Education Programme
(Secondary)
Techno

1991
Royal Television Society
Best Production Design
A Way with Numbers

Contact:

BBC Education Information
White City, 201 Wood Lane
GB – London W12 7TS
United Kingdom

Tel.: +44-81-746 1111
Fax: +44-81-752 4304

1991
Royal Television Society
Best Education Programme
(Adults)
Birthrights

1991
Royal Television Society
Best Education Programme
(Primary)
Watch

1991
City of Basle Prize
Sex Education

1991
**European Alliance for
Television & Culture Prize**
West Africa

1991
**Swiss Radio & Television
Society Prize**
Commendation
Music Time

1992
New York Film Festival
Gold Award
The Last Exodus

Appendix: Outline structure of the new directorate (January 1993)

Director of Education

Open University Production Centre

(Senior Management Team)

Senior Management	Head of Schools Programming	Head of Continuing Education & Training	BBC Select	Head of Multi Media Publishing	Chief Accountant	Head of Policy and Resources

Bimedia Business Unit — Bimedia Business Unit — Subsidiary company of BBC — Subsidiary company of BBC

Managing the following functions

Functions:

Producing programmes of high quality and educational effectiveness for transmission and as part of multi-media projects involving television/radio/video and print.

Commercial use of night hours. Subscription television service for a range of specialist audiences – both in clear and encrypted services.

Educational Publishing (commercial)
Audio/Video/Print/Multi-media
(partnerships, sponsorship and co-productions)
Information to Schools and Colleges
Support for general output programming
Developing Language Policy Unit and Commissioning through New Languages Unit
Research commissioning
World Service liaison
Commercial use of night-time hours

Co-ordinating finances of all areas of Directorate

Managing EBS – and its relationship with EBC Managing all 'shared services' or bought-in arrangements, relating to Directorate, eg. Personnel, Publicity Managing liaison with OUPC

237

British Broadcasting Corporation
Broadcasting Research Department (BRD)

The BBC's Broadcasting Research Department (BRD) — formerly Audience Research Department — was set up in 1936. It exists to provide a continuous measurement of audience size and audience reaction to both TV and radio output, and to undertake investigations associated with specific programmes or issues of more general interest.

The role of The Information Services section within the BRD is to exploit the department's continuous research sources. This involves the analysis, interpretation and presentation of both television and radio audience research to assist in BBC management's planning and decision-making.

Information services produce regular customised trend reports, carry out a wide range of ad hoc analysis and provide an enquiry service for both internal and external clients.

The types of analyses which can be done range from the straightforward to the complex:

- audience size for a programme or timeband;
- audience reaction to a programme measured as an Appreciation Index (television) or Reaction Index (radio);
- audience profile — composition of the audience in terms of age, sex and social grade;
- programme inheritance — the number of people already viewing/listening to the channel or station and the number who switched on, off or over as the programme started;
- audience overlap — the number of viewers or listeners who watch for example, the breakfast, lunchtime and evening news;
- audience loyalty — the number of viewers who see one episode of a series and also go on to watch the next;
- channel and station performance indicators such as share of viewing/listening, amount of viewing/listening and the proportion of viewers/listeners using BBC and competitive services over a day or week.

The research is used extensively throughout the BBC, from producers to controllers, to contribute towards tactical and strategic planning.

Audience Measurement

Television

This is carried out for the Broadcasters' Audience Research Board (BARB) by two independent market research agencies, i.e. AGB and RSMB. A panel of 4,500 households is maintained. It is designed to be a nationally representative panel selected using a range of demographic variables and recruited from an Establishment Survey of 40,000 interviews per year.

A meter is attached to each TV set in the panel household which records when the set is on and to which channel it is tuned. Each household member − usually four or more − records his/her viewing by pressing a personal button on a handset in the TV room. Data are fed down a telephone line each night and audience estimates processed at AGB.

The system covers all terrestrial channels and satellite and cable channels available from the Astra Satellite. The system also measures timeshift viewing: the playback of programmes taped on video recorder.

Radio

This service is currently carried out for BBC Radio by the Broadcasting Research Department. In the autumn of 1992 a joint industry service will start, i.e. Radio Joint Audience Research (RAJAR). Seven-day diaries will be placed in sample households and listeners will record their listening to each station by quarter hour. Twice-yearly studies will also be carried out to estimate local/regional radio audiences.

Special Projects

Special Projects section of the BRD produces tailor-made surveys for BBC Management, individual programme departments and decision-makers at all levels. The types of project cover a wide spectrum but can be divided into the following areas:

Projects for Production

- Feedback on programme ideas
- Testing pilot programmes, music preferences
- Evaluating particular programme or series
- Developing current output

Background Strategic Research, e.g.

- Daily Life in the Late 1980s
- Radio Waveband Use
- Corporate Image Research
- Channel Image/Branding
- Attitudes towards Funding

Broadcasting Developments, e.g.

- 24 hour Radio news
- Satellite Television
- Down-loading

Advice and Consultancy

- Commissioning Polls
- Integrating continuous and ad-hoc data
- Developing school audience measurement

Methods used

The particular research technique employed depends very much on the nature of the problem to be solved. Essentially the distinction is between quantitative research, where a large number of people are interviewed and generalisable conclusions about the opinions or behaviour of the population can be inferred, and qualitative research where more in-depth information is obtained in detailed discussions with a relatively small group of respondents.

For quantitative research studies there are three methods by which interviews may be carried out: face-to-face, by telephone, or by post. Each of these is used within Special Projects, but each has its own advantages and its drawbacks.

The drawback with any quantitative research is that the information collected is often superficial. In a number of cases exploratory qualitative research is needed to unravel the motivations behind people's opinions or behaviour. This takes the form of a more free-ranging discussion, usually among small groups, or occasionally with individuals, chosen to represent the target population, or a sub-section of it. The discussion is not totally unstructured, but is controlled by a trained researcher who guides it along pre-defined lines so that all the points of interest are covered and each member of the group is able to present his or her opinions.

The opinions from a few group discussions cannot be said to reflect the views of the population, but they do provide a valuable insight into how people are thinking about a particular issue. This information may be useful in its own right, or it may be used as input for a large scale study which subsequently quantifies the opinions expressed.

Other facilities

Other facilities within Special Projects include:

- *Television Opinion Panel* (T.O.P.)
  This is a nationally representative panel of 3,000 people aged 12 and over; questions are put to members each week about specific programmes shown that week, series/serials just completed or more general issues.

- *Radio Listening Panel*
  It consists of 3,000 listeners to BBC Network Radio, and is designed to give feedback on specific programmes or series, as well as more general issues.

Special Projects Research evaluating public attitudes to back-up activities has drawn on most of the methods mentioned above:

- face-to-face interviews with the general public,
- group discussions with people who had either sent for back-up material or had considered doing so,
- telephone or postal surveys among recipients of back-up.

Contact:

Mrs. Rosemary Bristow
British Broadcasting Corporation
Broadcasting Research Department
Woodlands, 80 Wood Lane
GB – London W12 0TT
United Kingdom
Tel.: +44-81-743 8000
Fax: +44-81-743 0906

Independent Television Commission (ITC) Educational Broadcasting

The situation in 1992/93

For some 35 years the *ITV Schools* service has been broadcasting alongside BB◄ School TV. Schools can and do choose freely from the alternative services. Aroun◄ 9 out of 10 UK schools use either or both sources. There is no formal cooperatio◄ in sharing out programme production but common sense dictates that there is rough complementarity between what is provided on both.

Channel Four, which has been broadcasting the ITV Schools service since Septembe◄ 1987, has contracted with the ITV Schools companies to continue their service unt◄ the end of the school year in June 1993. From September 1993 there will be a ne◄ *Channel 4 Schools* service. This is expected to broadcast for at least 340 hours year, and current plans for the school year 1993/94 are for some 84 hours of ne◄ production. The Commissioning Editor recently appointed to establish the ne◄ schools service is Paul Ashton.

Changes in Schools TV programming

In the last year or two Schools TV has set about a major reorientation of i◄ programming to match the new National Curriculum (implemented in England an◄ Wales). There have also been substantial developments in the separate and differe◄ curricula in Scotland and Northern Ireland.

An important effect of the National Curriculum has been to move away from liberal topic-based approach in primary education (5 to 11 year-olds), towards cle◄ subject strands, certainly from 8-year-olds onwards. At the same time there h◄ been increased programming for teacher training, particularly to help ◄ implementing the new curriculum programmes of study, and to show good exampl◄ of school management. This is likely to remain a strong area of demand with◄ the Schools TV output because other aspects of new legislation reduce the role ◄ the Local Education Authorities and the support services which they have bee◄ providing for schools.

242

upport services for ITV Schools

he ITV Schools service provides a teacher's booklet for every series, and
ipplements many of these with pupils' materials. Other print material may include
'all-posters, story books allied to the programmes, text books particularly on newly
eveloped areas of the curriculum, master copies of pupils' worksheets for each
rogramme topic. Beyond print there may be audio cassettes for story or language,
ut the most interesting recent development has been the production of a range
f software for use with school microcomputers. Some of this is role-play, narrative
r investigatory games. Much is based on pupils exploring data which is
omplementary to the TV programmes. The ITV Schools data retrieval package
EY is now the most widely used in UK schools.

he Educational Television Company (ETC)

he Educational Television Company has been given the contract to maintain the
iformation and support services for the new Channel 4 Schools service. As part
f the arrangement the ETC will also supply from its shareholder companies about
0% of the programming. This will be an important new force in UK school
elevision. The shareholders are some of the companies who have been supplying
ie ITV Schools service during the last 10 years, and the Chairman of the Board
Chris Jelley, Head of Education for Yorkshire TV.

ey appointments to the new ETC are Davina Lloyd as Chief Executive. She was
ormerly editor of the very successful journal *Practical Parenting*. As Senior
ducation Officer the ETC has appointed Simon Fuller, previously one of the BBC
lucation officer team. He will be administering a network of Education Officers,
ased in the larger regions of the UK. The ETC will be an active and entrepreneurial
ompany, also very much involved in the marketing of video and software packages
nked to the school television service.

valuating school television

he new legislative role of the Independent Television Commission (ITC) requires
to 'police' the output of the UK broadcasters it has licensed, and to intervene
the TV companies fail in any way to fulfil the requirements in their Licences.
enalties vary from substantial fines to abrogation of the broadcasting licence. How
in the principles of quality assurance be applied to a school television service?

Two main criteria are required by the Broadcasting Act – that the programme should be of high quality, and that they meet the needs of schools. The ITC has appointed a Schools Advisory Committee (SAC), and Channel Four, as the broadcaster, has agreed that this will be regarded as the prime source of advice. The SAC therefore provides an active interface with schools, education authorities and teachers. The members will be able to set criteria for high quality, and by examining and advising on the forward planning, they will try to ensure that the service meets the needs of schools.

Additionally, the ITC staff have begun to set up a network of professional monitors who will undertake to report on the perceived quality and effectiveness of the programmes as they are broadcast. The monitoring network is a hierarchy where the advisory or inspectorate team in a sample of Local Education Authorities undertake to organise specific tasks, and involve local teachers in monitoring and assessing programme value. It is highly likely that these reports will immediately influence the commissioning and making of programmes, and much less likely that ITC interventions will be hostile. Nevertheless the ITC has to fulfil its clear legal obligation to review the service and to ensure that quality and relevance continue to be delivered by the licensee.

Adult and community education

Mainline documentary educational programmes are broadcast on Channel 4. Each ITV regional station has a duty to provide community and social action programming for its region, sometimes within a co-ordinated national project and sometimes as a separate initiative. Each weekday morning there is an entertaining magazine *This Morning* in which there is a quota of short educational items for which follow-up services are normally available.

ITV can also broadcast programmes that are the start of a major project or event. Recent examples are:

The Last Cigarette

– an entertainment-led 90-minute programme on a familiar subject of health education. This reached an audience of nearly 3^1/$_2$ million and 15,000 people asked for the supporting literature.

Adult Learners Week

– the ITV part of the campaign combined network local programmes plus Community Service Announcements and local news. It also linked into the BBC *Second Chances* campaign.

hannel 4 have run several successful short campaigns or seasons, normally over single week or fortnight. These have included *Disabling World, Maps and Dreams, alestine* and *Israel*.

upport services for adult and community education

oth C4 and ITV adult and community education are supported by a network of ommunity education officers (a requirement under the 1982 ITV contracts) who aise with local organisations and initiate the support projects. Information about ll ITV and C4 education programmes has been co-ordinated during the past decade an IBA/ITC publication *TV take-up*.

oth the Independent TV broadcasters (C4 and ITV) and the BBC use the national roadcasting Support Services (BSS) organisation. Originally founded to provide telephone referral system, it has expanded to act as a major publisher of support aterials and co-ordinator of counselling and referral services. Particular projects ave also been undertaken, and database back-up compiled, by consultancies such s Independent Media Services, in this case founded by former ITV staff who had orked in community education and social action. With the radical changes in roadcasting it is likely that there will be a stronger role to be played by such onsultancies.

lajor changes in UK television

1 late 1990 the final version of a new Broadcasting Act became law. It forces the aost radical changes on independent broadcasting in the UK, and these are legally nplemented from January 1993. The Act expects educational programmes to ontinue on Channel Four, but removes any general mandate that might apply to ther channels. However a specific clause in the Act required the new Independent elevision Commission to secure a school television service on any of its terrestrial hannels.

hannel Three

'arly in 1991, the Independent Television Commission advertised 16 new licences or Channel 3 (currently the ITV service). These cover 15 geographical regions to *rhich is added a national breakfast-time service. Licences were awarded on three aain criteria:

- The ITC had to be satisfied of the financial viability of the company, and that its business plan could be sustained over the 10-year period of the licence.

245

- The programme plans, their diversity and the experience of the proposed staff must pass a quality threshold.
- Then the licence would be awarded to the highest bidder in what was in effect a blind auction on behalf of the government Treasury.

The licences were awarded in October 1991 and the successful licensees will commence their service on 1 January 1993. Current ITV companies who have lost licences are: TV-am – the national breakfast service; Thames Television – the London service; TVS – the service in Southern England; and TSW – in South West England.

These companies will be replaced by: Good Morning Television (GMTV) – as the national breakfast service; Carlton Television – for the London area; Meridian Television – for Southern England; Westcountry Television – for South West England.

All licensees have the responsibility for ensuring that their programming and services comply with the Broadcasting Act and the ITC Code and Programme Guidelines and where their applications promised educational or social action programming this has now been written into the individual licences.

Thames Television

Thames Television has been for many years a major provider of educational programming, and has produced a large quota of programmes for the ITV Schools service. It will now become a major independent production house. It has created an associated company *Tetra*, which will take on some of the continuing schools TV production, and which is a shareholder in the Educational Television Company (ETC). Thames, as an independent producer, also has a strong interest both in satellite services (it is a partner in the recently launched *UK Gold*), and is the only company that has bid for the new Channel Five licence.

Channel Four

At the end of this year Channel Four ceases to be a subsidiary of the ITC and becomes a Corporation which will hold the licence to broadcast on the fourth UK TV channel. The conditions in its licence spell out C4's obligations, which include providing a school television service and a substantial quota of other educational programming. For some years now, C4 has been carrying (but not producing) the ITV Schools service.

From September 1993 there will be a new Channel 4 Schools service. About half the output of the new Channel 4 Schools service will be commissioned from independent producers, and the other half from the newly-formed Educational Television Company, the consortium of several of the current ITV Schools producing companies mentioned above. The ETC is also contracted for three years to provide the education officer network and the essential support services of information and publishing.

Channel Five

The Broadcasting Act required the ITC to take responsibility for a fifth television channel, yet to be developed. Channel Five will cover about 70% of the UK, including major metropolitan areas, but excluding most of the south of England. One distinctive proposal is that C5 may in time develop towards being a network of city-focussed local TV stations, potentially providing an analogue of local radio. Applications for the Channel Five licence were invited in 1992 and a decision on whether or not to award the licence to the only applicant was expected by the end of 1992. C5 will not have any specific educational mandate, but the concept does seem to provide eventual opportunities for community education and social action in a more local context.

What the ITC is and will be

The ITC took over the duties of the Independent Broadcasting Authority at the beginning of 1991. For two years, until the expiry of the ITV contracts and their replacement by licensees, it has remained the constitutional broadcaster, responsible for programme content and quality and approving the schedules. But from 1993 it only has powers as a licensing body (the main work on this having already been done), which may intervene if the TV companies fail in any way to fulfil the requirements in their licences. Under the present EBU constitution the ITC will no longer qualify as a member of the EBU, though in some circumstances may be an observer.

The ITC has been through the process of re-organising its Programme Division to implement the legislative changes and its strictly limited mandate. Taking into account the new position of educational programming and the output of the licensees, the ITC education department will be reduced to only 4 staff by the end of 1992. Dr Robin Moss remains as Head of Department, assisted by one Senior Educational Broadcasting Officer, Eileen Allen, and two of the present administrative staff.

An archive of past documentation and research in educational broadcasting is being created, some of which will be available to interested institutions in microfiche format.

Future prospects

At the end of 1992, while the existing Independent system continued, there had been no significant changes in the amount of airtime devoted to education on ITV and Channel 4. All licensees have included plans for community education in their promises of performance from 1993. The funding background for Schools TV has been strengthened, but for Adult and Community Education cuts in budget and staff commitments for 1992/93 and beyond are likely to result from the changed circumstances.

Longer term broadcasting issues

International broadcasting treaties allocated frequencies and a 'footprint' for UK satellite broadcasting direct to the home. British Satellite Broadcasting (BSB) launched the five-channel high-power Marco Polo satellite, and subsequently merged with Sky Television. British Sky Broadcasting (BSkyB) is consolidating services on the Astra satellites, and the higher quality Marco Polo D-MAC broadcasts are expected to cease at the end of 1992. Current legislation will make it extremely difficult to reinstate other services on the Marco Polo transponders, although a number of expressions of interest, particularly from potential educational and ethnic minority services had been received by the ITC.

Research commissioned by the ITC from its former engineering division (now an independent company National Transcommunications Limited – NTL) have recently successfully demonstrated the technical possibility of broadcasting digital TV alongside the current analogue signals. One other possibility would be to subdivide any of the existing UHF frequencies to carry about four digital TV channels. Although not much more than two years old at the time of writing, the 1990 Broadcasting Act is already proving less than adequate to deal with the developing situation.

The UK government elected in 1992 created a Department of National Heritage, which among other matters has taken over responsibility for broadcasting.

Contact:

Independent Television Commission
70 Brompton Road
GB – London SW3 1EY
United Kingdom

Tel.: +44-71 462 59 88
Fax: +44-71 589 55 33

Central Independent Television (CEN)

Central Independent Television is one of the largest companies in Independent Television Network. It is licensed to provide a television service to viewers in the Midlands and to contribute to the networking of programmes throughout the United Kingdom.

The Education Department of Central is part of the public service activities of the Company, and is a requirement under the conditions of the Company's television licence. Central Television contributes approximately one quarter of the new productions required by ITV Schools, working in co-operation with Granada TV, Yorkshire TV and Thames Television.

Central (formerly ATV Network), has been producing programmes for schools since 1961, specialising in Mathematics and Science for primary and secondary schools, Geography, English, Religious Studies, and Health Education for primary and middle schools, and contributes to the professional in-service training of teachers, INSET. In a typical year Central prepares some 12 hours of new programmes for schools.

All the television series are supported by handbooks for teachers, prepared using the Company resources. Increasingly, series are complemented by books and computer software materials for pupils, prepared and distributed on the basis of joint ventures established between Central and specialist publishers of educational books and software.

Currently, Central is interested in co-operating with expertes in areas of new technologies and particulary interactive video systems. Arrangement would be by negotiation, but Central would hope to contribute television software – video and animation based images, and educational expertise.

The changes in indepentend broadcasting from January 1993 place the responsibility for a schools service on Channel 4. The Education Department at Central will contribute to this service as a shareholder in the Educational Television Company.

Contact:

Mr. Paul Martin
The Education Department
Central Independent Television plc
Central House
Broad Street
GB – Birmingham B1 2JP
United Kingdom

Tel.: +44-21-643 9898
Fax: +44-21-616 4259

Channel Four (4)

Channel 4 was launched on air in 1982 as the UK's newest terrestrial television channel with full nation-wide coverage. Though funded entirely from commercial revenue, the channel is not simply committed to public service broadcasting in abstract principle. It is required under the original 1981 Broadcasting Act to cater for tastes, interests and audiences not served by ITV (or other television channels) to innovate in the form and content of programmes and to devote a proportion of its airtime to educational programming.

The channel does not attempt to compete with the mass channels for a major share of viewing at all times, but it does attract large audiences at some points in the week with popular programming, which can include the best of American comedy and feature films. It can be distinctive and innovative as well, as in the case of the channel's own drama serial, *Brookside* (now thrice-weekly), or its own home grown comedy, drama or commissioned feature films in the *Film on Four* strand. These figures help to balance the smaller, more targeted audiences it serves at other times, whether with programmes for businessmen or jazz fans. In interpreting its remit, it has always made special provision to reflect ethnic interests with multicultural programming and to serve the youth audience that was largely neglected by British television before the advent of Channel 4.

All viewers are members of many diverse and overlapping minorities, and over 80% of viewers tune into Channel 4 each week. Altogether, the channel attracts up to – and occasionally beyond – a 10% share of all viewing.

In targeting specific audiences, Channel 4 can attract many 'light' viewers who do not watch much television at all, particularly on ITV, and it thereby gains an audience profile that tends to be younger and more 'upmarket' than other channels. This not only fulfils a function in offering viewers distinctive programming they could not find on other channels, it also provides a commercial opportunity and a way for advertisers to reach those viewers who watch little ITV.

Independent production

Unlike other existing British television channels, which previously made virtually all their programmes in-house with their own staff and facilities, Channel 4 was charged from its inception with *not* making its own programmes (except for one weekly programme, *Right to Reply*, which allows viewers to answer back). Instead Channel 4 was required to obtain its programmes from outside sources, with a 'substantial proportion' from independent producers. Rather than relying on package deals, output guarantees or – primarily – on pre-purchases it has chosen to do so through a process of 'commissioning'.

Channel 4's role as a 'publisher broadcaster' has attracted considerable world-wide interest as a model which other emerging channels have wished to adopt. It also stimulated the growth of an independent television production industry in the UK, and the success of independent production in all areas – including current affairs – has led to pressure on the BBC and ITV to offer a proportion of their own airtime to independent production.

Channel 4 purchases some of its programmes, series and feature films in a conventional way from producers or distributors around the world – drawing for instance on the strongest American sitcoms, the most distinctive American features, but also on the widest range of material from around the globe, including the Third World. However, for its original programming, the channel relies on commissioning, from independent producers, or from ITV companies.

The commissioning process

The commissioning process is centred around a team of commissioning editors, each addressing a specific area of programming or audience – Drama, Arts, Music, Sport, Education – and individual posts for youth programming and multicultural programming indicate the importance they hold in the channel's policy. The editors are arranged in three groups under the Controller of Factual Programmes (who doubles as Deputy Director of Programmes), Controller of Arts and Entertainment, and Head of Drama, all reporting to the Director of Programmes.

Each editor has a specific budget to allocate and a sense of the airtime and slots at their disposal, and either responds to proposals from potential producers or sometimes invites proposals for a specific strand of programming – occasionally with some form of limited tender. If the editor likes an idea, he or she might commission development work – a full script, a treatment, a research visit to a foreign location – or may wish to proceed straight to a commission. This involves negotiations with a programme finance manager from the channel's Programme Finance Department, and a negotiator from the channel's Acquisitions Department to agree a budget and contract, subject to approval by the channel's Programme Finance Committee.

If the channel commissions (or co-finances) a project, it requires a detailed and realistic budget and cash flow that allows for every aspect of production, including heat and light for the production office and other overheads for the period of the production, plus appropriate contingencies. Once this figure has been agreed, a percentage of that total (excluding overheads) is added on as a 'production fee' providing a recognised profit for the company.

This commissioning system means that the smallest conceivable production company – the proverbial 'man, dog and answerphone' can get a major commission provided the channel wants the idea and has confidence in the producer and the people he or she hires. A production company does not necessarily need enormous reserves to prepare a project beforehand, nor does it need the resources for 'deficit financing', as in some television industries, where the producer can only fully recover costs and make a profit with subsequent subsidiary sales either overseas or in syndication.

With this commissioning system, Channel 4 has not only encouraged the growth of an independent sector, but has helped to sustain its diversity, commissioning over 500 individual companies each year. While some companies may win several commissions in the year, the score or so who receive more than £1 million in the year do so either because they make a long-running strand, like a weekly political series, or a short series with higher unit costs, as with drama or situation comedy.

Relying on independent production also encouraged the channel to pioneer links between television and film, so that the channel has supported feature films that can be seen in the cinema first, gaining kudos and often a financial return, before their premiere on Channel 4.

Channel 4 also commissions from ITV companies in a broadly similar way. While current affairs is commissioned from many different sources, *Channel 4 News*, and other news summaries and the early morning *World News* is commissioned from Independent Television News (ITN), which supplies news to the ITV network.

Ownership and funding

The Channel 4 Television Company Ltd was originally established as a wholly-owned subsidiary of the Independent Broadcasting Authority, and ownership has now passed to its successor the Independent Television Commission. From 1 January 1993, the channel will be reconstituted – under the terms of the 1990 Broadcasting Act – as the Channel 4 Corporation. Its programming is regulated by the ITC, as it was previously by the IBA. From 1993, the channel will operate under a ten-year licence from the ITC and will be governed by its programme regulations.

From its inception and up to 31 December 1992, the channel is funded by a subscription levied on the ITV companies, currently amounting to 13.6% of the previous year's advertising revenue on both commercial channels. (Another 3.4% of total revenue goes in subscription to the Welsh Fourth Channel, making 17%

n total). In return for this subscription, the ITV companies have the right to sell airtime on Channel 4 in their own franchise area.

From April 1989, Channel 4 has broadcast an early morning service between 6.00 a.m. and 9.25 a.m. – on weekdays, this is *The Channel Four Daily*. This has been funded by a subscription from TV-am, which holds the ITV franchise nation-wide for that time period, in return for which TV-am sells the advertising.

From 1 January 1993, Channel 4 will sell its own airtime to fund its operation. The channel is beginning to recruit its own dedicated in-house sales, marketing and research team for the purpose, under a newly-appointed Director of Advertising, Sales and Marketing. This brings new opportunities and challenges. The channel now has the opportunity to sell its own particular range of programming to advertisers in its own way. Not only has the channel's mix of programming attracted for some years a larger share of the commercial audience than the 13.6% share of the previous year's revenue it currently receives as subscription, but its programming has attracted specific audiences – small but comparatively well-targeted – that could attract a premium price for its airtime. The channel will decide whether to sell its airtime from 1993 nationally or on some regional basis, according to whichever it estimates will maximise its income.

The channel faces new costs of selling its own airtime and a new degree of competition for advertising revenue with the post 1993 licence holders on ITV/Channel 3.

Along with these opportunities and challenges, Channel 4 will still maintain its statutory public service commitments, together with several new responsibilities, including schools broadcasts. Since 1987, Channel 4 has acted as a conduit for ITV's schools programming, which continues to be made and funded by ITV as it had been for the past 30 years. From 1993, Channel 4 will itself be responsible for commissioning and funding schools broadcasts and the essential apparatus of back-up and liaison.

Channel 4 is confident that from 1993 it can thrive commercially while maintaining its public service commitments and the range of programming its viewers have come to expect. Nevertheless, the 1990 Broadcasting Act has provided a limited safety net, designed to protect the channel against the worst financial dangers and to encourage commercial coexistence with ITV, without dulling its sales force's competitiveness. If the channel fails to attract 14% of the total terrestrial advertising revenue (TNAR), any shortfalls up to a maximum of 2% of that total revenue figure will be funded by the ITV/Channel 3 companies. Any surplus over this 14% figure will be divided up, with 50% going to the ITV companies, 25% into the channel's reserves (to be used to finance future shortfalls before calling on funding from ITV/Channel 3) and 25% available for enhancing Channel 4's future programme budget.

Organisation of Channel 4

Channel 4's Board includes six executive directors, led by the Chief Executive, each overseeing several departments. The Director of Programmes oversees the commissioning departments, general programme policy and programme planning.The Director of Finance oversees programme finance and financial accounts. The Director of Acquisitions and Programme Sales is responsible for the teams negotiating deals and contracts and safeguarding the legal content of programmes; also the sale of programmes and the channel's own feature films overseas, through its in-house operations, Film Four International, and Channel 4 International. The Director and General Manager oversees engineering, administration, personnel and industrial relations. The Director of Advertising, Sales and Marketing is establishing the team to sell the channel's advertising airtime from 1993. The Chief Executive himself oversees directly the Corporate Affairs Department (including press and publicity) and the Presentation Department dealing with on-air promotion.

Wales

In Wales the fourth channel frequencies are used by the Welsh Fourth Channel, S4C, which is run by an independent authority. It is charged with providing a Welsh language service during the night-time peak period and showing the majority of Channel 4's programmes at all other times, either simultaneously or rescheduled. SC4 is also funded by a subscription based on the advertising revenue of the ITV companies (and its funding unlike that of Channel 4 UK, will remain substantially unchanged after 1993). *Sianel Pedwar Cymru* is also a publisher/broadcaster like Channel 4 and commissions the majority of its programmes from the local Channel 3 contractor and from independent producers – about 20 hours per week, with the remaining 10 hours coming from the BBC, funded out of the licence fee.

Contact:

Mr. Derek Jones
Editor Support Services
Channel Four Company
60 Charlotte Street
GB – London W1P 2AX
United Kingdom

Tel.: +44-71-927 8939
Fax: +44-71-580 2617

The Learning Channel (TLC)

What is it?

The Learning Channel is an educational television service broadcast in the United Kingdom on cable only, seven days a week, and offers a wide variety of subjects.

The channel is owned by United Artists Programming, who also bring you *The Discovery Channel* − *Europe, Bravo* and *The Parliamentary Channel.*

What does it do?

A great deal of television can be said to be educational − watch it and you learn something. TLC aims to do more: we want to provide everyone, from teenagers to senior citizens, with programmes that are of practical educational value. By this we mean that the viewer should gain one or more of the following from watching the channel:

Information
  − that will enable people to do something; to be more assertive, eat more healthily, cook better, grow better vegetables.

Inspiration
  − to follow up on one's interest inspired by a programme − like joining a course, reading a book, developing skills.

Education
  − knowledge that will deepen people's understanding about themselves, their family, our society and world.

Broadcasting hours

The Learning Channel is broadcast seven days a week between 12.00 mid-day and 3.00 p.m. In some areas cable operators will extend the service by repeating the previous day's programmes.

Each day's programming is divided into three hour-long sections, each covering a different category of subjects.

First hour: 12.00 mid-day -1.00 p.m.

Family Health and Society

Programmes about personal matters – such as parenting, healthy eating, dealin
with stress, wider issues, too, such as caring for older people, women at work

Second hour: 1.00 p.m. – 2.00 p.m.

Leisure, Do-it-yourself, Hobbies

This is the "how to" hour – information and handy tips on cooking, photography
gardening, model-making, painting, cricket, golf.

Third hour: 2.00 p.m. – 3.00 p.m.

Science, The Arts, Politics

The study hour informs on great writers, the solar system, our bodies, Europea
culture, the AIDS crisis – with programmes to stimulate the mind. The study hou
is of special value to students in secondary schools and further education colleges
If you are not at college you may be encouraged to join a course or do some mor
reading.

Support of programmes

Wherever possible, we will provide written back-up for programmes, either a
booklet, programme notes or a reading list. The aim is to enable the viewer to follo
up the interest created by our programmes.

Contact:

Mrs. Jane Campbell
The Learning Channel
Twyman House
16 Bonny Street
GB – London NW1 9PG
United Kingdom

Tel: + 44-71-428 4824
Fax: + 44-71-284 2042

Broadcasting Support Services (BSS)

Broadcasting Support Services is a not-for-profit institution which was founded by the BBC in 1975. Its main task is to run telephone helplines and provide follow-up services for viewers and listeners on BBC, Channel 4, ITV and other media. BSS is an independent charity. Our Board of Trustees consists of senior broadcasters and professionals drawn from the statutory, voluntary and business sectors. Our staff have extensive experience in providing follow-up to broadcasts.

Viewers and listeners guides

These booklets and leaflets are trailed on air after a programme. We write, edit, design, publish and distribute them or undertake any one or more of these tasks. We publish some titles in a variety of languages, braille, large print and on tape.

Helplines

Using our 60-line phone systems in London, Manchester and Cardiff, we run 100 different helplines on topics ranging across the fields of health, social welfare, education, the environment and recreation. Our helplines are staffed by specialists in the particular topic of the broadcast.

Appeals

We provide administrative services to broadcast appeals such as the BBC *Children In Need* appeal and Capital Radio's *Help A London Child*. In addition, our donation taking telephone lines have brought in millions of pounds over the last few years for charities such as *Live Aid*, *Comic Relief* and many others that have appealed in broadcasts.

Letter answering service

Programmes commission our correspondence bureau to answer letters from viewers and listeners. These letters often require a specialist response.

257

Dial-and-listen and telephone discussion

Introduced in 1985, our telephone dial-and-listen services provide a 3-minute talking factsheet following a broadcast. Viewers or listeners can hear useful follow-up information immediately and in complete privacy. We are also developing telephone conferencing for viewers.

Community outreach

Broadcasters often wish their programmes to be shown to particular audiences. We set up viewing groups and community screenings. More recently we have established viewers clubs with Channel 4.

National AIDS Helpline

Devised in 1986 by BSS and BBC Radio, our National Aids Helpline offers confidential information, advice, education and referral to over 18,000 callers a week. It is free and is open 24 hours a day every day of the year. The service is funded by the UK Health Departments and is run in conjunction with Network Scotland.

International

Over the last few years BSS has undertaken a range of international work. With the One World Group of Broadcasters we produced follow-up for *One World 92* and with the Commission of the European Community we organised the recent European Drug Helpline Conference. We are now co-ordinating aspects of the media work for European Drug Prevention Week.

Evaluation

Over the last few years we have set great store by the evaluation of our services by independent researchers. Results are available on request but, as a taster, here are some of the main results:

Nine in ten respondents (the public) agreed that offering information after television programmes was a useful public service. (Source: *Public Attitudes Towards Back-Up Literature*; BBC, Channel 4 and IBA 1988).

Most callers to the helpline were very satisfied with the service they received. They did not know what they would have done without it; they were reluctant to turn elsewhere for help. (Source: Department of Health commissioned study on the National AIDS Helpline).

A large proportion of current tranquilliser users specified that the helpline had been the crucial factor influencing their decision to embark on withdrawal. (Source: Institute of Psychiatry).

Contact:

Mr. Keith Smith
Director
Broadcasting Support Services
252 Western Avenue
GB – London W3 6XJ
United Kingdom

Tel.: +44-81-992 5522
Fax: +44-81-993 6281

TVOntario, Canada

Facts, figures and highlights of activities

Since the organisation's creation in 1970 as OECA (the Ontario Educational Communications Authority), we have provided Ontarians with educational television programming and support materials in both English and French. Right from sign-on, day one, we have been opening Ontario's eyes to the possibilities and delights of lifelong learning via television. Through our 21 years of operation we have steered our ship by this guiding polestar of lifelong learning: our programming aims to promote learning through all stages of life, from wide-eyed childhood to clear-sighted adulthood, from the schoolyard to the arenas of business to the home, beginning with developing basic literacy but not ending with professional development.

Our programming has been recognised for its excellence from our 1970 beginnings, when the programme *What Do I Like about Tommy?* (from our sociology series *The Family Structure*) won the Prix Jeunesse in Munich, Germany, to our most recent successes, including the Gold Award won by the programme *Slicing the Cone* (from *Conic Sections*) at the 1991 International Film and Television Festival of New York.

As we look back on more than two decades of service to the province, we can see that the seeds of our initially small-scale (four employees) operations have blossomed into a full-size broadcasting organisation, renowned around the world for the excellence of our programming, for our investigation of the educational applications of technology, and for our research into learning. Of course, this growth has taken much dedication and work from TVOntario employees; on-going financial support from government, corporate, and individual stakeholders; encouragement from regulators; and interaction with the learners and learning institutions of the province.

TVOntario has developed into a team of over 500 employees supporting two programming networks (TVO and *La Chaîne*), each broadcasting 100-130 hours per week. In Canada, TVOntario is the only educational television organisation producing and broadcasting in both official languages, on two services, seven days a week. Canadian content is a substantial component of our broadcast schedule, from September 1990 to March 1991 reaching 69.2 per cent overall on TVO, 60 per cent overall on *La Chaîne*.

TVOntario is accessible to more than 97 percent of Ontarians via a hybrid satellite-based distribution system comprising 22 medium- and high-powered transmitters, 191 low-power transmitters, and 323 cable systems. This distribution system provides TVO and *La Chaîne* to many communities across the province. The latest Bureau of Broadcast Measurement (BBM) statistics show that nearly two million people view TVOntario at least once a week.

Throughout the province we have a network of 96,000 Public Members, who in 1990-91 contributed $3.5 million to TVOntario's programming; among the contributors are 125 francophone community groups and 800 individuals who participated in and raised money through the 24-hour on-air Téléthon. Our 90 advisory councillors throughout Ontario also offer input and feedback.

Over 80 percent of English- and French-language teachers have used television or video in the classroom and over 60 percent used educational television during the 1989-90 school year (the most recent for which statistics are available). Since 1970, our programmes and graphic designs have won over 565 awards at major international competitions. TVOntario also sells programmes across Canada and to 80 countries around the world; we are the largest foreign supplier of programmes to the United States' instructional television market.

The 1 January 1987 launch of our French-language service was of real significance to TVOntario and the learners of the province. *La Chaîne* provides French-language programming to all Ontarians who wish to learn in French. Although TVOntario has throughout our history created and broadcast educational programmes in French, before the launch of *La Chaîne* it made up at most only 17 percent of the broadcast schedule. The launch of our second channel marked the culmination of many years' work by staff, members of the TVOntario Board of Directors, community groups, and government funders: at last Ontarians may watch seven days a week of French-language educational programming and seven days a week of English-language educational programming.

Programming is the core of TVOntario's activities. In keeping with our lifelong learning orientation, TVOntario produces educational programmes for all ages, representing all kinds of educational experiences — formal (designed for use in elementary, secondary, or post-secondary courses), non-formal (structured part-time learning courses, independent of educational institutions), and informal (unstructured learning to expand personal well-being and increase general knowledge and life skills).

In the last 5 years from the 1986-87 season through to the 1990-91 year, TVOntario has produced more than 1,360 hours of English programming and 1,010 hours of French. Many of these hours have been captioned for the hearing-impaired. We are pleased that our captioning activities increase from year to year; from 1986-87 to 1990-91, we have captioned a total of 478.06 hours of English- and 181.75 hours of French-language programming for learners of all ages.

Children's programming

Children's programming is the heart and soul of TVOntario; well-loved favorites such as *Polka Dot Door, Today's Special*, and *Join In!* have set standards of excellence for children's programming around the world. Our programmes and series reach out to children both in school (in which case they are based on Ministry of Education guidelines) and at home. Each week, approximately 40 percent of all Ontario children aged 2-11 (a whopping 50 percent of the 2- to 6-year-old group) watch TVOntario at home. The most watched segment of our broadcast schedule (for both TVO and *La Chaîne*) is children's and family viewing programming from 5:00 to 9:00 p.m. on weekdays.

A focus of intense effort and activity, our programmes attempt to help children learn and develop physically, socially, culturally, emotionally, and intellectually. Programmers take pains to ensure that our fare for children and youth promote basic human values of tolerance and non-discrimination. The series *Many Voices* for example, helps students in grades 4 to 6 deal with race relations and diversity in the schools. Each of the open-ended dramas is presented by a child of the religion, race, or culture featured in the programme. *A la claire fontaine* also includes racial tolerance as a continuing theme.

Youth programming

TVOntario produces award-winning programming for youth in school. Based on the Ontario curriculum, it is also used with success and enthusiasm around the world to help young people learn. Our continuing senior science and mathematics series, *Concepts in Science* and *Concepts in Mathematics*, continue to be highly successful in the classroom, acclaimed as models of television's ability to concretise abstract concepts for easier learning. Youth programming also has special challenges, such as preparing young people for the world of work. Series such as *Skills* and *Work The Inside Story*, and *Au travail!* help teens understand what a particular job is like and the skills it requires, encouraging students to stay in school to get the training they will need.

La Chaîne's Jeunesse programming has taken up the special challenge of validating the French language and Franco-Ontarian culture for the province's young (13-25) francophones, whether the programmes they watch relate to secondary and post secondary curricula directly or to less formal learning at home. A major TVOntario research study indicates that this age group is particularly vulnerable to assimilation and so becomes a priority for *La Chaîne's* education activities. To demonstrate *La Chaîne's* strong commitment to this special audience group, the Jeunesse sector was established in January 1991.

Distance education

Through Home Studies and the French-language distance education courses of *La Chaîne*, Ontarians participate in television-based courses that help improve their professional skills, widen their knowledge, and enrich their leisure time. Course components can include television broadcasts, videos for home use, audiocassettes, texts, workbooks and other print support materials, as well as telephone tutoring.

TVOntario considers these courses a linchpin of our lifelong learning and an increasingly important element in the province's spectrum of training possibilities. When Home Studies was launched in 1982 as Part-Time Learning, its six courses received more than 7,500 registrations. By 1990-91, TVOntario offered more than 100 Home Studies courses, 13 of which earned university credit, and received 35,127 registrations – the most ever, producing revenue of $1,456,200. The most popular series were *Foundations of Taoist Tai Chi, The Successul Landlord*, and *Chinese Brush Painting*.

One focus of Home Studies/Formation à distance programming is language training, answering the needs for basic skills training and for work skills oriented to the global marketplace. The popular series *17, rue Laurier* helps francophones improve their French-language skills; *How Do You Do?* has been acclaimed by the community of teachers of English as a second language as an excellent resource for newcomers to the language; *Ciao Italia's* two versions assist francophones and anglophones in learning Italian; and *French in Action, Deutsch direkt!* and *España viva* are all second-language courses for English speakers.

The new technologies of The Box and Studio F (in each case, a self-contained studio, control and edit room) facilitate the production of quick-response, low-cost interactive programming -- rapidly becoming a core component of student- and teacher-oriented programming.

Adult programming

Audience-accessible programmes

TVOntario has also begun to strengthen the responsiveness and interactivity of our adult education programming. *Between the Lines* provides topical panel discussions on current issues and viewers are encouraged to respond with written letters or video mail. For French-speaking viewers, *Le Lys et le trillium* continued its live-to-air phone-in format, for example, exploring Jewish and Arab points of view during the Gulf War. Other on-going series such as *Imprint* and *The Science Edition* rely upon continuing audience feedback to ensure that programmes remain relevant and topical.

Ontario-specific programmes

Just as our interactive programmes give Ontarians a chance to speak out about issues of concern to them, so does our Ontario-specific programming deal with issues of special concern to people of the province. For example, TVOntario's own arts productions for adults – *Imprint, Hands over Time* (about Ontario crafts) and *Jay Scott's Film International* – explore issues and present themes of concern to Ontarians, frequently in a multicultural perspective.

In addition, *A comme artiste* often presents artists from various cultural heritages, including story-tellers of Tunisian and Senegalese origin in a special about oral history. International acquisitions, such as the drama miniseries *Shalom Salaam* and the feature film *Train d'enfer*, help give Ontarians a broader scope for understanding race relations.

Science and technology programmes

This is also emphasised by TVOntario. Whether through original productions, such as *The Science Edition* and *Science amateure*, or through international co-productions created under the auspices of the *Scienceview* consortium or our bilateral agreement with NHK-Japan, or because of high-quality international acquisitions such as *National Geographic*, TVOntario has become the Ontario source for exceptional science programmes. In 1990-91, TVO brought Ontario viewers more then 100 programmes on environmental issues.

Partnerships, alliances and co-ventures

Cooperative activities have become increasingly important to TVOntario, serving a threefold purpose: cooperative ventures allow us to bring Ontario viewers top-quality programming at a reduced cost; participation with other public and educational broadcasters and independent producers enables us to contribute to other programmers' viability while helping our own; and international activities improve TVOntario's status in and access to the global market-place, essential at this time of internationalisation:

- In May 1990, TVOntario signed a three-year partnership agreement with NHK Japan, the world's largest public broadcaster.
- In September 1990, TVOntario launched a major international initiative to explore new sources of international funding and co-production.
- In October 1990, TVOntario, with NHK Japan and ZDF (Germany) co-produced *Our Beautiful Planet / S.O.S. Terre*, one of the most extensive co-productions about environmental issues ever mounted.
- In November 1991, TVOntario co-hosted with NHK Japan in Toronto the Public Broadcasters International symposium, a three-day meeting of senior executives to establish international links and discuss concrete projects geared to sharing resources and technology.

Research, education and community activities

TVOntario's Policy, Research and Planning sector provides research data and analyses that assist the broadcaster in making programming decisions that will satisfy educational and home audience needs.

The TVOntario Videotape Program Service (VIPS) allows educational institutions and non-profit organisations in Ontario to purchase the rights for the non-broadcast use of videotape copies of educational programmes and series. More than 12,900 programmes (French and English) are available through VIPS.

In 1990-91, TVOntario's English Educational Services and French Utilisation and Planning sector conducted professional-development courses and workshops for nearly 13,200 Ontario educators.

Revenue-generating activities

Each year, TVOntario receives base grants from the Ministry of Culture and Communications, totalling approximately 70 percent of its gross operating revenues.

Funding is also received from the Ministry of Colleges and Universities for post-secondary credit courses and from the Department of the Secretary of State for French-language programming aimed both at francophones and persons learning the language.

TVOntario generates revenue through the sale of broadcast and non-broadcast rights to its programmes.

Membership donations totalling $3.5 million (Canadian) from nearly 86,000 members in 1990-91 go directly to assist the production and acquisition of programmes.

TVOntario receives additional support for programming from other Ontario and federal ministries and agencies, as well as corporations.

Contact:

Mrs. Judith Tobin
Director General
International Affairs
TVOntario
Box 200, Station Q
Toronto, Ontario M4T 2T1
Canada

Tel.: +1-416-484 2654
Fax: +1-416-484 7771

Nippon Hoso Kyokai (NHK) Educational Broadcasting

Nippon Hoso Kyokai (NHK) is the sole public service broadcasting organisation in Japan, and it is financed with fees collected from its audience. Thus NHK's educational broadcasting has a strong public service character, with nation-wide networks.

NHK now operates four television channels, including its new satellite broadcasting channel, and three radio networks, including the FM network. Educational programmes are broadcast mainly on the Educational TV channel (ETV) and Radio I Network.

Educational broadcasting is prescribed as follows in the Broadcasting Law of Japan:

"The Corporation (NHK) shall, in compiling and broadcasting educational programmes, clearly indicate the persons for whom such broadcasting is intended. Programme contents should be systematic and have continuity, as well as being instructive and appropriate for the target audience. At the same time, means shall be provided for the general public to learn the plans for and the contents of such broadcasting in advance. If the programme is intended for schools, its contents shall conform to curricular standards as provided in the laws and regulations relative to school education."

School Broadcast Programmes on Educational TV
(Numbers of broadcasts and hours per week)

	First Broadcasts		Repeats		Total	
	Progr.	Hours	Progr.	Hours	Progr.	Hours
Kindergarten and Nursery School	6	1:30	12	3:30	18	4:30
Primary School	32	8:00	41	10:15	73	18:15
Secondary School	8	4:00			8	4:00
Junior High School	1	0:20			1	0.20
Senior High School	1	0:40				0:40
Total (excluding Senior High School Courses)	48	14:30	53	13:15	101	27:45

Apart from the above, 19 programmes, equivalent to 4 hours and 50 minutes including the repeats, are broadcast on Radio II Network.

Use of NHK's school television broadcasts

The majority of schools at all levels make use of NHK's school programmes. Th following illustrates such utilisation:

	Utilisation rate	Number of schools using broadcasts (rounded off)
Kindergartens	71.6%	10.700
Nursery Schools	76.4%	17.900
Primary Schools	94.0%	23.100
Junior High Schools	53.9%	6.000
Senior High Schools	54.3%	3,000

Education by means of broadcasts is especially widespread at primary schools, with 94% of them using NHK's school programmes in 1989. It is estimated that about 8.8 million primary school pupils in Japan viewed NHK's school television during that year.

The most commonly used series of all school programmes is *First Grade Science*, with a utilisation rate of 81.1%, equalling some twenty thousand schools. This series consists of 36 programmes, and more than ten thousand schools reported that they used 'almost all' of them. Clearly, NHK's school broadcasting now plays an indispensible role in Japan's school education.

NHK started to broadcast school television in 1953, and school broadcasting has since spread steadily, thanks to close cooperation between NHK and school teachers engaged in education through broadcasts.

Expansion of educational broadcasts

When NHK began public television broadcasting in Tokyo in February, 1953. Programmes intended for primary and secondary schools were broadcast at the rate of one a day, on six days a week.

A number of commercial television services were launched soon after the inauguration of the NHK TV station in 1953. As commercial television programmes

– even programmes intended for children – contained few if any educational elements, concern began to spread over the possibly harmful effects of television on children. Responding to public needs, NHK began in 1959 its channel devoted entirely to educational programmes.

This newly established Educational TV Channel took over the school broadcast programmes, which NHK had previously presented on its general channel, thus leading to systematic school broadcast programming.

School broadcasting on the educational channel is obliged to observe certain rules and conditions. For instance, it must be in accordance with the goals of education specified in Japan's Fundamental Law of Education; its programmes must be produced in line with the Course of Study prescribed in the School Education Law Enforcement Regulations, and they must be compiled for a specific target audience; the contents must be made public in advance; and, to promote equal opportunity in education, broadcasting must be available everywhere in the country.

On the basis of such guidelines, NHK's school programmes have come to be presented as series closely related to school teaching materials and targeted at specific school grades or levels. NHK's school broadcasts are distinguished by the fact that they are compiled as course series by groups of specialists, in ways that use to the full the advantages of broadcasting media. In addition, NHK has worked out its own broadcasting curriculum for presenting year-long series. NHK's high-quality course programmes have been awarded the grand prize a number of times at the Japan Prize International Educational Programme Contest.

Contact:

Mr. Yoshiyuki Fukushima
Director
NHK Educational Programme Production Centre
Shibuya-ku,
Tokyo 150-01,
Japan

Tel.: +81-3-5478 2889
Fax: +81-3-5478 2902

Appendix A: List of Acronyms

A2 (A2F)	Antenne 2 (now France 2), France
ABC	Australian Broadcasting Corporation
ARD	Arbeitsgemeinschaft der öffentlich-rechtlichen Rundfunkanstalten der Bundesrepublik Deutschland, Germany
BBC	British Broadcasting Corporation, United Kingdom
BBC/OUPC	BBC Open University Production Centre, United Kingdom
BR	Bayerischer Rundfunk, Germany
BRF	Belgisches Rundfunk- und Fernsehzentrum der Deutschsprachigen Gemeinschaft, Belgium
BRT	Belgische Radio en Televisie, Belgium
BRTN	Belgische Radio en Televisie, Nederlandse uitzendingen, Belgium
CEN	Central Independent Television, United Kingdom
C4	Channel Four, United Kingdom
CNDP	Centre National de Documentation Pédagogique, France
CPB	Corporation for Public Broadcasting, United States
DR	Danmarks Radio, Denmark
DRS	Radio- und Fernsehgesellschaft der deutschen und der rätoromanischen Schweiz, Switzerland
DW	Deutsche Welle, Germany
EAC	Education Advisory Council, United Kingdom
EBC	Education Broadcasting Councils, United Kingdom
EBS	BBC Educational Broadcasting Services, United Kingdom
EBU	European Broadcasting Union
ERT	Elliniki Radiophonia Tileorassi SA (Greek Radio and Television), Greece
ETC	Educational Television Company, United Kingdom
FR3	France Régions 3 (now France 3), France
GTV	Granada Television, United Kingdom
HR	Hessischer Rundfunk, Germany
IBA	Independent Broadcasting Authority, United Kingdom
IETV	Israel Educational Television, Israel
ILEA	Inner London Education Authority, United Kingdom
ITV	Independent Television, United Kingdom
ITC	Independent Television Commission, United Kingdom
ITN	Independent Television News, United Kingdom

ZI	Internationales Zentralinstitut für das Jugend- und Bildungsfernsehen, Germany
RT	Jugoslovenska Radiotelevizija, Yugoslavia
MBA	Malta Broadcasting Authority, Malta
MTV	Magyar Rádió és Televízío, Hungary
N3	"Nordkette", Norddeutscher Rundfunk (NDR), Germany
NDR	Norddeutscher Rundfunk, Germany
NHK	Nippon Hoso Kyokai, Japan
NOS	Nederlandse Omroepprogramma Stichting, Netherlands
NOT	Nederlandse Onderwijs Televisie, Netherlands
NRK	Norsk Rikskringkasting, Norway
OECD	Organisation for Economic Co-operation and Development
OIRT	Organisation Internationale de Radiodiffusion et de Télévision, Czechoslovakia
ORF	Österreichischer Rundfunk, Austria
OFRT	Organismes Français de Radiodiffusion et de Télévision, France
PBS	Public Broadcasting Service, United States
PRT	Polskie Radio i Telewizja, Poland
RAI	Radiotelevisione Italiana, Italy
RB	Radio Bremen, Germany
RTB	Radiotelevizija Beograd, Yugoslavia
RTBF	Radio-Télévision Belge de la Communauté Française, Belgium
RTE	Radio Telefís Éireann, Ireland
RTP	Radiotelevisão Portuguesa, Portugal
RTSR	Radio-Télévision Suisse Romande, Switzerland
RTVE	Radiotelevisión Española, Spain
RUV	Rikisutvarpid-Sjonvarp (Islandic State Broadcasting Service – Television), Iceland
RVU	Radio Volks Universiteit; Educatieve Omroep, Netherlands
SDR	Süddeutscher Rundfunk, Germany
SFB	Sender Freies Berlin, Germany
SR	Saarländischer Rundfunk, Germany
SR	Sveriges Radio Ab (Swedish Broadcasting Corporation), Sweden
SRG	Schweizerische Radio- und Fernsehgesellschaft, Switzerland
SSR	Société Suisse de Radiodiffusion et Télévision, Switzerland
STV	Scottish Television, United Kingdom
S3	Südwest 3, Germany
SWF	Südwestfunk, Germany
TELEAC	Stichting Televisie Academie, Netherlands

TRT	Türkiye Radyo-Televizyon Kurumu, Turkey
TRU	Kommittén för television och radio i utbildningen, Sweden
TSI	Televisione della Svizzera Italiana, Switzerland
TSR	Télévision Suisse Romande, Switzerland
TVE	Televisión Española, Spain
UKIB	United Kingdom Independent Broadcasting, United Kingdom
UER	Union Européenne de Radiodiffusion (EBU)
UR	Utbildningsradion, Sweden
UTV	Ulster Television, United Kingdom
W3	West 3, Westdeutsches Fernsehen (WDF), Germany
WDF	Westdeutsches Fernsehen, Germany
WDR	Westdeutscher Rundfunk, Germany (FR)
YLE	OY Yleisradio Ab, Finland
YTV	Yorkshire Television, United Kingdom
ZDF	Zweites Deutsches Fernsehen, Germany

Appendix B: Press Release, Conference Programme

Internationales Zentralinstitut
für das
Jugend- und Bildungsfernsehen
(IZI)

Bayerische Landeszentrale
für
neue Medien
(BLM)

PRESS RELEASE

International Symposium
**Cultural and Educational Programmes on Television –
Deficiencies and Chances in a Competitive Media Environment**
held at MediaNet '92,
July 8th – 10th, 1992,
at the Munich Trade Fair and Exhibition Centre.

he 'Internationales Zentralinstitut für das Jugend- und Bildungsfernsehen' (IZI)
t the Bavarian Broadcasting Corporation, jointly with the 'Bayerische Landes-
entrale für neue Medien' (BLM), the umbrella organisation under public law of
te private broadcasters in Bavaria, is holding an International Symposium on the
tbject "Cultural and Educational Programmes on Television: Deficiencies and
'hances in a Competitive Media Environment" within the framework of MediaNet
2.

is the aim of this event

- to stimulate discussion on the chances of cultural and educational programmes
  in dual broadcasting systems;
- to exchange information on the experience and activities of European and non-
  European broadcasting organisations in a competitive situation;
- to propose support measures and activities to enhance the awareness for, and
  acceptance of, educational programmes, especially those relevant for attaining
  objectives of national or regional educational policies.

a almost all European countries, broadcasting legislation has undergone substantial
tanges – following on technological innovations and political developments. As
result, both the public service broadcasting corporations and the state-controlled

273

broadcasting organisations have lost their monopoly and are now forced to compet
for the public's favour with private programme companies.

For many broadcasting organisations, however, no changes have taken place i
the programme assignment with its division into the three sections information
entertainment and education, which for decades has been typical in Europea
broadcasting. On the other hand, similar demands are being increasingly made o
private companies. Some of the questions arising from this are:

- How can cultural and educational programmes, often conceived only for specifi
minorities, carry on in this dual system with a competitive character?
- What strategies and methods have been and are being developed in the productio
departments to reach the target groups they are aiming at, i.e. culturally intereste
minorities or groups with special information needs?
- What chances do cultural and educational programmes have on the market o
the audiovisual media?

Speakers have been invited, among others, from the USA (Discovery Channel)
Canada (TVOntario), France (CNDP), Britain (BBC Education, Independen
Television Commission; Channel 4, Broadcasting Support Services), the Netherland
(NOT, TELEAC), Sweden (SR/UR), public and private broadcasting organisation
in Germany, as well as renowned researchers and education experts.

It is planned to hold sessions on the following subject areas:

- Culture and Education on Public and on Commercial Television
- Public Service Broadcasting and the Market Situation
- Strategies for Improving the Acceptance and Effectiveness of the Educational
Programmes for Schools
- Programmes for Continuing and Community Education: Media Integration,
Cooperation and Partnership
- Alternative Ways of Offering and Financing Cultural and Educational
Programmes
- A Look at Future Developments of Cultural and Educational Television in Dual
Broadcasting Systems. A Panel Discussion

Participation in the conference and access to all satellite events is free of charge
for visitors to MediaNet '92. Entrance fee for MediaNet is DM 28, – for a daily
ticket, DM 98, – for a full-time ticket. A preliminary programme and an application
form will be sent on request to anybody interested.

Please contact:
Bayerischer Rundfunk
Internationales Zentralinstitut für
das Jugend- und Bildungsfernsehen

Bayerische Landeszentrale
für neue Medien
Press Department

Internationales Zentralinstitut
für das
Jugend- und Bildungsfernsehen
(IZI)

Bayerische Landeszentrale
für
Neue Medien
(BLM)

**Cultural and Educational Programmes on Television –
Deficiencies and Chances in a Competitive Media Environment**

An international symposium jointly organised by the Internationales Zentralinstitut
für das Jugend- und Bildungsfernsehen (IZI) at the Bayerischer Rundfunk and the
Bayerische Landeszentrale für neue Medien (BLM)

July 8 – 10, 1992
Munich, Exhibition Centre, Messeplatz

on the occasion of
MediaNet '92

Programme

Wednesday, 8th July, 1992

10.00   Opening

10.15   Subject of the Session:
        Cultural and Educational Programmes and the Dual System
        Chairman: Wolf Feller, Director of Television,
        Bayerischer Rundfunk, Munich

        On the Situation of Public Service Broadcasting in Dual Systems
        Prof. Albert Scharf, Director General of the Bayerischer
        Rundfunk; President of the European Broadcasting Union (EBU)

        Private Television and Public Responsibility
        Dr. Wolf-Dieter Ring, President of the Bayerische Landeszentrale
        für neue Medien (BLM), Munich

11.00   What Do the Media Want? – What Does the Audience Want?
        Alfred Payrleitner, Head of Main Department Science and
        Education, Österreichischer Rundfunk (ORF), Vienna

12.30   Lunch

        Subject of the Session:
        Public Service Broadcasting and the Market Situation
        Chairman: Armin Veihl, EBU Working Party for Educational
        Programmes, Geneva

275

14.30   BBC Education and the New Broadcasting Environment
         Brian Wright, Head, Educational Broadcasting Services,
         Jean Nunn, Head, Educational Developments and Information,
         Robert Seatter, Manager, Information and Promotions;
         British Broadcasting Corporation (BBC), London

16.00   Coffee

16.15   Culture, Education and Training: New Challenges to Public Service
         Broadcasting
             Léa Martel, Controller Educational Broadcasting, Belgische Radio
             en Televisie (BRTN), Brussels

         Reaching a Market of Millions: TVOntario's Educational
         Programming
             Olga Kuplowska, Director, Policy, Research and Planning;
             Judith Tobin, Director, International Affairs, TVOntario, Canada

20.00   Reception given by the Lord Mayor of Munich,
         Dr. Georg Kronawitter (on invitation)

Thursday, 9th July, 1992

         Subject of the Session:
         **Strategies for Increasing the Acceptance and Effectiveness of
         Educational Programmes**
             Chairman: Manfred Meyer, Internationales Zentralinstitut (IZI),
             Bayerischer Rundfunk, Munich

10.00   Back-up Services of Independent Television Companies in the UK
             Christopher Jones and David Lee, Education Department,
             Independent Television Commission (ITC), London

         Promoting and Marketing Schools Programmes
             Henk Jakobsen, Nederlandse Onderwijs Televisie (NOT),
             Hilversum

11.00   Coffee

11.15   Activities in Support of Educational Programmes in Japan
             Yoshiyuki Fukushima, Head,
             School Broadcast Programs Production, NHK, Japan

         Learning Foreign Languages by Television:
         The Role of Back-up Material
         Rolf Horneij, Utbildningsradion (UR), Stockholm

Support Activities for Science Programmes
Paul Martin, Central TV, Education Department, Birmingham

3.00   Lunch

Subject of the Session: **Cooperation and Partnership: Media Integration and Shared Responsibility**
Chairman: George Fleeton, President, Educational Media Association of Ireland, Belfast

4.30   The Multi-media Conception of Teleac
Henny van der Eng, Programme Support Department, Teleac, Utrecht

Cooperation with German Broadcasting Organisations: Experience of the Adolf Grimme Institute
Dr. Hans Paukens, Adolf-Grimme-Institut, Marl

6.00   Coffee

6.15   Commissioning Television Programmes and Back-up Material: The Model of Channel 4
Derek Jones, Editor Support Services, Channel 4, London

Broadcasting Support Services: A Joint Enterprise of the BBC and Private Competitors
Keith Smith, Director,
Broadcasting Support Services (BSS), London

Public Attitudes Towards Back-up Activities
Rosemary Bristow, BBC Broadcasting Research, London

Friday, 10th July, 1992

Subject of the Session: **Alternative Ways of Offering and Financing Cultural and Educational Programmes**
Chairman: Prof. Dr. Karl-Friedrich Reimers, Munich Film and Television Academy and Leipzig University

9.45   European Cultural Channel – Cultural Programming without Borders?
Dietrich Schwarzkopf, Vice-President, ARTE, Strasbourg

Technology Support for the French Educational System:
The Centre National de Documentation Pédagogique
Pierre Trincal, Director General, Centre National de Documentation Pédagogique (CNDP), Paris

11.00	Coffee
11.15	The Learning Channel and Discovery Europe Nick Comer-Calder, Director, The Learning Channel, London
12.30	Lunch
14.30	Cultural and Educational Programmes on Public Service Broadcasting and Private Television – A Programme Analysis Prof. Dr. Hans-Jürgen Weiß, Göttingen University
15.00	Panel Discussion **A Look at Future Developments of Cultural and Educational Programmes in Dual Broadcasting Systems** Chairman: Prof. Dr. Karl-Friedrich Reimers, Munich Film and Television Academy and Leipzig University Participants: Dr. Walter Flemmer, Coordinator, Programme Group Culture and Family, Bayerischer Rundfunk, Munich Werner Honal, Chairman, BLM Television Committee, Munich Karl-Otto Saur, Agency for Culture and Communication, Munich Prof. Dr. Alfons Silbermann, Professor of Sociology, Cologne Dr. Johannes Willms, Chief Editor "Aspekte", ZDF, Mainz
16.00	End of the Conference

Appendix C: About the Contributors

Rosemary Bristow spent most of her working life in audience or broadcasting research. It began in the mid-60s in the Australian Broadcasting Commission, followed by nearly 22 years in the BBC's Broadcasting Research Department, where she has been a Technical Organiser looking after sampling, Senior Researcher responsible for weekly programme evaluation via Listening and Viewing Panels, Senior Researcher and currently Manager in Special Projects. Recently she has been reviewing ways of measuring schools' use of Radio and Television as well as helping evaluate audience response to Continuing Education broadcasting.

Nick Comer-Calder who holds a BA in Development Studies and a MPhil in Urban Studies started his broadcasting career as a researcher at Granada and went on to join the BBC's Continuing Education and Training Department, where he worked, among other things, as a producer on the award-winning "Business Matters" series and on the highly successful "Play It Safe" child accident prevention series. In 1992 he joined United Artists as Programme Manager of The Learning Channel, in which capacity he was responsible for its launch and initial development.

Henny van der Eng worked in the graphic and publishing business before joining the Teleac Foundation, where now he is Head of the Programme Support Services with its various sections, i.e. the Publishing Department, the Audio and Video Department, the Telematic Department and Marketing & Sales. His special interest is the development, making and selling of multi-media packages.

Wolf Feller has been BR's Director of Television since 1987, and Deputy Director General since January 1993. He joined Bayerischer Rundfunk in 1958 as a radio journalist for economic affairs programmes. In 1966 he became Head of Television Economics Department. From 1976 to 1983 he was Head of the ARD studio in Rome, in which position he reported on the latest news from Italy, Greece, Malta and the Vatican. In 1983 he was elected Editor-in-Chief/Television at BR.

Yoshiyuki Fukushima, Head of School Broadcasts Production of Japan Broadcasting Corporation (NHK), joined NHK in 1963 and worked for the NHK branch stations in Kumamoto, Osaka and Hiroshima. Then he moved to NHK School Broadcasts Production in Tokyo, where he has strived to develop and improve educational broadcasting by producing numerous educational programmes. Now he is developing new multi-media programmes and High Definition TV programmes in the field of educational programme production.

Rolf Horneij is Head of Programmes at the Swedish Educational Broadcasting Corporation, where he has specialised in foreign languages. He has been the project leader of many multi-media projects including TV, radio, printed material, teletext, in collaboration with study organisations.

Henk Jakobsen started as a school television producer in 1981 (current affairs) and is now Manager of Magazines with NOT, i.e. he is, as a member of the NOT management team, responsible for all the magazines broadcast by NOT. His special interests are children's television, educational television in Europe and overseas and consulting the Caribbean and Namibia, Africa.

Christopher Jones has been Deputy Head of Educational Broadcasting for the ITC (previously IBA) with responsibility for the ITV Schools service since 1973. He has also had a particular interest in the development of pre-school programmes and resources using new information technology in schools. Since 1989 UK broadcasting has been undergoing extensive political change and recently he has been involved in research and planning for the future Schools TV service.

Derek Jones, Editor, Support Services at Channel 4 since 1982, was formerly active in community development and arts funding. From 1973 – 76 he was Co-ordinator of the North Devon Project (TV and the people) and from 1976 Assistant Chief Social Development Officer in Warrington New Town.

Olga Kuplowska, who holds an M.A. degree in Applied Psychology, is presently the Managing Director for Policy, Research and Planning at TVOntario, responsible for determining research policy and priorities and for developing strategic research plans in support of TVOntario's mission and corporate plans. She was previously Director of Evaluation and Project Research – a department she helped to set up when she first arrived at TVOntario in 1974.

David Lee worked as a teacher in primary and secondary schools, as a lecturer in speech and drama and as a teacher trainer before joining the IBA in 1976. As an accredited expert of the Council of Europe in the field of media and in-service training, he has served on a number of projects run by the Council, OECD and various European governments. He has particular interest in modern languages, multicultural education, creative and expressive arts, economic awareness and education for enterprise and capability.

Léa Martel is Managing Director of BRTN Educational Broadcasting. She studied Politics and Diplomatic Science at the Brussels University and started her career as a radio journalist. Her interest lies in economics, environment, women's studies, new technologies and broadcasting in relation to education. In 1989, she was elected Chairperson of the EBU's Working Party for Educational Programmes.

Paul Martin M.A., B.Sc., has been a producer in the Education Department of Central Independent Television plc for some twenty years, specialising in the production of television programmes and associated computer and print packages to support the teaching and learning of science and mathematics in school. Formerly a science teacher with the Inner London Education authority, he has acted as a consultant to UNESCO in Africa and held the Imperial Relations Trust Bursary for a study of multi-media in Australasia. He has been nominated for outstanding achievement by the British Academy of Film and Television Arts on three occasions and holds awards from a number of scientific and educational organisations.

Manfred Meyer is information specialist and Deputy Head of the Internationales Zentralinstitut fuer das Jugend- und Bildungsfernsehen (IZI), a documentation and information centre at the Bayerischer Rundfunk (Bavarian Broadcasting Corporation), founded in 1965. His main interests are: forms and functions of educational television and radio programmes, educational broadcasting research, television for children and young people, research into the effects of broadcast media.

Jean Nunn is Head of Educational Developments and Information which promotes all of the BBC's educational activities and publishes educational and training resources. She joined the BBC in 1970 as a producer of Mathematics, Science and Teacher Education programmes with the Open University Production Centre. Then she tranferred to the central policy unit of BBC Education as Chief Assistant to the Controller of Educational Broadcasting.

Dr. Hans Paukens, following his studies in Educational Science, Sociology, Psychology and Media Science, became head of department at an Adult Education Institute. Since 1977 he has been at the Adolf Grimme Institute, where he is now a specialist for radio, media, education, and culture. He is the author of several specialist works and essays on media development, media education, radio, and audience participation.

Alfred Payrleitner has been Head of the Main Department Science and Education at the ORF since 1984; one of his department's activities is reporting on historical themes. Under his aegis new series such as *Wissen Aktuell* (Science Today), *Wissen*

Spezial, featuring special scientific topics, and *Universum* have been launched. From 1969-74 he was Head of the Main Department Politics and Current Affairs in television, and from 1979 Head of the Main Department Documentation. Payrleitner, author of many specialist publications, was awarded in 1991 the Special State Prize for his achievements in the cultivation of scientific journalism in the field of television.

Dr. Wolf-Dieter Ring, lawyer, began his career in 1975 as the Personal Adviser to the Director of Bavarian Radio. Three years later he was appointed Head of the Media Policy Department of the Bavarian State Chancellery. From 1986 to 1989 he was Managing Director of the Bayerische Landeszentrale für neue Medien (supervisory authority for privately organised broadcasting in Bavaria); from 1987 he chaired the Conference of the directors of all German supervisory authorities for private broadcasting. Since 1990 he has been President of the Bayerische Landeszentrale für neue Medien (BLM).

Albert Scharf was elected Director General of Bayerischer Rundfunk in 1990. After completing his studies in law at the University of Munich, joined the Bavarian State Ministry of Finance from 1962 to 1966. In 1966 he became the Legal Director of Bayerischer Rundfunk. During his career he has occupied a number of important positions: Chairman of EBU Legal Committee from 1972 to 1982, Chairman of EBU Finance Committee from 1979 to 1982, and President of EBU since 1983. Moreover, he is Honorary Professor of Media Law at the Film and Television Academy Munich and Dean of the Department for Communications and Media Research.

Dietrich Schwarzkopf previously worked as a journalist and Bonn correspondent for various newspapers and broadcasting corporations (mainly the NDR and the WDR). In 1962 he became Head of the Bonn office of Deutschlandfunk in Cologne; after four years he was appointed Television Programme Director of the NDR in Hamburg. In 1974 he became Deputy Director of the NDR, and since 1978 he has been Programme Director of Deutsches Fernsehen (ARD's joint channel First German Television and the satellite channel EINS-PLUS). In April 1991 he became Vice President of the newly founded European culture channel ARTE.

Robert Seatter, formerly teaching English as a foreign language in France and Italy, pursued a career in EFL publishing, working for both Cambridge University Press and Oxford University Press. Since 1989 he has been Manager of Information and Promotion, with specific responsibility for campaigns to both the schools market and adult learners' sector. Other areas of activity include press, extension print, advertising and exhibitions.

Keith Smith, who previously worked as a book publisher and consultant, is the Director of Broadcasting Support Services (BSS), a not-for-profit organisation which runs helplines and provides follow-up services for viewers and listeners serving BBC, Channel 4, ITV and other media. As director of the BSS, he is also consultant of many partners of public broadcasting organisations in Europe.

Judith Tobin joined TVOntario in 1982 as a researcher in Planning and Development Research, becoming Head of the Department in 1984. She has coordinated over 50 studies on media in education, distance education, public broadcasting and learning needs. From 1984-87, Tobin served as the Canadian coordinator of two UNESCO studies on technology in education. In 1990, Tobin became Director General of International Affairs, with special responsibility for United States initiatives, relations with French-language broadcasters and cooperation with educators internationally.

Pierre Trincal, previously assistant private secretary at the Ministry of National Education, has been Director General of the CNDP since March 1990. After leaving the ENA (college for senior civil servants) in 1965, he chose to devote his administrative career to education. He has occupied responsible posts, notably in the university sector (creation of autonomous universities, libraries, the provision of welfare meals and accommodation for students).

Brian Wright was until recently the BBC's Head of Educational Broadcasting Services – as such he was responsible for the advisory and policy services for all of the BBC's educational broadcasts. As a former teacher and government administrator he joined the BBC over 24 years ago and has spent all of his BBC career in educational broadcasting. Now he is Special Assistant to the Director of Education working on a number of projects relating to the establishment of the new Education Directorate.

COMMUNICATION RESEARCH AND BROADCASTING
A publication series of the Internationales Zentralinstitut
für das Jugend- und Bildungsfernsehen (IZI)

No. 3
**Women, Communication,
and Careers**
Edited by Marianne Grewe-Partsch
and Gertrude J. Robinson
1980. 138 pages. Paperback
ISBN 3-598-20202-4
(Available from the IZI free of charge)

No. 5
**Health Education by Television
and Radio**
Contributions to an International Con-
ference with a Selected Bibliography
Edited by Manfred Meyer
1981. 476 pages. Paperback
ISBN 3-598-20203-2
(Available from the IZI free of charge)

No. 6
**Children and the Formal Features
of Television**
Approaches and Findings of
Experimental and Formative Research
Edited by Manfred Meyer
1983. 333 pages. Paperback. DM 42.–
ISBN 3-598-20205-9

No. 7
**Children and Families Watching
Television**
A Bibliography of Research on
Viewing Processes
Compiled by Werner Müller and
Manfred Meyer
1985. 159 pages. Paperback. DM 28.–
ISBN 3-598-20206-7

No. 8
Television and Young People
A Bibliography of International
Literature 1969 - 1989
Compiled by Kurt Aimiller, Paul Löhr
and Manfred Meyer
1989. 225 pages. Paperback. DM 32.–
ISBN 3-598-20207-5

No. 9
**Media Communication in Everyday
Life**
Interpretative Studies on Children's
and Young People's Media Actions
Edited by Michael Charlton and
Ben Bachmair
1990. 224 pages. Paperback. DM 48.–
ISBN 3-598-20208-3

No. 10
Aspects of School Television in Europe
A Documentation
Edited by Manfred Meyer
1992. 596 pages. Paperback. DM 56.–. ISBN 3-598-20209-1

K·G·Saur München·New Providence·London·Paris
A Reed Reference Publishing Company
Postfach 70 16 20 · D-81316 München · Tel. (089) 7 69 02-0